MY SUCCESS IS YOUR

SUCCESS

Questions, Reflections & Answers

Germain Decelles
Change management strategist

MANAGEMENT and PUBLISHING

Author: Germain Decelles, o.s.j.
Editor: WebTech Management and Publishing Incorporated
Revision: Patricia Goodrum Decelles
Cover photo: WebTech Collection, Managing Change
Page layout: WebTech Management and Publishing Incorporated

Print and distribution: http://www.lulu.com/

MY SUCCESS IS YOUR SUCCESS

ISBN 978-1-7388000-0-1

Copyright: first quarter 2023
National Library of Quebec
National Library of Canada

17, Marien Avenue, Montréal, Québec, Canada H1 B4T8
www.webtechmanagement.com
www.webtechpublishing.com

MY SUCCESS IS YOUR
SUCCESS

Questions, Reflections & Answers

Germain Decelles
Change management strategist

Hard times create strong men,
strong men create good times,
good times create weak men and,
weak men create hard times.

G. Michael Hopf
American writer.
Veteran,
Marine Corps,
United States

WebTech
MANAGEMENT and PUBLISHING

This book in our series on managing change is for students, parents, workers, educators, artists, athletes, scientists, managers, politicians, retirees, writers, or coaches, whether they work alone or belong to a team or organization whose goal is destined for success.

Our goal is to bring out new intellectual capital in everyone through the sharing of ideas.

In short, we aim to publish a book that disrupts the present, so that success manifests in every reader's life.

WebTech
MANAGEMENT and PUBLISHING

TABLE OF CONTENTS

Contents

Contents

Contents

Contents

Germain Decelles

Contents

Contents

Contents

WISDOM - 393
1. Be honest with yourself:
2. Be honest with others:
3. Focus on the process rather than the result:
4. Listen to the changes in yourself:
5. Learn from your mistakes:
6. The power of time itself:
7. Believe that you have a contribution to make:
8. Be kind to others:

RELIGION AND SPIRITUALITY - 397
Human beings can live without religion, but they cannot live without spirituality.

RELIGION - 398
1. Cultural identity:
2. The values and ethics:
3. The Spiritual Bond:
4. The idea of wellness:

SPIRITUALITY - 399
1. Spirituality means:
2. Spirituality entails:
3. Spiritual journeying involves:
4. The development of spirituality:
5. Religion formalizes:

BIBLIOGRAPHY, PHOTO CREDITS & NOTICE OF USE

We suggest that the reader consult the works listed throughout the book to learn more about certain specifics for successful use. Reading these reference documents helped the author in his quest for information related to the various topics contained in « My success is your success. »

By providing references throughout the book, the author urges the reader to further deepen their knowledge of the various topics covered. We cannot guarantee the validity, accuracy, completeness, or timeliness of the information contained in the documents offered. Most of the authors of these documents have developed an international reputation in their fields.

Various books and electronic formats inspired the quotes and texts contained in this book. Most of the biographical information and quotes are unpublished. We cannot, however, guarantee their authenticity.

All quotes, short texts and photographs contained in the book have been included to encourage the reader to reflect on the educational content provided by each author. The purpose was to provide introductory information on each topic.

All quotes, short texts and photographs remain the property of the authors concerned. Most of the images are from the Wikipedia website and are marked « public domain, » that is, material which is not eligible for copyright or for which copyright has expired. Images, such as book covers, and official photos have been taken from various websites that promote the work of the authors in question. The purpose was only to correctly identify the authors of quotes and short texts. Other photos were taken from the WebTech photo collection.

Finally, we urge the reader to consult with a professional or other authority in the appropriate field to contextualize particular needs before using any information we provide in « My Success is Your Success. »

The information in this book is provided for informational purposes only.

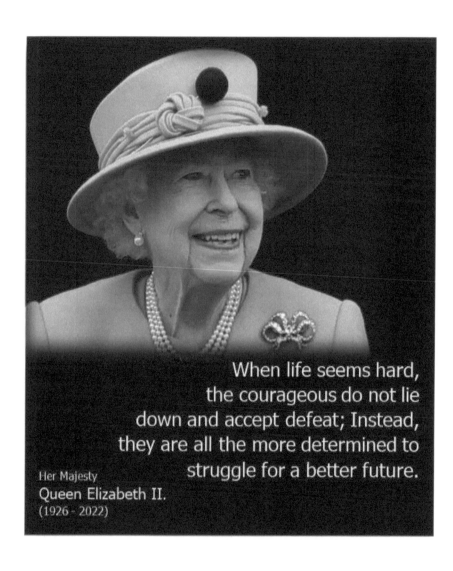

When life seems hard, the courageous do not lie down and accept defeat; Instead, they are all the more determined to struggle for a better future.

Her Majesty
Queen Elizabeth II.
(1926 - 2022)

FOREWORD

Want to discover how to be successful in life!

Of course, we all want to be successful in life. We all want to be able to live our dream life away from all the struggles and constant worrying about our day-to-day problems.

We all have different definitions of success, but for most people, success can mean that you want to live a happy, wealthy, contented and overall better life than the one you are currently living in, especially if it is far from the life you expected.

If right now you are not there yet, or you would like to be there and you feel within yourself that you will succeed by putting in the necessary effort to achieve your goals, then it will eventually happen.

Whatever good you attract or offer in your life, if you focus and work hard at it, just know that it has a good chance of coming true.

Now however you define success, be it financial, spiritual, physical, mental, emotional, philanthropic, community or family, the most important thing you need to know about success to be successful is that success matters, and you are solely responsible for it.

Most will agree regardless of culture, race, religion, economic or social background that success is important and vital to the well-being of the individual, family unit, workplace, and social environment. And, certainly, for the survival of these elements in the future.

Understand that those who downplay the importance of success are usually confused or have given up on their own chances for success.

Success brings confidence, security, a sense of well-being, the ability to contribute hope, and leadership at a higher level.

Without success, you, your environment, your goals, your dreams, and even entire civilizations may be in jeopardy.

Just think that without continued success, entire races ceased to exist, as was the case with the Vikings, Romans, Greeks, Native Americans and then an endless list of businesses and products. Success is important in the sense that it is necessary to continue to subsist and thus ensure its survival!

If you are unable to take care of your children, they will be looked after by the state. For an individual or a group to continue, they must actively achieve their goals and targets, otherwise they will cease to exist.

For a company or an industry to continue, it must be successful in creating new products, bringing them to market, satisfying customers, employees, and investors, and repeating this cycle over and over.

Regardless of the goals you are trying to achieve, success is important. Stop succeeding and you will stop winning. Stop winning long enough and you will give up!

Success is not only important, it is vital. It should never be reduced to anything less than necessary for life.

I wrote « My Success is Your Success » because I have great excitement seeing people from all walks of life experience success.

I wanted to help people like you discover their potential, so they can help themselves grow in life and help those around them.

« My Success is Your Success » lets you take the ideas from the book and apply them to your personal development.

This will enable you to become a more effective, efficient, and authentic person, a person who can grow and change from within to achieve a better future.

Becoming a genuine person requires hard work!

To become great at any endeavor, whether in your career, family, or community, you must use the unique strengths you were born with and develop them to the fullest, while recognizing and learning from your shortcomings.

Above all, remember that in most cases, individuals must work hard to shape their future.

They endure disappointing defeats and rejections and search for many years to find the right place to thrive.

Each of them is required to take the journey to their own soul, discover who they are, where their true passions lie, and how they can become more effective in shaping their future.

Personally, I didn't have a distinct reference text like this book to help me when I was young, so I built my evolution plan as I went along, with the help of my father, employers, close friends, my wife, my son, and mentors throughout my journey.

After many years of looking for role models, I learned that I could never truly become myself by trying to emulate someone else or minimize my flaws.

If you aim to look like someone else, you'll just be an impersonator, because ultimately, you'll think that's what the people around you want you to do.

You will never be a real person with that kind of thinking. However, you could be a real person, following your passions.

Many self-help books offer a quick fix or provide the reader with, say, seven or easy steps to follow and you're done.

Unfortunately, the development and evolution of a person does not usually happen this way, and one rarely becomes a fulfilled person simply by reading a book. Much more is needed!

To realize your potential in life, you need a detailed development plan that will allow you to shape your future.

This is the goal of « My Success is Your Success » which will help you to develop a clear and detailed plan for your personal growth, your success, and your happiness in life.

I encourage you to have as many experiences early in life as possible.

Do not sit around waiting for these experiences to come to you. Look for them!

Then, after each experience, you should compare it to your evolutionary plan to see what changes you need to make or determine what future experiences you should explore.

Remember the fundamentals in this book because they will help you change your future.

You will have to discover your authentic self as soon as possible.

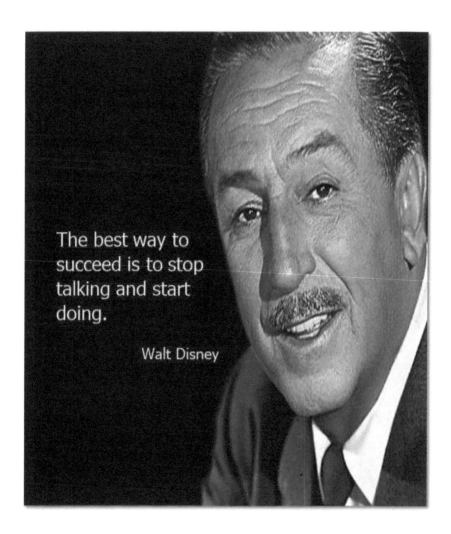

The best way to
succeed is to stop
talking and start
doing.

Walt Disney

You will have to remember that you don't have to be born with certain characteristics to be able to shape your future.

You won't have to wait for someone to tap you on the shoulder to get started.

You won't have to wait until you're at the top of an organization to get started, and most importantly, you'll have to remember that you're never too young or too old to grow to change your future.

I encourage you to be completely open and transparent with yourself as you answer the difficult and challenging questions you will ask yourself about where you think you should be in the future.

You must explore your life story in depth to understand who you are as a human being, where you fit into this world, how you can positively impact the world, and how you can leave a lasting legacy.

I hope you and many others can transform businesses, institutions, governments, society and revalue education and religion, bringing authenticity and encouraging others to do the same.

At this point, it is important to keep in mind that changing your life for a better destiny is solely up to you!

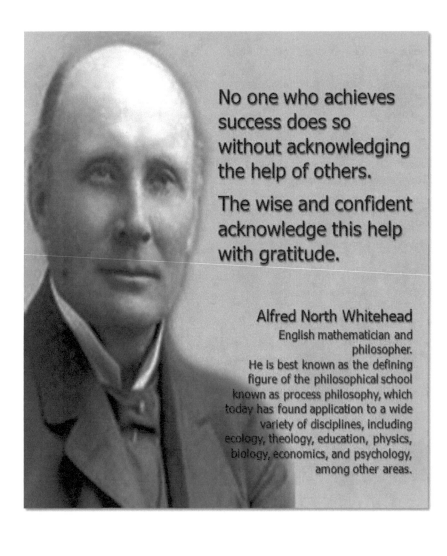

No one who achieves
success does so
without acknowledging
the help of others.

The wise and confident
acknowledge this help
with gratitude.

Alfred North Whitehead
English mathematician and
philosopher.
He is best known as the defining
figure of the philosophical school
known as process philosophy, which
today has found application to a wide
variety of disciplines, including
ecology, theology, education, physics,
biology, economics, and psychology,
among other areas.

ACKNOWLEDGMENTS

This book is the result of forty years of experience acquired with local and international organizations and businesses and during consulting services in change management and marketing.

I would especially like to thank all our customers, business relations, colleagues and friends for their friendship and support.

In particular; Sister Marie-Salomé and Mr. Dugas teachers, Bernard Berthiaume, Normand and Mario Forgues from the automotive industry, Claude Marcoux CPA, Jean-Louis Richard CMA, Georges Klein international business consultant, Gilles Paul, Michel Kwas and Albert Lasry senior management advisors, The Honorable Gerry Weiner Canadian Secretary of State, numerous small and medium-sized business entrepreneur clients, and our associated Information Technology and Change Management partners over the past forty years.

We had many discussions with them on many of the topics covered in this book. Their advice and suggestions helped make this project a reality.

Acknowledgment would not be complete without mentioning my wife, Patricia, who supported my career and my son, Frédéric-Alexandre, who served, during his university years and until today in business development, as a test subject. to confirm many of the questions, thoughts and answers when writing « My Success is Your Success. »

Germain Decelles, o.s.j.
President & Senior Partner
WebTech Management and Publishing, Inc.

Special thanks for their wisdom and support:
Mr. & Mrs. Leonard J. Messineo
Grand Chancellor,
Sovereign Order of Saint John of Jerusalem ®
New Jersey, U.S.A.

Sovereign Order of Saint John of Jerusalem ®
※ Knights of Malta ※

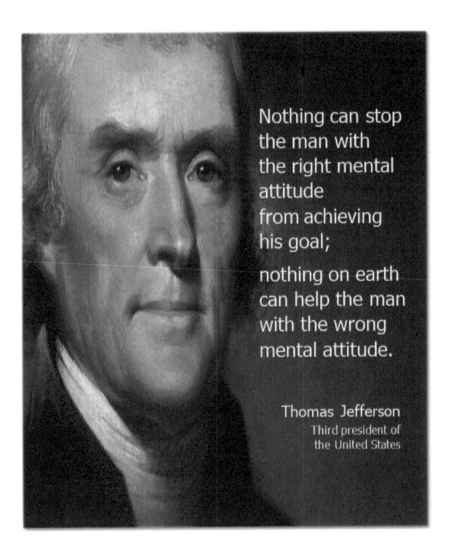

Nothing can stop
the man with
the right mental
attitude
from achieving
his goal;

nothing on earth
can help the man
with the wrong
mental attitude.

Thomas Jefferson
Third president of
the United States

INTRODUCTION

We can all achieve success!

You have a tool in your hands that can change your life. The following pages will guide you in determining the path necessary to explore your desire for a better future.

This book is for people who are actively engaged and open to questioning their own assumptions and listening to their deepest inner voice, because it is only through this kind of listening that a future of success will be « graspable. »

Your motivation for using this book may be that you are looking for new ways to fulfill yourself in life. You may be 17 or 18 and want to explore ways to advance your career. Or maybe you'll be retiring in a few years and can't wait to help the next generation take over from you.

Perhaps you are 40 years old and confronted by aggressive young colleagues and feel compelled to consider ways to deal with such situations. Or maybe you are 70 years old and want to leave a good impression by helping younger people face the challenges surrounding success by sharing your experiences.

If you want to grow and progress in your life as well as in your career, you obviously need to equip yourself with the skills and knowledge to be a proactive person in the face of threats and ready for the future, to achieve success.

Our survival and well-being depend on our ability to perceive, evaluate, and control the effects of our actions to imagine and create more desirable ways to achieve success in our lives.

This book describes how to improve your ability to reach your goals for success. Success is the only part of our lives that we can achieve by what we do or don't do.

Particularly, being authentic to ourselves is the most important thing in order to achieve success!

The secrets of success?

If you define a secret as simply an unknown fact or an undiscovered detail of a fact you already know, then the "secrets" to success abound.

On the other hand, if you define a secret as a magic bullet that can guarantee success, that magic bullet or success secret can only be yourself.
Your convictions, your actions, your personal, professional, and relational qualities as well as your determination to carry out your projects will ultimately determine your success.

Others can make your path to success easier or harder, but they don't have the final say on whether you succeed in life.

Simple, we are all we really have. Any current possessions could go away for a variety of reasons. The same is true with any ongoing relationship.

If we define ourselves through our possessions or our relationships, we will be devastated if they are lost. Fundamental autonomy is therefore *one of the keys to success.*

While support from others is welcome, it is not guaranteed. Self-confidence is another key to success, and it starts with being your biggest « groupie. »

Others can influence or persuade you, but they cannot "make" you act in a certain way without your permission.

Recognizing and using your ZONE of control, which is part of overall self-control, empowers you to take charge of your actions, reactions, emotions, and attitude to the best of your ability.

Only then will you be able to take control of each situation.

What is success?

Achieving wealth, fame, a perfect body, respect from our peers and our community, or winning a marathon could be one of those things, because success irretrievably includes achievement.

However, truly satisfying success also includes a degree of inner peace, joy, and self-fulfillment in terms of the dreams you can contemplate and the goals you set for yourself.

Therefore, success could be defined as an accomplishment that involves personal development and growth, as defined by the individual.

But remember that what one person defines as personal achievement, growth, or development may mean nothing to another person.

Real and lasting success comes from within. It is not something "far away" that must be found.

It is something that we create ourselves by developing our basic life skills to their full potential and putting those skills into action.

Now the question that always comes up, is there a secret to success?

The answer is yes and no. It's always fun to dream up magical and even mystical success secrets that guarantee instant happiness.

Many people dream of how they could change the world if they could just win the lottery.

Realistically, a secret could be defined as a fact we haven't discovered yet, or an exciting new detail of a fact we already know.

In this sense, the secrets of success, most certainly exist and may well lead to increased success and happiness.

This is especially true in areas such as autonomy, self-control, and self-esteem.

How do you measure success?

Just as the meaning of success is subjective, so is how we measure success. Developing strong foundational skills helps us create realistic benchmarks to measure personal success.

Remember that other people's point of view really doesn't matter. The most important thing for you is to know if you have the feeling of wanting to succeed or not.

Why are the basic skills important?

Let's first define basic life skills. They could also be called life management skills. These are the strengths and skills that make us unique as individuals.

These skills take us from one moment in our lives to another. Indeed, they are the ones who help us survive and thrive by increasing our self-esteem and confidence.

Fundamental life skills help us be resilient and allow us to bounce back from difficult situations.

If we are not resilient, we cannot survive. If we truly believe that we cannot overcome our current situation, we might stop trying and give up altogether.

Strengthening skills not only gives hope for the future, but also increases the chances of success.

Seeing ourselves as strong, confident individuals allows us to see mistakes and setbacks, no matter how small, as challenges, not failures.

Practicing life skills gives us more control over our lives and our future.

They allow us to improve our relationships and provide a solid foundation for overcoming challenges, for example, managing our anger during an argument or conflict, dressing appropriately to speak in a group.

In order to assess the first step to achieving success, you need to assess your current strengths.

There is also the importance of overcoming current obstacles to personal growth.

Then, determine what additional skills will be needed to develop your life plan.

This plan will be used to put your old and new skills into action.

To get started, start flipping through « My success is your success. »

What should I consider?

In « My success is your success. »

I tried to make every page count. Each page contains at least one piece of practical information that can help you improve your skills to achieve success for a better life.

It is important that you be comfortable with the material, so please start where you feel the most relaxed.

Recommended reading and references

We suggest that you consult the works identified below in order to learn more about the particularities contained in this chapter.

BOUTIN, Gérard & JULIEN, Louise. L'OBSESSION DES COMPÉTENCES. Éditions Nouvelles. ISBN 2-921696-56-8.

BUTLER-BOWDON, Tom. 50 PSYHOLOGY CLASSICS: Who we Are, How We Think, What We Do. Gildan Media. ISBN 1-59659-119-6.

SILLS, Judith. OSER CHANGER. Stanké Publication. ISBN 2-7604-0481-1.

WALKER, Harold Blake. POWER TO MANAGE YOURSELF. Harper & Brothers. Library of Congress catalog card number: 55-8529.

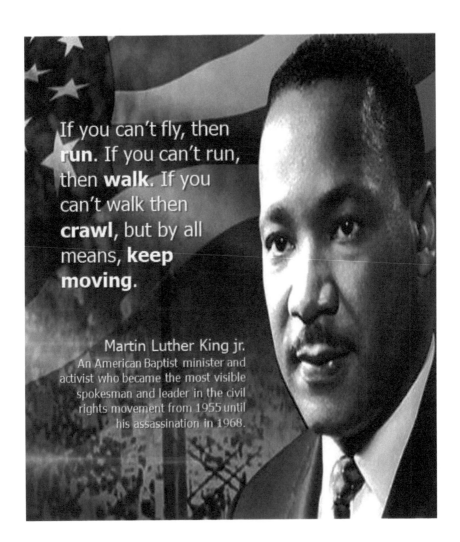

If you can't fly, then **run**. If you can't run, then **walk**. If you can't walk then **crawl**, but by all means, **keep moving**.

Martin Luther King jr.
An American Baptist minister and activist who became the most visible spokesman and leader in the civil rights movement from 1955 until his assassination in 1968.

A MEANINGFUL LIFE

What makes a life meaningful?
It is difficult to give a definitive answer to the question.

Simple, because everyone has their own ideas of what a meaningful life should be. What may give purpose and meaning to one person may be completely different from another.

In general, a meaningful life is a life of happiness and self-fulfillment, a life surrounded by loved ones and activities that are enjoyed.

If a person is satisfied with what he is doing with his life, then for him his life has meaning. To have a meaningful life is to wake up each morning with a sense of appreciation for the opportunity to live another day.

Everyone is here for a reason. Finding that reason can be difficult, but to find it, you must pursue your passion. Doing whatever it takes to accomplish something you love makes your life worth living.

Whether it's caring for people, excelling at your job, or creating something new, your passion creates an inner joy unlike anything else.

Some people seem to spend their whole lives unsatisfied in search of the ultimate goal. However, we all have what we need to live a meaningful life.

When you know you are working towards that passion every day, you feel a sense of purpose. You are drawn into this state of self-fulfillment. And until you can achieve this goal, you are dissatisfied, and you feel a void in your life.

Self-fulfillment should be a lifelong goal for everyone.

The whole process gives meaning to your life, but you can't stop when you think you've reached your goal. You must continue to set higher goals for yourself, so that your life will always have a meaning.

A meaningful life is above all the accumulation of success for which you have set the goals. To do this, you must set goals and achieve them, you must motivate yourself.

Motivation is a powerful energy that determines the way we work, the vigor with which we approach our lives, and a greater sense of purpose derived from what we do.

Motivation is, in short, the incentive we need to wake up in the morning, get dressed and get to work.

To help us understand what the motivation for success is, we must first focus on the basic needs of life and the exploration of self through, the will to achieve.

Once you have a good understanding of basic needs and their hierarchy, you will be better able to motivate yourself while avoiding unrealistic expectations with an action plan that will need to consider the passion and vocation.

THE NEEDS OF LIFE

To do this, let's look at Maslow's hierarchy of needs theory. Abraham Maslow was a mid-20th-century American psychologist working in the field of humanistic psychology, who introduced the concept of self-realization, highlighting our innate need for fulfillment.

According to Maslow's theory, an individual begins by focusing on the lower order needs of physiology and safety.

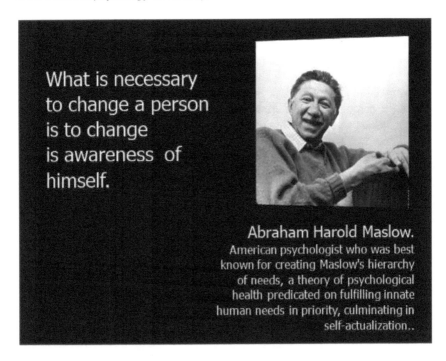

What is necessary to change a person is to change is awareness of himself.

Abraham Harold Maslow.
American psychologist who was best known for creating Maslow's hierarchy of needs, a theory of psychological health predicated on fulfilling innate human needs in priority, culminating in self-actualization..

A person who has just started their career will be more concerned with physiological needs such as a stable income and security needs. Once these basic needs are met, she or he will now focus on social needs.

Once these needs are met, she or he will want to meet higher-level needs such as self-esteem needs.

These needs are linked to the person's image and their desire for respect and recognition from others. Even if the person doesn't want to move into a higher role, they probably don't want to continue doing the same job for their entire life.

Maslow's theory is based on five basic types of needs. Often represented, as levels in a pyramid, the needs residing in the lower levels must be satisfied before those of the higher levels can be met.

1. *Physical:* the need for air, water, food, sleep.
2. *Security:* the need for security, shelter, stability.
3. *Social:* the need for intimate relationships, to be loved, to belong.
4. *Self-esteem:* the need for self-esteem, prestige, recognition of achievements.
5. *Self-realization:* the need to develop, to be creative, to realize one's full capacities.

The first four levels are considered « deficiency needs. » If we lack any of these levels, we can become distracted, anxious, or depressed. If all these needs are met, we are free to explore our « growth needs » or our unique human need to grow as individuals.

1. *Physical Needs:* our biological needs « air, water, food, shelter » are simple, but vital for survival, and when they are not met, put all other needs on hold.

   For instance, you must take a lunch break, but you are delayed for half an hour at the end of a meeting. Your body and brain react biologically and emotionally to the need to eat.

   When you are « hungry » your ability to focus on your work steadily decreases as the urgency to meet your hunger increases.

2. *Security needs*: security can mean feeling physically secure, but it can also mean a desire for stability, order, predictability, and control regarding, for example, in the workplace, pay, working hours, structures, team building, workload and performance monitoring, to name a few.

All these circumstances lead to feelings of conflict, instability, and a lack of confidence in the ability to meet needs.

3. *Social needs*: the ease with which we feel welcome in a group or in finding people « like us » has a huge impact on our performance at work and in life in general.

    Feeling like an outsider means, you're less likely to engage, offer ideas, or go the extra mile for fear of being ridiculed.

    When we feel welcome, we are more likely to trust those around us and trust ourselves to be ourselves. Our ideas and efforts are validated, motivating us to do and be better.

    If you can't express yourself authentically and adapt to it, it may be best, to leave the environment altogether.

    The goal is not to have everyone get along with each other all the time. The important thing is to find harmony within your group while allowing individuals to be themselves to form an engaged and motivated group.

4. *Needs of self-esteem:* when we learn to ride a bike, we start with training wheels for support and balance. We build self-esteem by mastering this task.

    Once we mastered the technique, the training wheels come off and a steady hand on the back of the seat helps us learn to balance the bike while moving. Eventually, that hand lets go, and you ride alone.

    Like riding a bicycle, to meet the needs of our ego both at work and socially, we must develop self-esteem through an ability to perform tasks independently.

    We also need a support system that helps us achieve our goal and a recognition system that validates our accomplishments.

    For example, to motivate ourselves in this way at work, we need to look for work that showcases our abilities while challenging us to master new skills.

    However, it is suggested to place at the top of your list, the mastery of observing the people around you as well as your communication skills.

5. *Needs for self-realization*: Maslow defined self-realization as the desire to « become all that one is capable of becoming. »

    The need for self-realization can materialize when you have « harnessed » all the experiences and knowledge in each circumstance, but you know that you can do more, and you can do better. The awareness of this needs to grow comes to the fore because all other needs have been met.

    Free from distractions, you can take a broad look at the sum of your efforts and decide what really makes you feel fulfilled. This level of freedom has its own motivating power, making it easier for you or the people around you to take the next step on a personal development journey.

    To support this, find continuing education opportunities, higher-level certifications, or resources that help pursue these passions.

Over time, you will recognize that your needs overlap or change in importance based on individual circumstances.

Awareness and constant communication around your needs and those of the people around you are the essential component to meet these needs, whatever their order.

MOTIVATION

Motivation is what drives us to achieve our goals, feel more fulfilled, and improve our overall quality of life.

Understanding and developing your personal motivation can help you take control of many other aspects of your life.

To improve your personal motivation, you could think of achieving an ambition, or placing yourself in a state of mind. To be more specific, there are two types of mindsets, the fixed and the evolving.

For people with a fixed mindset, they believe talent is ingrained and they cannot change their level of ability. And there are those with an evolutionary mindset who believe they can improve their skills through hard work and effort.

People who believe they can improve themselves have an evolutionary mindset above all else, and they are much more likely to succeed in any field they choose.

A growth mindset is therefore an important element in a personal desire to succeed. Other elements of personal drive include organization, especially good time management and avoiding distractions.

There is plenty of evidence, albeit largely anecdotal, that goal setting is important for our overall well-being.

For example, Albert Einstein reminded us; if you want to live a happy life, tie it to a goal, not to people or things.

Most of us need to aim for something in our lives. Knowing where you want to go and understanding how you plan to get there is the key to staying motivated.

To do this, it is necessary to consider helping you in your quest for success, to develop a spirit of initiative.

Initiative is, in fact, the ability to take advantage of circumstances when they arise, and it is too easy to hesitate and then the opportunity may be lost.

However, the old saying, look before you jump, makes perfect sense. It's important to think things through and make sure you're making the right decision for you, while considering the other people involved.

The initiative can therefore be seen as a combination of courage and good risk management.

Risk management is necessary to ensure that you identify the right opportunities to consider, and that they present the appropriate level of risk for you.

Courage is needed to overcome the fear of the unknown inherent in new circumstances.

However, the initiative cannot take place without a touch of optimism accompanied by resilience.

Optimism is the ability to see the bright side of things or to think positively. Resilience is the ability to bounce back from setbacks or stay positive in the face of challenges. The two are closely related, although not exactly the same.

Resilient people use their thinking skills to manage negative emotional reactions to events. In other words, they use positive or rational thinking to examine and, if necessary, overcome reactions that they understand, may not be entirely logical. They are also willing to ask for help when needed, as well as generously offering their help to others in need.

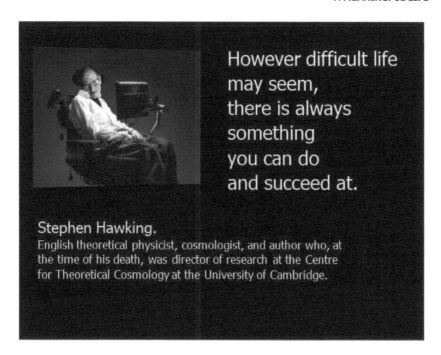

However difficult life may seem, there is always something you can do and succeed at.

Stephen Hawking.
English theoretical physicist, cosmologist, and author who, at the time of his death, was director of research at the Centre for Theoretical Cosmology at the University of Cambridge.

On the other hand, it helps to understand what motivates you to do things. There are two main types of motivators, intrinsic and extrinsic.

In their simplest form, you can consider these two types of motivation: intrinsic, which is related to what you want to do, and extrinsic, which is related to what you must do. To be more precise:

- *Intrinsic*: Performing an action or task based on the expected or perceived satisfaction of performing the action or task. Intrinsic motivations include pleasure, interest, and personal challenge.

- *Extrinsic*: Performing an action or task to gain some sort of external reward, including money, power, and good grades.

Also, consider that different people are motivated by different things and at different times in their lives.

The same task can have more intrinsic motivations at certain times and more extrinsic motivations at others, and most tasks combine the two types of motivation.

Remember, we all tend to work better when we love what we do. It's easier to get out of bed in the morning, we're happier at our jobs, and happier in general.

Research shows that this is especially important when we are under stress. It is much easier to deal with stress and long hours if we generally enjoy our work. Intrinsic motivators therefore play a big role in personal motivation for most of us.

What if a task has no intrinsic motivations or extrinsic motivations?

The obvious conclusion is that we are unlikely to do so, as it would serve no purpose.

We all know it doesn't always work that way. There is another problem, the feeling of obligation.

Obligation motivations are not strictly intrinsic or extrinsic but can still be very powerful.

Obligation itself result from our personal ethics and our sense of duty, of what is right and what is not.

For example, you may feel compelled to go to a party because someone you know has invited you. There will be no obvious extrinsic or intrinsic benefit to attending, but you may fear offending or upsetting your friend if you don't.

However, you are more likely to enjoy the party if you go with a positive and open attitude, expecting it to be fun.

As a result, it adds intrinsic motivation, allowing you to have fun and consequently derive some satisfaction from it.

Here, we must understand that wishing to be motivated, or even to improve your personal motivation a little, will not happen overnight.

There are a lot of skills involved and you can't expect to develop them all instantly.

However, a better understanding of the elements of motivation, and especially their combination, should help increase your skills.

Just remember that Rome was not built in a day: think about progressing over a long period and in small steps!

People who have achieved extraordinary success in life are extremely motivated people. They live a passionate life, they work tirelessly on their goals, and they are always on the move no matter what.

So, have you ever wondered if you are someone who is highly motivated, or someone who is not?

Motivated people come from all walks of life. It can be anyone who is driven by a clear goal and has a burning desire to achieve their dreams.

And, to achieve exceptional results in life, you must develop the characteristics of a highly motivated individual:

- You must detach yourself from the ordinary to achieve the extraordinary.
- You must choose to move on when others give up.
- You must work harder and dare to pursue your dreams while the rest of the world is still comfortably in its cozy bed.
- You must have a clear and useful purpose rather than living your life without a purpose.

So, what are the characteristics of motivated people and how can you become one?

1. *They are absolutely clear about what they want:* first of all, motivated people are absolutely clear about what they want in life. They are goal oriented and driven by their goal. If you want to be motivated, you need to know why you're doing what you're doing. Your purpose is the energy that sustains you when you encounter difficulties and challenges.

2. *They always live their purpose*: knowing what you want from your life is just the beginning. What you need to do next is to live your life according to your purpose. There's no point in dreaming about what you want, if you don't do anything about it.

   Motivated people are motivated most of the time because they have programmed what they want to accomplish into their subconscious. Therefore, they can't help but constantly think about their dreams, goals, and what they want to achieve in life. You should do the same.

   Make your goals and dreams your dominant thoughts for you to think about at all times. Remember, you will become what you think about most of the time.

   If you are constantly thinking about enjoying life, watching a movie, and playing games, guess what, that will be exactly what will make your life. However, if you consistently hold on to the idea of achieving your goals, living your dreams, and achieving great success, you will reap great benefits.

You become goal-oriented. You will become more motivated and take action to achieve them. So be like all successful people, keep the things you want to accomplish in mind, and you will bring them into your life.

3. *They ignore detractors*: another trait of motivated people is that they ignore naysayers. They are so driven that they ignore the rest of the world. So ignore the naysayers and chase your dreams.

    That is, if you want to be a driven person, don't listen, to what other people tell you about how to live your life. Instead, choose to listen to yourself.

    Follow your heart and chase your dreams and let the rest of the world admire your success once you've done it.

4. *They are always passionate and full of energy*: what are the common characteristics of motivated people?
    They are always passionate and dynamic.

    Do you live your life with passion and energy?
    If not, re-examine your goals and think about what you really want in your life.

    Highly motivated people always live their lives with passion and seem to have all the energy in the world.

    Your work is going to take up a large part of your life, and the only way to be truly satisfied is to do what you believe to be a great job. And the only way to do great work is to love what you do.

    If you haven't found it yet, keep looking. Do not be discouraged.

    Therefore, if you want to be highly motivated, align your goals and dreams and live with passion!

5. *They act massively and keep progressing*: yes, motivated people are constantly on the move. They are taking massive and consistent action every day. They are constantly progressing towards their goals.

    They don't just talk about their dreams; they make them come true. They dare to persevere, and they always progress.

    Does that mean they make no mistakes or will never fail?
    Not at all. Successful people fail, but they don't stop there. They make a mistake, they learn from it, and then they keep moving forward. They don't dwell on their mistakes and failures.

Take the time to study successful people in their respective lives, you will see that they don't just talk, they act. They act despite many difficulties and challenges.

This is the kind of persona you need to embrace if you want to be a driven person who strives to achieve their dreams. Progress all the time. Get into the habit of always taking at least one step to reach the goal.

6. *They dare to sacrifice and take risks*: yes, motivated people dare to sacrifice themselves and they are ready to take risks.

The key to achieving the success you want in life is figuring out what you want and then getting busy paying the price to get there.

Unsuccessful people understand what they need to do to get there, but they're not willing to pay the price. Successful people, on the other hand, understand this and are willing to sacrifice themselves and pay the full price.

Those who have achieved extraordinary results in life are those who don't complain and choose to do so even when they don't feel like it.

They are motivated to achieve their goals and are absolutely committed.

Successful people are clear about the « why » of what they do. The « why » provides the deeper meaning responsible for maintaining their motivation.

They understand that they can get almost anything they want out of life, if they're willing to pay the price.

So, are you ready to do more?
Are you ready to do the hard work where most people don't want to?

When you are absolutely determined to achieve what you want, you give yourself no excuses, you just accomplish. And only then will you become a motivated person who makes things happen.

7. *They take full responsibility for everything that happens to them*: motivated people have an « it's up to me » mentality.

They know that whatever is happening to them right now is only temporary and they are in control of changing their lives because they oversee their lives.

They are the ones who are responsible for their lives. That's why it's normal that they can be born into a poor family, but that doesn't mean they have to be poor for the rest of their lives.

They believe they are the ones who can change their destiny. And so, they make choices and decisions based on the future they want.

Of course, there are things we cannot control, such as weather, gravity, nature. But that doesn't mean we can't be responsible for what happens to us.

Even if you can't control the event, you can still control your responses.

Like this saying: I can't change the direction of the wind, but I can trim my sails to always reach my destination.

Motivated people understand that blame, excuses, and justifications are not going to help them reach a higher level. And if they want to win the game of life, they must take full responsibility for their lives.

You too should do the same. Don't blame or make excuses. Take responsibility for your life from this moment on.

8. *They defer instant gratification*: yes, highly motivated people know the power of gratification. When given the choice between partying and making their dreams come true, they always choose to make their dreams come true.

They understand that if they work harder now for what they want, they can enjoy it later.

Success is about making the right choices and doing the things that will get you where you want to go.

Often people choose to have instant pleasure rather than sacrifice themselves and work towards their goals.

Motivated people understand that they must work hard now and sacrifice for their future.

Remember this quote: Success is living a few years of your life like most people won't, so you can spend the rest of your life like most people can't.

Therefore, learn to defer gratification. Choose to work on what is important and not on something that gives you immediate pleasure.

So choose to defer gratification.

Work on the essentials. Work on your goals and dreams. And when you get there, you can taste the victory of your own hard work, which in itself will be far more fulfilling and enjoyable than the small gratification of the moment.

9. *They work very hard:* should I explain more?
    Motivated people are people who work extremely hard. They choose to work on their dreams and goals whenever possible.

    Rather than wasting time checking their friends for updates on Facebook, Twitter and the like, they choose to work on their goals.

    They don't just waste time for anything, but they enjoy working towards their goals and chasing their dreams.

    That's not to say, highly motivated people don't enjoy or don't have free time. They just work harder so they can enjoy later.

    Therefore, do not be lazy. Keep doing, pushing yourself, and eventually your hard work will pay off.

10. *They make mistakes and fail, but don't give up*: motivated people are people who will never give up. A winner will never quit, and a quitter will never win.

    The only way to achieve victory is to not give up, no matter how difficult the situation. No matter what happens, choose not to give up.

    You may face failures and experience dramatic setbacks, but whatever you do, don't give up.

    Motivated individuals know they are working for a greater purpose.

    They don't work for the money or the car, they work for a higher purpose that motivates them internally.

    And, because they are working for a purpose greater than themselves, they will not give up. They make mistakes and they fail, but they keep moving forward.

UNREALISTIC EXPECTATIONS

A new job, a new relationship, we've all been there. We are so eager to get things done. All the ideas swirling around in our heads now have the chance to come to life.

However, this impatience never ends well. What usually happens in such a scenario is that we start out with unrealistic expectations.

We always want to be perfect and never make mistakes. However, that just doesn't happen.

To achieve this, we must not forget that we must spend a lot of time and energy. Therefore, we inevitably fall short of expectations.

As our illusion of perfection crumbles, our self-esteem tends to follow the movement. So, to save ourselves, we give up. We stop trying, as much as possible so that the next failure doesn't sting so much.

If this is something that's been undermining, you then maybe it's time to adopt a longer-term strategy of pursuing success. It should always be remembered that the best things come to those who are patient and above all ready to invest themselves fully.

When our purpose is clear, it leads to success and if we are successful, it leads to more options and opportunities.

However, when you have more options and opportunities, it leads to diffused efforts and scattered efforts undermining the very clarity that led to your success in the first place.

So, it is suggested to focus on the most important things. Take the time to evaluate and put into a perspective to focus your energy on the goal to be achieved.

It's about making the wisest investment of your time and energy, so you can be most efficient by doing only what's essential.

YOU NEED A PLAN

We always need a plan. When we're too excited to start something new, we often don't come up with a plan.

We go headlong into it thinking we can catch up as we go along, but, from experience, it ends up making us inconsistent.

Not having a plan leaves a lot of room for things to go wrong. And, after a while of struggling in the dark, the work becomes too overwhelming and then you end up giving up.

Taking the time to develop a plan allows you to take appropriate action and when to execute it.

Such an elaboration allows us to put into perspective, to follow our progress over time to obtain success.

Additionally, people tend to rely on external positive validation and praise to keep them going.

Here it must be understood that we give up so easily, because we are subconsciously programmed to survive through external validation.

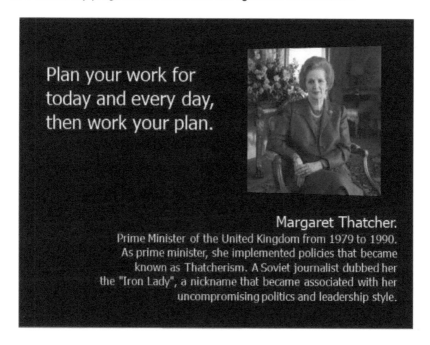

Plan your work for today and every day, then work your plan.

Margaret Thatcher.
Prime Minister of the United Kingdom from 1979 to 1990. As prime minister, she implemented policies that became known as Thatcherism. A Soviet journalist dubbed her the "Iron Lady", a nickname that became associated with her uncompromising politics and leadership style.

Humans are an extremely social species. For millennia, it was genetically advantageous to be socially approved of by those around us.

Even though we like to think we've evolved, things are still the same. To this day, we thrive on positive reinforcement from others.

It is easy to see this. It's about a boss telling you that you're doing a good job, and immediately you experience joy.

However, if that's the only thing that motivates you to go to work in the morning, then you're simply giving them complete control of your happiness.

Another aspect of having your life controlled by others is when you pay too much attention to negative comments. Don't get me wrong, we should always take the advice of others into consideration.

We are not perfect, but we can do better.

However, once the feedback becomes only negative from one source, it becomes problematic. It won't work.

Why do you persist in trying?
You should give up. These are powerful messages that are slowly but surely beginning to fester within us.

If, external negative talk is something you struggle with, then I highly recommend that you start using positive affirmations first thing in the morning.

For example, I'm good enough, I'm worth it, I'll be fine. Repeating statements like this, to yourself will be a game changer in terms of changing your perspective on your life.

So, when you remove all the positive and negative outer voices, what are you left with?
If the answer to this question is nothing, you have a problem on your hands. You need to be able to find your « why. »

Why do I want this so badly?
What do I gain from it?
Why am I here?

These are undoubtedly difficult questions to answer. However, you will have to complete this challenge.

A good way to put it all into perspective is to document your feelings whenever you're about to start a new project.

This will allow you to dig deeper into your subconscious, allowing for inner criticism, to debate situations. You will be surprised at how much you can learn about yourself when you give yourself the space to open.

This introspection will allow you to realize that you did not deserve it. This point hits a little too close. It all boils down to one thing, low self-confidence.

So, like many, we display a façade of trust. We don't want those around us to think that we are not insecure, because that would be seen as a sign of weakness.

So, when we fail, a large part of us expected it to happen.

I'm not smart enough. I knew it would be like this.

It is the negative thoughts directed by our inner critic that run amok in our brain. If you're stuck in this negative spiral, the best thing you can do is put less pressure on yourself.

You must become the biggest supporter of yourself. For example, it is about taking long walks to reflect, to put into perspective, to rekindle your positivism. You could also treat yourself to a few pleasures of life.

When negativity sets in, you tend to lie to yourself all the time. You mask yourself to pretend to be someone you think people will like.

While you might end up attracting a fake crowd, the main downside will be that you'll end up forgetting who you are under fake guises.

Have you ever been surprised to start a task because of social pressure, then six months later wondering why you're still there?

Here it is important to consider that self-knowledge is one of the greatest skills necessary for success. You can fake a personality for months or even years.

However, if that's not who you are, you will eventually give up. Instead, find out what your strengths are, then focus on them. Be the best at what you are, and success will follow!

You must understand that motivation will only take you part of the way. There will be days when you need all your energy to get out of bed. Days when it feels like the entire universe has conspired against you. These are the days when you will need consistent discipline.

Once motivation is accompanied by a good foundation of discipline, giving up becomes much more difficult.

However, it must be remembered that there is no success without failures and that you will always have to consider the factor of failure in the management of your discipline, to favor your success and thus benefit from a meaningful life.

IT NEEDS PASSION

If you could do one thing to transform your life, I would highly recommend finding something you're passionate about and doing it for a living. Learning to find your passion may not be as easy as it sounds, but it's worth the effort.

If you dread going to work, find yourself constantly lacking motivation, or find what you're doing boring and repetitive, it might be a good idea to start looking for a new job that matches your aspirations.

If you stay in your current job, not only will you feel stuck and unhappy, but you will not realize your full life potential.

Instead, imagine this.

You get up early, jumping out of bed, excited to go to work. You can put in more hours than the average person, but it doesn't seem difficult because you don't see the time spent.

You are often in this state of mind, often called « flow, » where you can lose track of space and time, getting lost in the task at hand.

Work is not seen in the ordinary sense, but as something fun, interesting, and exciting. It is not a « job, » but a passion that leads to a fulfilling life.

If you have a job that you don't like, or even hate, it will seem like a pretense. And if you never strive to find what you are passionate about, it will never be possible.

However, if you dare to ask how to find your passion, imagine the possibilities, and actually pursue what you love, because it's not just a possibility, but a probability.

How do you learn to find your passion in life?

Here are some suggestions:

1. *Is there anything you already like to do?* Do you have a hobby or like something you loved to do as a kid but never considered a job opportunity?

   Whether it's reading comics, collecting something, crafting, or building, there's probably a way to do it for a living. If there's already something you love to do, you have a head start. Now all you have to do is look for the possibilities of making money from it.

2. *Discover your passion:* when you're passionate about something, read books and magazines about it and scour the internet for more. There may be a few possibilities that will emerge for you to find possible career paths.

   Above all, do not close your mind to these subjects. Go through them until you've exhausted each topic and are happy with it. It will help you in your reflections to find your passion.

3. *Ask around:* the more possibilities you find, the more likely you are to learn how to find your long-term passion. It may mean that you spend time talking to friends and family, colleagues, or even acquaintances in your free time.

4. *Don't quit your job just yet:* if you find your calling, your passion, don't just hand in your resignation right away. It's best to keep your job while you investigate the possibilities.

   If you can exercise your passion on the side and build up some income for a few months or a year, that's even better.

   This gives you a chance to accumulate funds and if you are going into business, you will need this cash reserve.

   Also, this period will allow you to obtain or strengthen the skills you will need.

5. *Try it out first:* it is best, to actually test your new idea before embarking on a career when you are still seeking confirmation that it is indeed your true and ultimate passion.

   Do it first as a hobby or as a side job, to see if it's really your true calling.

   You may be passionate for a few days, but are you sure?
   If you're passionate for a logical period, you've probably found it.

6. *Never stop trying:* you may not be able to find your passion quickly. However, if you give up after a few days, you are sure to fail.

   Keep trying, for months if necessary, and eventually you will find it. You may have thought you had found your passion but found out months later that it wasn't for you.

   Start from scratch and find a new passion. There may be more than one passion in your life, so explore all the possibilities.

You have found your passion, but you have not managed to make a living from it?
Keep trying, and try again until you succeed.

Success doesn't come easily, so quitting early, is a sure way to fail.

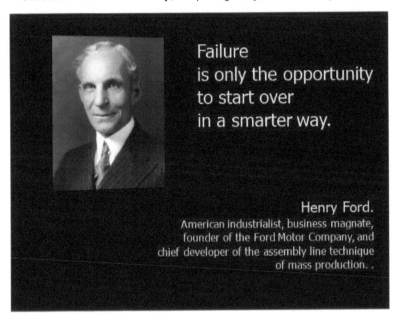

Failure
is only the opportunity
to start over
in a smarter way.

Henry Ford.
American industrialist, business magnate,
founder of the Ford Motor Company, and
chief developer of the assembly line technique
of mass production. .

The main thing, remember that all of this will take a lot of hard work, but it will be the best investment you've ever made to help you succeed and enjoy a meaningful life.

Take the time to learn how to find your passion and you will find that your days are more fulfilling and produce more happiness and long-term well-being.

VOCATION IS NECESSARY

Finding your vocation is the key to a meaningful life because it answers two timeless questions:

Who am I? Why am I here?

You see, when you understand your identity and your purpose, life takes on meaning. It is your personal vocation, the bridge between, your identity and purpose.

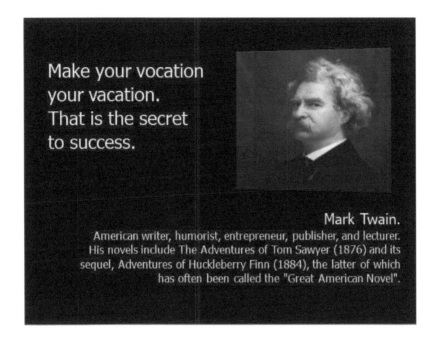

Make your vocation your vacation. That is the secret to success.

Mark Twain.
American writer, humorist, entrepreneur, publisher, and lecturer. His novels include The Adventures of Tom Sawyer (1876) and its sequel, Adventures of Huckleberry Finn (1884), the latter of which has often been called the "Great American Novel".

How do you find your vocation? Here are a few points to guide your journey.

1. *Your vocation is what you are, not what you do:* we start here, because nothing else matters if you miss this point. Your job or career is not something you're calling. For some, this news is a disappointment. For many, however, this news is liberating. You have to constantly remember that a job or a career does not define you.

2. *A vocation is to do things in their totality:* whether working as an engineer, raising a family, pastoring a church, being a politician or writing, this theme is consistent. Once you discover your calling, you let go of this naïve notion of only one way in your life. Your vocation determines your path, not the other way around.

3. *Your vocation leaves you with an aftertaste of being unqualified or outdated*: your vocation will not be the easiest. Many people miss their calling because they believe that a meaningful life is easy. The two great partners of well-being, comfort and safety tell many lies. Anything worthwhile requires sacrifice.

   When you review the most meaningful endeavors of your life, work, marriage, family, and situations in your social life come to mind. All those wounds inflicted weigh on you, demanding a lot of time and energy.

Therefore, these experiences make you a better person, more sensitive and compassionate, less prideful, and self-centered. You can have an easy life or a meaningful life, but you can't have both.

4. *A vocation always advances the world and contributes to the common good:* your vocation will do the same. Success and accomplishments are not indicators of a vocation. It is possible to be on top of the mountain with an empty heart. Most of the time you find your calling in the valley, in those spaces where the spotlight does not shine, in those areas where hope, beauty and justice are most needed.

5. *A vocation involves a community:* because your vocation always involves both receiving and giving. You can only love your neighbor if you love yourself. And you can't really love yourself unless you love your neighbor. Your vocation will inspire others, fill people with hope, or free others from the chains of injustice. In other words, your calling is never about you.

In a nutshell, a vocation is a person's response to a call beyond themselves to use their strengths and gifts to make the world a better place through service, creativity, and leadership. A call beyond oneself. To speak of a « vocation » or a « calling » is to suggest that your life is a response to something that is beyond you.

Don't forget Mark Twain and make your vacation your vocation. This is the secret of success.

Recommended reading and references
We suggest that you consult the works identified below in order to learn more about the particularities contained in this chapter.

CHURCHILL, Randolph S. WINSTON S. CHURCHILL: Young Statesman 1901-1914. Houghton, Mifflin co. 1967.

FILLIOZAT, Isabelle. L'INTELLIGENCE DU CŒUR : Confiance en soi, créativité, aisance relationnelle, autonomie. Marabout. 40-2625-8.

HUSTON, John. 50 FAÇONS DE CHANGER VOTRE VIE. Amerimag. ISBN 0-65385-575451-1.

KEEGAN, John. L'ART DU COMMANDEMENT; Alexandre, Wellington, Grant, Hitler. Editions Perrin. ISBN 2-262-00615-6.

LINOWES, F. DAVID. STRATEGIES FOR SURVIVAL: Using Business Know-how to Make our Social System Work.
AMACOM: American Management Association. ISBN 0-8144-5326-0.

PETERS, Thomas J. THRIVING ON CHAOS/ A PASSION FOR EXCELLENCE.
Random House. ISBN 0-517-14816-1.

ROBINS, Stephen. PRENEZ LA BONNE DÉCISION.
Pearson Éducation France. ISBN 2-7440-6067-4.

TRUMP, Donald J. THINK BIG AND KICK ASS.
Harper Collins. ISBN 978-0-06-154783-6.

D'ADAMO, Peter Dr. LIVE RIGHT FOR YOUR TYPE.
Putman Publisher. ISBN 0-399-14673-3.

MYERS, Marc. HOW TO MAKE LUCK: 7 Secrets Lucky People Use to Succeed.
Renaissance Books. ISBN 1-58063-058-8.

PATTON, Arch. MEN, MONEY AND MOTIVATION. McGraw-Hill, New York, Library of Congress Catalog card number: 61-7845.

POTTER, E.B. NIMITZ. Naval Institute Press. 1976

ROBBINS, Anthony. UNLIMITED POWER.
Simon & Schuster. ISBN 0-671-62146-7.

THE NEW YORK TIMES. GUIDE TO ESSENTIAL KNOWLEDGE.
St-Martin's Press. ISBN 0-312-31367-5.

TRACY, Brian. CHANGE YOUR THINKING, CHANGE YOUR LIFE. How to Unlock Your Full Potential for Success and Achievement. Willey & sons. ISBN 0-471-73538-8.

STANLEY, E. PROJECT MANAGEMENT FOR DUMMIES.
Portny. ISBN:0-7645-5283-X

TOUS PSYCHOLOGUES. Les grandes idées tout simplement.
ERPI books. ISBN : 978-2-7613-4873-7

TOUS PHILOSOPHES. Les grandes idées tout simplement.
ERPI books. ISBN : 978-2-7613-4125-7

I think
temperament
is my single
greatest asset.

I have a winning
temperament.
I know how to win.

Donald J. Trump
American politician, media
personality and
businessman who served
as the 45th president of
the United States.

DISCOVERING YOURSELF AS TO BETTER UNDERSTAND OTHERS

Whether you are an employer, an employee, coveting a position in a social organization, or cultivating family respect, you will face technical and especially social assessments.

What does evaluating a person means?

If you evaluate someone, you consider them in order to make a judgment about them. Likewise, you must go through the same process before you even consider examining another person.

This requires looking for qualities such as clear and direct communications, a sense that the person is following their own agenda rather than responding to ours, thoughtful and plausible answers to our questions such as personal and organizational background, that the person thinks of himself and transparency.

Simple, to discover yourself in order to understand others is above all to examine your own life and then when you come into contact with others try to examine their life without, however, including non-factual values such as prejudices.

During your own introspection, find what is missing, in order to take steps towards fulfillment.

This exercise will allow you to discover yourself and put yourself in a better position to understand others, because you will already have had a first experience of interpreting.

UNDERSTANDING TEMPERAMENTS

A person who is motivated to understand himself and to improve himself must distinguish among his qualities, those which generally arouse positive reactions. These are likely to improve the personal image.

However, we must analyze all our characteristics and especially those that cause excessive behavior that offends others, because if knowing our qualities and being able to use them wisely gives us an exceptional advantage, we also have all our weak points.

Understanding others and realizing that just because someone is different from you, doesn't automatically mean they're wrong.

Each temperament has strengths and weaknesses.

No one alone has all the characteristics of the same temperament. To help you explore this important aspect of temperament, ask yourself the following questions:

Do you get angry easily?
Are you resentful, shy, or too talkative?

Now review the definition of each of the four temperament types below, to familiarize yourself with this facet of human behavior assessment.

Each temperament has strengths and weaknesses. No one possesses all the characteristics of a single temperament. Everyone has their own temperament, there is no distinction between men and women.

Being able to identify the person facing you in one of the four categories will allow you to get to know them better quickly.

1. *The sanguine*: emotions are on edge. He is demonstrative and transforms each task into a pleasure.

    He loves the company of others, and each new experience has a stimulating effect on him. He does not fail to embellish reality at the first opportunity. He bonds easily and is an optimist.

    The sanguine temperament engages in lively conversation under any circumstances. It is a natural tendency for him. But, if he overdoes it, we will say that he is talkative, that he monopolizes the conversation and that he constantly interrupts others.

2. *The melancholic:* is a thoughtful person. Whether male or female, he takes everything seriously and his life is subject to order, method and the appreciation of beauty and intelligence.

    He does not rush in search of celebrations but analyzes how he could best, organize his life.

    The natural quality of the melancholic temperament is its analytical mind. This is an undeniable advantage for him. However, when this analytical mind is accentuated, it generates worries and can lead to depression.

    Sanguine and melancholic are very similar. They are both emotional, but differently; the sanguine person goes through ups and downs that last a minute, while in the melancholic ups and downs can last a month.

3. *The choleric:* is an ambitious person who normally achieves the goals he has set for himself. While the sanguine spends his time telling stories and the melancholic spend his thinking, the choleric, do what he must do.

    One can easily understand and get along with him if one observes the guidelines. Leadership is an important quality in the choleric. Considered a major asset, it can generate a tyrannical and manipulative being, when too important.

    The choleric resemble the sanguine, as they both possess open and optimistic personalities.

    However, the ambition of the choleric gives him leadership qualities and greater productivity. He speaks only when he is sure he is right. He likes to face obstacles and friends hold little place in his life. He prefers emergencies.

4. *The phlegmatic:* adapt to all situations. This is the temperament that is easiest to get along with. He attenuates the outbursts of the sanguine, refuses to be impressed by the brilliant decisions of the choleric and does not take the complicated plans of the melancholy too seriously.

    In the middle ground, the phlegmatic walk quietly alone, avoiding conflicts and decision-making. The conciliatory nature of the phlegmatic earns him the respect of all, but if he becomes too good a prince, the others will decide for him in his own life.

    While the choleric want to command everything, the phlegmatic tend to wait to be asked to act and does not seek to show off. He has many friends because his qualities lead him to maintain positive human relationships. He knows how to listen and is generally calm and in control.

Each temperament has its own unique qualities. When pushed too far, these may turn into a defect.

The person motivated to understand and improve himself must distinguish among his qualities, those which generally lead to positive reactions. These are likely to enhance his personal image.

However, it is necessary to analyze all our characteristics; especially those that cause excessive behavior and offend others, because if knowing our qualities and being able to use them wisely gives us an exceptional advantage, we also all have our weak points.

KNOWING YOURSELF

To progress and be happy, it is fundamental to know oneself. Here are some questions to ask yourself. There are many others and during your introspection you will surely add more.

- Are you a spoiled child?
- Are you self-centered?
- Do you know right from wrong?
- Are you logical?
- Do you have a critical mind?
- Are you resourceful?
- Do you take everything for granted?
- Are you ready to make the first effort?
- Do you have a sense of organization?
- Do you know how to manage priorities?
- Are you comfortable in teamwork?

You have to take a critical look at yourself and recognize that sometimes you can be wrong. This skill is the very basis of career development potential, because by knowing our weak points, we are able to find ways to improve.

In this quest for ourselves, others can be useful to us. The perspective and opinion of colleagues and clients help to get the facts straight about our work. Annual reviews as well.

Do the same comments come up every time?
What links can we make between them and what can we deduce?

We must be attentive to what the environment tells us. Personal strengths are very important in the intellectual growth of a person.

These are the attributes that define us as individuals.

Positive attributes can include being honest, kind, patient, respectful, motivated, confident, and self-disciplined. While negative attributes can include being dishonest, impulsive, cruel, selfish, and obnoxious.

Overall, personal strengths are the personal skills we use to achieve goals. These are also the skills that help us survive.

With that in mind, it's easy to see why some people see negative attributes as strengths. However, these « strengths » rarely lead to positive relationships and high levels of satisfying and lasting success.

If we really want to change our lives and take more control over our future, personal strengths are the starting point to start developing basic skills.

Generally speaking, positive attracts positive and produces better results. Thus, our main goal should be to acquire and develop positive attributes. However, since no one is perfect, allowing time to minimize weaknesses is also a good idea.

A personal inventory is a good starting point. Before acquiring and developing the skills that will allow us to succeed, we must first identify these specific skills.

A good way to do this is to create a personal inventory that outlines current strengths and weaknesses. This personal assessment will help develop an overall plan for developing the skills needed.

1. *Honesty and trust are the most important:* honesty is probably the greatest personal strength. It is also a crucial element of good character.

    - If we are not honest with ourselves, reality can become a fantasy.
    - If we are not honest with others, we cannot expect them to be honest with us.

    As mentioned before, the positive tends to attract the positive. Honest people tend to attract honest people and dishonest people tend to attract dishonest people.

    Who do you think will have the easiest path to success?

2. *Self-confidence makes us progress:* the fear of failure often holds people back. If we don't believe we can accomplish something, we may not even try.

    Nothing will change if we don't find the courage and self-confidence to overcome our fear. Keeping a positive attitude is an essential part of self-confidence and very important for finding true happiness and success.

    By focusing on what we can do rather than what we can't, it will be easier to answer the question:
    what is success as it relates to our personal life?

    Start small. Slowly gain confidence by completing a series of small tasks, remembering to acknowledge those accomplishments as successes and move on.

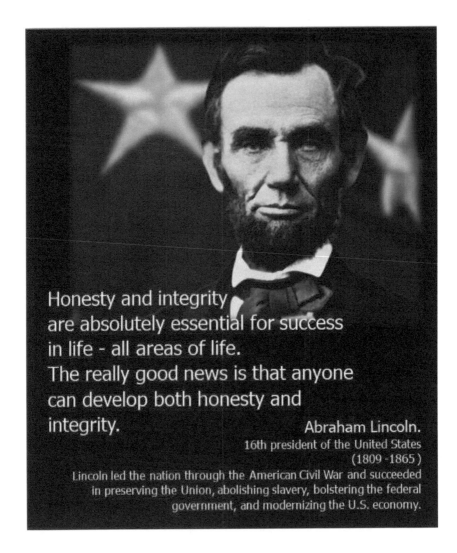

Honesty and integrity are absolutely essential for success in life - all areas of life. The really good news is that anyone can develop both honesty and integrity.

Abraham Lincoln.
16th president of the United States
(1809 -1865)

Lincoln led the nation through the American Civil War and succeeded in preserving the Union, abolishing slavery, bolstering the federal government, and modernizing the U.S. economy.

3. *Self-control empowers us:* self-discipline is empowering. By recognizing and using our « zone » of control, we learn to take charge of our actions, reactions, emotions, and attitudes to the best of our ability.

   This allows us to gain a stronger position in almost any situation. If others dictate our actions, reactions, emotions, and attitudes, we give up that power.

4. *Stress control keeps us focused on the important things:* stress management skills can help us take at least some control over every situation.

   The decrease in stress in a given situation allows us to think more clearly.

5. *Setting goals keeps us moving in the right direction:* setting personal goals not only gives us a roadmap for success, but also increases our determination and self-confidence.

   If the goal is realistic and well defined, we will be more determined to achieve it. And every step taken along the way will build the confidence to keep going.

6. *Limits keep us safe:* we have the right to set limits on our time, our energy, our money, and our emotions. Boundaries protect individuality and are a very important part of successful relationships.

7. *Personal strengths form a basis for other skills:* the strength of our people skills and our project skills are highly dependent on the strength of our personal attributes.

   - If we have self-confidence, then assertiveness and project management will become easier.
   - If we have self-control, then conflict resolution and quality work will be easier to achieve.

   On the other hand, if we are obnoxious or intimidating, cooperation with others will be more difficult. Always keep in mind that dishonesty can easily destroy relationships and lead to dismissal.

   Organization can also be difficult if we tend to be impulsive.

   Undoubtedly, personal strengths provide a solid foundation for developing both relationship skills and project skills.

NAIVETY

Naivety is not a static concept. What may seem like naivety to some people may seem like kindness to others, or among other things, optimism, good faith, and innocence.

But maybe you feel as if you have a tendency to be naive in life and you fear that it will cause you problems?

You don't want to become distrustful or pessimistic, but you can't carry on as you are, because it hurts you.

- Maybe you are naive about relationships in the blind belief that they will magically work out or do you fall in love in the blink of an eye?
- Maybe you find it hard to read others and always think the best of them no matter what.
- Maybe you tend to think that things in life are just sunshine and rainbows, when the world, unfortunately, doesn't quite work that way.
- Maybe you have even been scammed in the past.

Either way, your naivety has gotten you in trouble, and you want to become a little more knowledgeable and more informed in the face of adversity in the world, without losing that wonderful optimism and innocence you have now.

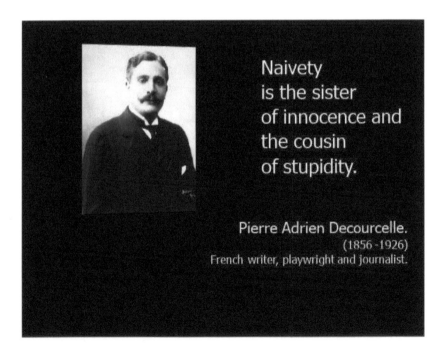

Naivety
is the sister
of innocence and
the cousin
of stupidity.

Pierre Adrien Decourcelle.
(1856 -1926)
French writer, playwright and journalist.

Here are some tips to help you say goodbye to gullibility and educate yourself a little more, without disillusioning you.

1. *Think before you speak or act:* if you think you're naive, your problem may be that you don't stop to think before you speak or act.

   You say the first thing that comes to mind or follow your instinctive reaction without taking a moment to really think about the situation.

   So, the first thing to do is to consciously slow things down and take some time to think before you say or do anything.

   It's easier said than done so start with a day. A day when we make it our duty to take a moment to reflect and look at the issue from another point of view before reacting to any situation.

   Then a week. If you keep forcing yourself to take that time and think first, sooner or later, that will become your default reaction.

2. *Don't be afraid to sit on the fence:* the fence is underrated. In our modern world, you're often expected to choose sides from the start, and if you sit on the fence, you're seen as weak or indecisive.

3. *Be overly cautious:* if you tend to be naive, then to solve a particular problem, you will have to deliberately behave too cautiously.

4. *Be more present:* naivety can often result from having your head in the clouds and not really paying attention to what is happening here and now. So, make sure you try to be more present in your day-to-day life.

5. *Listen attentively:* being a good listener is a trait to develop, but it can also be a great way to learn about a new person without revealing too much about yourself.

   Ask them questions and show them genuine interest, rather than wanting to share details about your life right away.

6. *Do research:* well-informed and conscious people can, of course, remain naive.

   But their knowledge of the world makes them less likely to take things at face value. So, try to educate yourself on the things you don't understand.

   - If you're financially naive, read up on what you need to know or even consider taking a course.

- If you have been the victim of a scam, always make sure to confirm things directly with the company or institution involved before acting. For example, if you have received a pseudo-email from your bank that you are suspicious of.
- If your problem is being naive in your relationships, examine the psychology behind why people act a certain way.
- Whenever you are unsure of something, go and research before making a decision. Life is a long lesson, and the more you learn, the more realistic and practical you will become.

7. *Keep Trusting Others:* whatever you do, don't start blaming yourself for having a confident nature. Trust is a beautiful thing.

   To be less naive is not to distrust people. It's about not making decisions quickly. It is a question of thinking well and reading situations between the lines.

   That doesn't mean you can't trust the people around you and keep looking for the good in them. Assuming someone is trustworthy, until proven otherwise should always be your default reaction, and that doesn't mean you're naive.

   Of course, there are many people in the world who are bad, but the vast majority of human beings are essentially good.

8. *Learn to recognize when someone is being dishonest:* if you often get tricked by liars, learn to spot the most common signs of being lied to.

   Most human beings are naturally confident until something happens to change that. As a general rule, and especially if we are honest with ourselves, it is in our nature to believe what others tell us, especially our loved ones.

   The most cynical would say that's gullible, but there's nothing wrong with trust being your default setting.

   Although we should trust people, and most people are inherently trustworthy, we will all encounter a serial liar at some point in our lives.

   Being able to spot one can save you from serious disappointment whether in a personal situation or in a work environment.

   We all tell white lies every day, whether for practical reasons or because no one really needs to know.

It can even be about making the other person, feel better about themselves, although this has been proven to be more of a feminine trait, whereas men are more likely to lie to feel better.

While it's a good policy to try to be honest as often as possible, being completely honest can sometimes end up hurting people's feelings or causing problems.

However, it's when bigger lies start in an important relationship, whether it's with a partner, close friend, or family member, that things can start to fall apart quite quickly.

Lies can also be a big problem in business situations and professional environments.

We're normally pretty good at naturally spotting the signs of lying, but we put those instincts aside and convince ourselves we've been wrong.

If you're worried that someone is trying to cheat on you, here are some signs you can watch for that will confirm they're not being honest with you:

a. *They begin to fidget:* when we lie, we get nervous, no matter how many times a day we do it.

   Nervous energy can be detected when someone plays with their hair, fidgets with their feet, taps their fingers on the table, or suddenly moves in their chair. This is because he subconsciously prepares to run away in case their lies are discovered.

b. *They repeat themselves:* a great way to tell if someone is telling lies is for the liar to repeat what they've already said while adding a lot more detail than you asked for. In his desperation to prove to you that he is telling the truth, he will go too far.

   A good test is to stay quiet longer than usual to see if he keeps talking. Thus, long silences will make it uncomfortable.

   Your silence will make them think you don't believe them, so they'll try harder to convince you.

   Repeating what he has already said is a sign that he is trying to fill the time while he is trying to update his lie in his head or just embellish his story further.

c.   *They are incoherent:* all that chatter they do. If they keep changing details about their story, that's your clue.

Granted, none of us has incredible memories, but if there are glaring inconsistencies in their story and it keeps changing and evolving, then you can be sure they're not being honest with you.

d.   *They cover vulnerable parts of the body:* as you probably know, lying can make you feel exposed and vulnerable.

The feeling that you might be attacked may cause you to cover your head, neck, or abdomen to protect yourself. You might also see them covering their mouths, ashamed of their words and trying to cut off communication.

e.   *Body language and words don't match:* he's telling you a sad story, yet he's smiling and cheerful, so you'll notice their body language is on high alert. Your alarm bells should ring immediately!

It is very easy to lie with words, but only the liar will be able to remain aware of their body language as they can emit signals that correspond to their lying.

f.   *Breathing changes:* when we lie, our body reacts. Our heart rate and blood flow change, which means we breathe more heavily.

Obviously, if your interlocutor has just walked up a flight of stairs, that's not an indicator you can rely on, but if he's sitting on the couch or behind his desk and his breathing changes, you have reason to suspect him.

g.   *They do not make eye contact:* some people are terrible with eye contact, but if someone who is usually happy to look you straight in the eye suddenly avoids your gaze, they may be lying between their teeth.

On the other hand, if he's making too much eye contact or more eye contact than he normally would, it could be a deliberate and quite aggressive attempt to convince you that he's being completely honest with you.

h.   *They are looking for an escape:* there is more to their eyes than just whether or not they are looking directly at you.

For example, people's eyes will look in a certain direction when they lie, but unfortunately it can be up and right, or down and right.

You need to know their typical eye pattern before you can identify the situation. So, you'll probably only notice it in people you know well.

Normally it doesn't matter what they are looking at, except if they are looking at the door it is a sign that, even if they are unaware of it, they are checking their escape route if they need to.

No one in their right mind really likes to lie or feels comfortable doing so, so their subconscious is looking for the fastest way out of the conversation.

i.   *They are getting ready to flee:* it's not just their eyes that will give you a clue. Their whole body will likely be tilted towards the door, and if they're standing, you might notice them slowly and gradually moving towards it.

If they were relaxed when you started talking to them and become tense when a certain topic is brought up, or if they tense up as soon as they see you, this is also a sign that they subconsciously prefer really to be somewhere else, and their bodies are about to flee.

j.   *They have an aggressive behavior:* if someone is getting angry or confronting you, that's a sign to take note of.

If someone starts behaving aggressively without provocation, their unconscious defense mechanisms are kicking in.

Always remember to look at the big picture.

Not all these signs will be true for everyone you meet depending on the circumstances.

If it's someone close to you, use what you know about their normal character before deciding whether you think they're lying or not.

If it's someone you're not that close to, be sure to consider the context.

For example, psychopaths don't get nervous when they lie because they won't show that they really feel guilty for the lies they tell.

Ultimately, just as you instinctively act in certain ways when lying, you are also able to instinctively pick up on signs in others.

Listen to your intuition and you can rarely go wrong.

9. *Listen to your instincts:* even if you tend to be naive, gullible, or innocent, there's probably often a feeling deep inside that tells you something's wrong.

Rather than just putting it aside, it's important for you to check out that feeling and think about where it is coming from.

Don't be afraid to let your instincts guide you from time to time. It might not always be right, but it's there for a reason.

10. *Be open to meeting new people:* your naivety may be due to the fact that you have led a rather sheltered life, surrounded by many people who think exactly the same way as you.

If this is your case, you should be open to making friends with people from different backgrounds or cultures.

If you don't live in a very diverse community, it may be more difficult, but the internet can be a great way to mingle with people, different from you.

And if you live in a multicultural place with people from all sorts of socio-economic backgrounds and with different beliefs, then take advantage of that and be open to making friends with those who don't look like you, don't speak or don't think like you.

11. *Go ahead and find out about life:* naivety is often a trait of people who lack life experience. If you don't experience the world firsthand, it's inevitable that you'll be a little gullible or innocent.

Normally people become less naive with age, but you can help yourself by simply saying, yes to life.

Try new things, volunteer to help those less fortunate than you, and learn about new cultures.

Learn about the history and realities and injustices of the society you live in, look at things from the perspective of others, and embrace all things in life whether good or bad, so that you can have a perspective on life.

PERSONAL INVENTORY

A personal inventory is not complete without an introspection regarding your contribution to work and in your social environment.

Depending on whether you belong to the private sector or the public service, whether you are an employee or a boss, you must assess your own performance by asking yourself the following questions:

1. Study the quality of your work as a whole and its constant improvement.
2. Study the degree of creativity according to the level of leeway, in order to have the effect of encouraging participation and above all of increasing your contribution.
3. Investigate customers, citizens, and peer feedback.
4. Study reactions to negative and positive comments.
5. Study reactions about accepting responsibilities.
6. Study the income generated by sales or the quality of service provided to citizens.
7. Study your social behavior and the value you bring to your family and to society in general.

Your current successes and your future successes stem from your life experiences that you have developed through prolonged disciplined effort. You have spent so much time focusing on these areas of your life.

Assessing your personal strengths allows you to adjust your skills at work and in your life environment, in order to be able to perform certain tasks and activities at a higher level to add value to your life.

Now, how can you use your strengths to your advantage and how can you turn your weaknesses into strengths?

To do this, it is essential to recognize and accept your weaknesses. You can't turn a weakness into a strength if you're busy denying that the weakness exists. To help you, get advice from someone you trust.

Knowing your own strengths and weaknesses gives you a better understanding of yourself and how you function.

For example, if you're considering career options, you'll be able to narrow down specific job fields based on areas you know you're good at. It also helps you grow more.

Also, knowing your strengths and weaknesses can help you, better manage others during exchanges.

COMPETENCE

In order to fully understand the meaning of the word « competence, » it is necessary to focus on two elements, namely psychological competence and technical skills.

One does not go without the other.

Often, we focus on technical skills and neglect psychological skills for fear of creating an atmosphere of instability in the moment.

A person is psychologically competent as long as they can understand the rights, responsibilities, risks, or benefits of decisions and the potential consequences of what they decide.

Also, she has the ability to understand or communicate with others, verbally or otherwise.

Technical skills are the abilities and knowledge needed to perform specific tasks. They are practical and often relate to mechanical, computers, mathematical or scientific tasks.

Some examples include knowledge of programming languages, design programs, mechanical equipment, or tools to accomplish tasks.

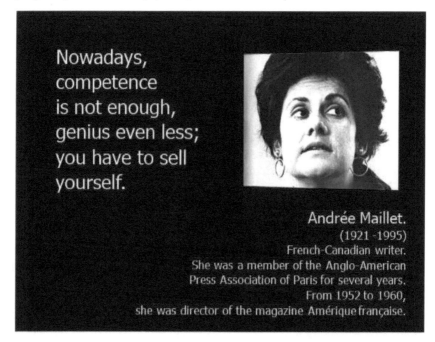

Nowadays, competence is not enough, genius even less; you have to sell yourself.

Andrée Maillet.
(1921 -1995)
French-Canadian writer.
She was a member of the Anglo-American
Press Association of Paris for several years.
From 1952 to 1960,
she was director of the magazine Amérique française.

Whether you're an employee or a boss, well-defined psychological and technical skills can help foster a strong company culture to build a better-aligned workforce to establish key competitive differences.

They also help ensure consistent performance standards and a good working atmosphere, which can help with employee recruitment and retention.

Psychological skills, or mental skills, are tools for the mind.

This includes skills such as positive self-talk, confidence building, goal setting and achieving the most productive mindset along with many other skills.

Improving your psychological skills can improve your job results and your overall well-being.

Psychological skills commonly examined in social and work settings are motivation, self-reliance, positivism, realism, being calm and relaxed in the heat of the moment, ready for action, high energy, determined, alert, focused, confident and responsible.

BEHAVIOR CHANGE

A change in behavior can be triggered by a lack of valid information, an unpleasant situation, a change in the work process, a personal situation, or a different social context than usual.

When faced with a situation that undermines the workplace, it is always important to take the time to assess whether you are an employee or a boss.

Behavioral changes are not only aimed at the workplace, but also at social and family activities.

If there is some level of overflow, one should be aware of the situation and contact a medical professional or even the public authorities.

Just think of certain mentalities and personalities, of hot tempers, of states of mind and soul, of the particular personal reaction to an action of another person.

A change in behavior must be evaluated by those in charge and the person leading the change in behavior.

A person wishing for success following a behavioral lapse will want to put things into perspective and quickly rectify the situation. The observation of a problem in good faith usually initiates the acknowledgment of the error followed by apologies and a return to the ranks.

However, rudeness, physical and verbal brutality never has a place and must be addressed immediately, in order to protect moral and social integrity.

If the person causing the behavior change challenges the situation, the approach to assessing this should be a tricky task.

To do this, it is necessary to consider a structured approach, in order to identify the problem. Confrontation without relevant information will only add fuel to the fire. Here, it is a question of taking a step back by mentioning to the people involved that all points of view will be considered shortly.

It is essential to be open-minded and understand the situation well from the beginning regarding the problem to be solved. We must first put into perspective the event that requires the intervention.

What kind of behaviors needs to change and why is it necessary?

To do this, it is necessary to examine the circumstances of the behavior guided by evidence of what works, and which is based on previous positive experiences.

However, while maintaining a perspective of the situation, the assessment in question should consider that it measures the actions taken by the person concerned, are based on evidence put into context.

Therefore, it is necessary to ensure an understanding based on existing data, but also on the context of the situation, in order to plan an intervention.

Often there is a rush to conclude when dealing with superficial data, without taking the time to examine the context of the situation, the interactions of other work processes, of colleagues involved, of personal and social situations.

Once this analysis of the facts has been completed, it is important to evaluate the effects of this change in behavior on the anticipated success you want for the company and the social peace to be maintained.

Before initiating the intervention, it is always preferable to ask questions, on the relevance of the intervention, the coherence of the measurement of the intervention, if the intervention will help the objectives of success and the impact on the environment.

During the intervention meeting, it will be important to mention that the meeting must be friendly and that the goal put forward must be focused on the success of the company, the people involved and social peace.

SELF-SABOTAGE

Have you ever somehow found yourself in the same place repeatedly?
Why do I keep doing this?
Why does this keep happening to me?

Do you ask yourself these questions, when you feel trapped in situations that create problems in your life and prevent you from achieving your goals?

If this sounds familiar, you might be sabotaging yourself.

Self-sabotage refers to behaviors or ways of thinking that hold you back and prevent you from accomplishing.

Self-sabotage happens when you do certain things that were appropriate in a context but are no longer necessary.

In other words, these behaviors helped you adapt to a past situation, such as a traumatic childhood or a toxic relationship, in order to survive the challenges you faced.

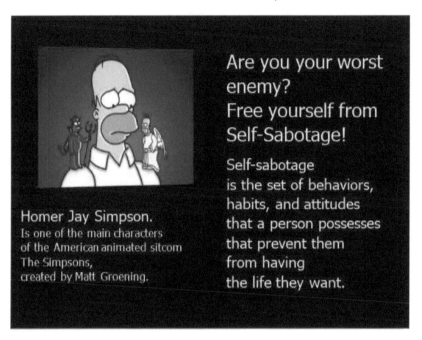

Homer Jay Simpson.
Is one of the main characters of the American animated sitcom The Simpsons, created by Matt Groening.

Are you your worst enemy?
Free yourself from Self-Sabotage!

Self-sabotage is the set of behaviors, habits, and attitudes that a person possesses that prevent them from having the life they want.

They may have appeased you or defended you at the time. However, these methods of adaptation, when situations and circumstances evolve or simply change, they can cause difficulties.

Some of the major contributing factors, for example, experiences established in our early relationships are often repeated in relationships throughout life. We are attached to these experiences. They mean something to us and it's hard to let them go.

Now suppose you had parents who never paid much attention to you unless they were angry.

You know it's not a good thing to make people angry, however, this experience for you is compelling because of this parenting. For you, making people angry is the only way to generate interest, so you feel stuck in this life experience where it is tempting, even attractive, to make people angry with you.

This can appear, for example, in your work, where you fail to show up on time. At first, your supervisor forgives and encourages you, but as time goes on and you're still not on time, your supervisor gets angry and eventually fires you.

There is also the dynamic of past relationships.

If you haven't felt supported or heard when asking for what you needed in past relationships, romantic or otherwise, you may struggle to communicate effectively in your present relationships.

Whether you had an abusive partner or a partner who simply didn't care about your thoughts and feelings, you may not have felt able to express yourself.

You have remained silent to protect yourself from anger, rejection, and other negative experiences. But as a result, you have not learned to defend your needs and rights.

You need to put everything into perspective, because present situations are different from those of the past. It can be difficult to get out of destructive situations that are similar or not, but it is always better to ask for help than to continue the destruction of your life.

FEAR OF FAILURE

Everyone hates to fail, but for some people, failure poses such a significant psychological threat that their motivation to avoid failure outweighs their motivation to succeed.

This fear of failure leads them to unconsciously sabotage their chances of success in various ways.

Failure can elicit feelings such as; disappointment, anger, frustration, sadness, regret, and confusion which, while unpleasant, are usually not enough to trigger a full-fledged fear of failure.

Indeed, the word is somewhat of a misnomer, as it is not a failure per se that underlies the behavior of those who suffer from it. On the contrary, the fear of failure is essentially a fear of shame.

People who fear failure are motivated to avoid failure not because they cannot handle the basic emotions of disappointment, anger, and frustration that accompany such experiences, but because failure also makes them feel deep shame.

Shame is a toxic psychological emotion, because without feeling bad about our actions « the culpability » or our efforts « the regret, » shame makes us feel bad about who we are.

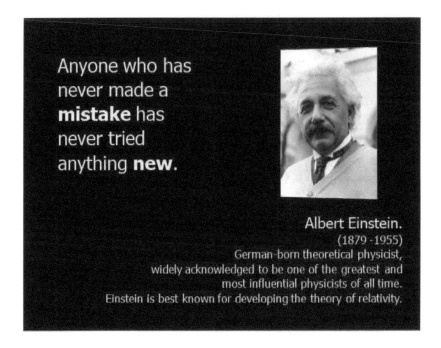

Anyone who has
never made a
mistake has
never tried
anything **new.**

Albert Einstein.
(1879-1955)
German-born theoretical physicist,
widely acknowledged to be one of the greatest and
most influential physicists of all time.
Einstein is best known for developing the theory of relativity.

Shame is central to our ego, our identity, our self-esteem, and our feelings of emotional well-being.

The damaging nature of shame makes it urgent for those who fear failure to avoid the psychological threats associated with failure by finding unconscious ways to lessen the implications of potential failure.

For example, buying unnecessary new clothes for a job interview instead of researching the company. This allows them to use the excuse of simply not having had time to prepare well.

There are several signs to help you grasp the meaning of the fear of failure.

We experience all these things to some degree.

1. Failing causes, you to worry about what other people think of you.
2. Failure makes you worry about your ability to pursue the future you want.
3. Failing makes you fear that people will lose interest in you.
4. A failure makes you worry about your intelligence or your abilities.
5. Failing makes you fear disappointing people whose opinion you value.
6. You tend to tell people in advance that you don't believe you can succeed, in an attempt to lower their expectations.
7. Once you fail at something, you find it hard to imagine what you could have done differently to succeed.

8. You often have last-minute headaches, stomach aches, or other physical symptoms that keep you from finishing your preparation.
9. You are often distracted by tasks that prevent you from completing your preparation and which, in hindsight, were not as urgent as they seemed at the time.
10. You tend to procrastinate and run out of time to complete your preparation properly.

You may want to investigate further through further reading on this topic or speaking to a mental health professional.

What to do when you fear failure?
The main problem with fear of failure is that it tends to operate at an unconscious level.

For example, you might think it's essential to finish writing your month-end report because you promised to send it by the end of the weekend, even though you're also on the point of completing a sale that will positively affect this month-end report.

To help you overcome and conquer failure, it is important to be willing to believe that failure makes you feel both fear and shame. Also, finding people you trust with whom you can discuss your feelings will help.

Bringing these feelings to the surface can prevent you from expressing them through unconscious efforts. Getting comfort from people, you trust can boost your sense of self-esteem while minimizing the risk of disappointing them.

Also, another good way is to focus on the aspects under your control. Identify the aspects of the task or preparation that you have control over and focus on those.

Think about ways to reframe aspects of the task that seem out of your control so that you can regain control.

Self-sabotaging behaviors can also arise from your need to control a situation. When you are in control, you may feel safe, strong, and ready to face anything that comes your way.

Certain types of self-sabotage provide this sense of control. What you're doing may not be good for your mental health or your relationships, but it helps you stay in control when you're feeling vulnerable.

Take the example of timing. Maybe you want to postpone a research paper because deep down you're worried that you won't write it as well as you hoped.

You know, writing it at the last minute, won't help quality, but it will give you control over that outcome because you chose to write it at the last minute.

It can also happen in relationships. Opening up to someone emotionally can feel extremely vulnerable.

By keeping things in, you hold what seems to have the upper hand. But in the end, you don't reap the rewards of building intimacy by not sharing your vulnerabilities.

EMBRACE YOUR EVOLUTION

Behaviors that have worked for you in the past usually don't help you once your circumstances change. In fact, they often cause harm. But you keep doing them because they've already worked well for you.

The good news is that self-sabotage patterns can be disrupted with a little effort.

It's not always easy to examine your actions deeply enough to notice patterns of self-sabotage.

Admitting that we sabotage ourselves is painful. No one is rushing to that conclusion. We tend to avoid it for as long as possible until we have no choice but to face it.

If you feel comfortable examining your behavior for factors, it helps to examine situations in your life where things seem to be going wrong on a regular basis.

Are there any common factors that stand out?

For example, maybe you pull away from a relationship once your partner says, I love you, starting to look for futile arguments. Or maybe you usually quit your job just before the annual review.

Find out what triggers these situations. Once you figure out how you're sabotaging yourself, take note.

What makes you feel compelled to act?

Perhaps an angry tone in the voice of your partner, boss, or co-worker reminds you of a shouting match in your youth. Or maybe you withdraw into yourself, even though that anger is not directed at you.

It is also suggested to observe other triggers that often set in motion self-sabotaging behaviors, such as boredom, fear, or when things are going well.

Practicing mindfulness or becoming non-judgmentally aware of your present-moment thoughts and behaviors can also help.

Whenever you discover a trigger, try to find an interesting reaction or two to replace that self-sabotaging behavior.

Train yourself to be comfortable with failure. It is normal to fear rejection, failure, and other emotional pain. These things aren't usually fun to deal with, so you need to take steps to avoid them.

This becomes problematic when the actions you take involve self-sabotage. You may avoid unwanted experiences, but you may also miss out on things you really want, like strong relationships, close friends, or career opportunities.

To manage this fear, strive to accept the realities of failure and pain. This is a difficult task, and it will not happen overnight.

Start small by trying to recognize the next setback, whether it's a relationship that's soured or an opportunity for advancement you might miss at work.

Maybe the end of that relationship means you can finally start a new relationship, or a missed work opportunity means you'll have a little more free time to get back to your hobbies.

If you notice certain situations keep popping up in your relationships, talk about them with people you trust.

Also, you could try telling your partner that you want the relationship to work, but you are afraid it will fail.

If you seem to be closing in on yourself or pulling away, it's because you're worried about losing her. Mention that you're trying to get by, but you don't want it to sound as if you don't care, in the meantime.

Another tip is to simply talk out loud to yourself when you're alone, this will help put the self-sabotage situation you're concerned about, into perspective.

This could cause this action, not to occur. Also, the result of this reflection certainly can become a powerful learning experience in a precarious situation and thus put you on the avoidance path of self-sabotage.

Self-sabotage can occur when looking for a way out. It is important to identify what you really want. Ordinarily, self-sabotaging behavior suggests that something in your life is not working for you.

Getting to know yourself better and exploring what you really want out of life can help prevent this kind of self-sabotage. It's not enough to know what you want; you also need to respect and support yourself enough to work for it.

It's not always easy to recognize and stop certain self-sabotaging behaviors, especially in situations that you've been inflicting on yourself for years.

If your efforts to rectify certain behaviors have worked for a while or simply have not worked, it is suggested that you seek help. Therapy may be a good option.

There is no shame in needing professional support. Therapy can be particularly useful for self-sabotage, as at some point you might even unwittingly begin to sabotage the therapy process.

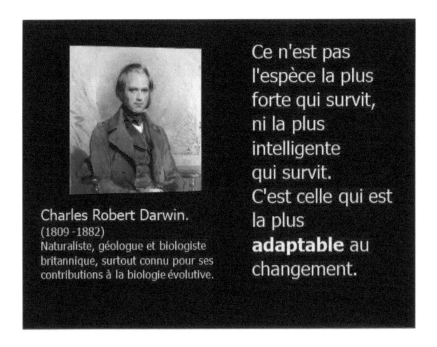

Charles Robert Darwin.
(1809 - 1882)
Naturaliste, géologue et biologiste britannique, surtout connu pour ses contributions à la biologie évolutive.

Ce n'est pas l'espèce la plus forte qui survit, ni la plus intelligente qui survit. C'est celle qui est la plus **adaptable** au changement.

A good therapist will notice this and help bring the problem to the surface, which you were probably unaware of.

Self-sabotaging behaviors are often deeply rooted and difficult to recognize. Once you recognize them, notice how you come to terms with a situation that may be difficult to accept.

In all faith, keep in mind that by recognizing these behaviors, you have taken the first step towards change. And you don't have to do it alone. Friends, relatives, and trained therapists can all offer support.

UNDERSTAND OTHERS

We need to go beyond visual and superficial judgments.

How do we assess a person's character?

In general, people first assess themselves visually, not only by skin color, but also by height, weight, gender, hair and eye color, eye shape, car driving, the inhabited house, etc.

It is our simplest and default way of forming an opinion about the qualities of others.

Second, we look at superficial aspects like a person's education, relatives, job, people they associate with, where they live, the church they belong to, their political party.

In the third line, what we find out when we talk to a person. Usually, we react emotionally to people when we talk to them. This emotional reaction is not always helpful.

Often, we feel positive and warm towards people who are outgoing, energetic, sometimes loud, or invasive.

It's about our automatic emotional reaction to how they present themselves and what we learned in childhood about how to conduct relationships.

We may decide that these people have high levels of integrity, reliability, and kindness, all from our automatic emotional reactions, when in fact, they may not possess any of these attributes.

On the other hand, shy people, who are less exuberant, low-key, and quieter, may evoke a different emotional reaction, making us feel untrustworthy.

Always put yourself in the other person's shoes.
Give up your opinions, your judgments for a while in order to understand it.
Many conflicts can thus be avoided.

Dalaï-Lama.
Tenzin Gyatso, 14th Dalai Lama.
Spiritual leader of the Gelug or "Yellow Hat" school of Tibetan Buddhism, the newest and most dominant of the four major schools of Tibetan Buddhism.

Automatically and emotionally evaluating them as cold, less kind, and having lower integrity, when this may be an inaccurate assessment.

Since our discernment of the character of others is automatic and emotionally driven, we fail to consider the realities of another person's situation or circumstances.

So, if we only use the emotional approach to judge others, it can often result in assessments that can be more or less biased. Because living automatically under emotional conditioning, shapes our lives and our relationships without some level of filtration.

To assess the character of another, we must recognize the personalities that we and the others have.

Once we know this, we can predict our future reactions, thoughts, and behaviors with high levels of consistency and probability. We will have a way of judging the character reasonably well.

To better determine the character, we can do better with another approach. We can look at people as they really exist in their personality. To make your life easier, let's base ourselves on two types of personalities: « omnipotent » and « powerless. »

Below, you will find seven-character traits that allow you to evaluate people more accurately:

1. *Attitude:* the attitude of people with omnipotent type personalities reveals that they have a great sense of pride and can also be pretentious.

   People with helpless personalities display arrogant attitudes and may show outrage when questioned.

2. *Personal standard:* the personal standard of omnipotent personalities is to strive for perfection. Nothing less will do. They demonstrate strong problem-solving skills and try to think through how to control and resolve various situations that arise.

   Powerless personalities display personal standards of opportunism. They take the path of least resistance. They focus on their personal needs and desires.

3. *Support requests:* omnipotent personalities avoid dependence on others and enjoy others' dependence on them. As a result, such omnipotent personalities rarely ask others for help.

   Their mantra, I can do it myself. They are looking for relationships that feel no appreciation for the benefits received but give much to others.

   Helpless personalities love to be looked after by others and depend on others to get things done for them.

   In fact, they excel at demanding that others meet their needs and may not be grateful when others meet their needs.

4. *The value system:* people with omnipotent personalities may put themselves down and have inflated esteem for people who demonstrate few true attributes or accomplishments. Powerless personalities value themselves highly and place a lower value on others.

5. *Self-esteem:* the self-esteem of omnipotents can suffer despite a fierce work ethic and their own accomplishments. Powerless personalities show high and even inflated self-esteem, even when they have few real accomplishments.

6. *The way to commit to others:* omnipotent personalities are steadfast and display a way of commitment to others that is so loyal and, devoted that those commitments endure even when relationships fizzle out.

Powerless personalities engage conditionally. Based on changing whims, they will end their relationship at the slightest disappointment.

7. *Scope of interests:* omnipotent personalities have an extremely broad field of interest. They have many and varied passions, especially those that perceive any injustice done to others.

The range of interests of powerless personalities is much narrower. Their passions are uniquely personal and reflect a unique vision.

Now you have a way to gauge another person's character unfolding by measuring these traits. You can observe the values, thoughts, interests, functioning and style of interaction of your interlocutors.

Also, you can circumvent your instinctive and emotional reactions that stem from what you see, what you learn superficially, and your automatic and emotional way of judging people.

This effort will allow you to go beyond visual and superficial judgments.
You will be able to replace these unnecessary and inaccurate instinctive and emotional reactions by meticulously observing and evaluating people's standards for their attitudes, their desire or refusal of emotional support, their value system, their self-esteem, their way of being, commitment to others and the extent of their interests in life.

Recommended reading and references
We suggest that you consult the works identified below in order to learn more about the particularities contained in this chapter.

ABRASHOFF, Michael D. IT'S YOUR SHIP. Warner Books. ISBN 0-446-52911-7.

BLIWAS, Ron. THE C STUDENT'S GUIDE TO SUCCESS.
MJF Books. ISBN13: 978-1-56731-952-1.

BYHAM, W. C., Ph.D. & COX, Jeff Heroz. EMPOWER YOURSELF, YOUR COWORKERS, YOUR COMPANY. Harmony Books. ISBN 0-517-59860-4.

FERNANDEZ-ARMESTO, Felipe. IDEAS THAT SHAPED MANKIND. Oxford University. Barnes & Noble's Publishing. ISBN 0-7607-7826-4.

GEORGE Bill. FINDING YOUR TRUE NORTH. Willey. ISBN:978-0-470-26136-1

PETERS, Thomas J. & WATERMAN, Robert. LE PRIX DE L'EXCELLENCE : Les secrets des meilleures entreprises. Inter Éditions. ISBN 2 7296 0025 6.

PETERS, Thomas J. RE-IMAGE! Business Excellence in a Disruptive Age.
Dorling Kinderly. ISBN 0-7894-9647-X.

PETERS, Thomas J. TALENT: Essentials. DK Publishing. ISBN 0-7566-1056-7.

PETERS, Thomas J. DESIGN: Essentials. DK Publishing. ISBN 0-7566-1054-0.

PETERS, Thomas J. TRENDS: Essentials. DK Publishing. ISBN 0-7566-1057-5.

PETERS, Thomas J. THE LITTLE BIG THINGS: 163 Ways to Pursue Excellence.
Harper Studios. ISBN 978-0-06-189408-4.

PEACH, Robert W. THE PROJECT MANAGEMENT Handbook.
CEEM Information Services, Fairfax, Virginia, 1995. ISBN 1-88333.7.

PORTNY, Stanley E. CPMP: PROJECT MANAGEMENT FOR DUMMIES.
Hungry Minds. ISBN 0-7645-5283-X.

RIES, Al & TROUT, Jack. MARKETING WARFARE.
McGraw-Hill, 1986. ISBN 0-452-25861-8.

ROGERS, David. LES STRATÉGIES MILITAIRES APPLIQUÉES AUX AFFAIRES.
Press Pocket. ISBN 2-266-03266-6.

SAMSON, Guy. L'ENFANT-TYRAN, SAVOIR DIRE NON À L'ENFANT-ROI.
Québécor. ISBN 2-7640-0851-1.

SCHWARTZ, J. LA MAGIE DE VOIR GRAND. Éditions Sélect. ISBN 2-89132-214-2.

SMITH. Hyrum W. THE 10 BEST NATURALLAWS OF SUCCESSFUL TIME AND LIFE
MANAGEMENT. Warner Books. ISBN: 0-446-51741-0

For success,
attitude
is equally
as important
as ability.

Walter Scott, 1st Baronet.
(1771 – 1832)
Scottish historical novelist, poet, playwright and historian.
Notably the novels Ivanhoe, Rob Roy, Waverley, Old Mortality and
the narrative poems The Lady of the Lake and Marmion.

A QUESTION OF ATTITUDE

Even though you love your job and your family, sometimes things get negative. You can get bogged down by an angry customer or a mischievous child, a miscalculation, or a feeling of lack of productivity.

While it's easy to fall into a slump based on a negative experience, it can be just as easy to redirect your thinking to a more positive experience.

Having a good attitude means being optimistic about situations, interactions, and yourself. People with a good attitude remain hopeful and see the best even in the most difficult situations.

In contrast, those with bad attitudes may be more pessimistic and disagreeable and generally expect the worst outcome in difficult situations.

The attitude you choose will determine your chances of success both at work and in your personal life.

A POSITIVE ATTITUDE

Your attitude determines how you live your life. Even if, at a given time, your choices of action are limited, your choices regarding your attitude are not. Always opt for a positive attitude and thus you will better manage the stress of life.

If you have a positive mental mindset, you can deal with stress and negative situations in a much healthier way. A positive attitude makes you happier and more resilient, it improves your relationships and even increases your chances of success in any endeavor.

Having a positive attitude naturally leads to a more optimistic outlook on life. Rather than thinking the grass is greener on the other side of the fence, you'll feel as if like you're already on greener grass. You will see the positive side of most situations.

Surely you will face disappointments and failures more easily. They'll still be tough, but you'll get through it and bounce back. Not only that, but you'll be able to accept that things happened the way they did, rather than being in denial.

Those with a negative attitude will dwell and ruminate on negative events.

The positive thinker
sees the invisible,
feels the intangible,
and achieves
the impossible.

The Right Honourable
Sir Winston Churchill.
(1874 – 1965)
British statesman, soldier and writer who served as Prime
Minister of the United Kingdom from 1940 to 1945, during
the Second World War, and again from 1951 to 1955.

Also, you will be more sensitive and understanding towards others. With a positive attitude, you learn to see the thoughts behind people's actions and why they may have acted the way they did. Rather than jumping to a harmful conclusion, you will be able to understand where people are coming from.

You will be more grateful. A positive attitude will teach you to be grateful for the good things in your work and in your life. You will approach each day with an appreciative mindset.

Obviously, having a positive attitude is hugely beneficial, but it's easier said than done. Having a positive attitude makes you more creative and can help you make better decisions.

To top it off, there are studies that show that people with a positive attitude live longer than their embittered counterparts.

Below, you will find some tips for creating and maintaining a positive attitude:

1. *Get into a morning routine:* how you start your day sets the tone for the rest of the day. Make sure you have a morning routine that boosts your attitude and puts you in a good mood so you can start your day off right.

You can start your day by dragging yourself out of bed at the last minute, rushing to get ready, then running out the door with a donut in one hand and your briefcase in the other.

Or you can start your day with good morning habits. Wake up early. Early risers reap many benefits. Some of these benefits include:

- Being able to follow your morning routine calmly and quietly instead of being rushed.
- Take time to review the planned milestones for the day and get in the right frame of mind. The quiet morning hours are a great time to get things done.
- Exercise daily, it will wake up your body and mind.

2. *Carry an attitude of happiness with you:* instead of waiting for outside things to make you happy, be happy and then watch how that influences the things happening around you.

   That is, instead of telling yourself that something good must happen first, and then you will be happy, be happy first. Happiness is an attitude, not a situation.

3. *Taste the little pleasures:* life is made up of small victories and simple pleasures. With the right mental mindset, watch the sunset, eat an ice cream cone, and walk barefoot on the grass are all you need to be filled with joy.

4. *Smile:* a little smile will give you an instant boost. Try smiling for a minute while thinking about a happy memory or the last thing that made you smile.

   The smile releases endorphins and serotonin, also called well-being hormones. It is much easier to adopt a positive attitude when the chemicals released by your body promote well-being.

5. *Transpose positivity in your brain:* read books with a positive message, listen to music with uplifting lyrics, and watch movies in which the central character's optimism helps him overcome obstacles and win, despite difficulties. Improve your attitude for the better by downloading as much positivity into your brain as possible.

6. *Take your responsibilities:* at any moment, your attitude can be one of a victim or a creator. The first step in moving from the victim mode to creator mode is to take responsibility.

This is the attitude of a creator; I create my life, I am responsible for myself, and I am the master of my destiny.

7. *Have a Zen attitude:* think of life not as something that happens to you, but as something is happening for you. Look at every difficult situation, person or event as a lesson that has been introduced into your life to teach you something.

   The next time you ask yourself: Why is this happening to me? Choose a Zen attitude instead. Ask yourself: am I supposed to learn or take advantage of this? How will this help me grow and become a better, more enlightened being?

8. *Be proactive:* a reactive person lets others and outside events determine how they will feel. A proactive person decides how they will feel no matter what is happening around them. Be proactive in choosing your attitude and maintaining it throughout the day, regardless of what the day may bring.

9. *Change your thoughts:* positive thoughts lead to a positive attitude, while negative thoughts lead to a negative attitude. Changing your attitude is as simple as hitting the « pause » button on what you're thinking and choosing to have different thoughts.

10. *Have a purpose:* having a purpose in life gives you a fixed point on the horizon to focus on, so you can stay stable amid life's fluctuations and challenges. Giving meaning and purpose to your life by knowing why you are here will do wonders for your attitude.

11. *Focus on the good:* in order to have a positive attitude, focus on the good. Focus on the good in yourself, the good in your life, and the good in others.

12. *Stop expecting life to be easy:* the truth is, sometimes life gets tough for all of us. It can even be painful. But you are brave and resourceful, and you can handle it. Know that sometimes things won't be easy and embrace the attitude that you have what it takes to face whatever life throws at you.

13. *Keep your enthusiasm:* enthusiastic people have a positive attitude towards life. Have a list of ways to boost your enthusiasm, for times when you feel your zest for life is running out.

    For example, positive thoughts lead to a positive attitude, while negative thoughts lead to a negative attitude. Changing your attitude is as simple as hitting the « pause » button on what you're thinking and choosing to have different thoughts.

Being enthusiastic will help you maintain the attitude that life is good, and you are lucky to be alive.

14. *Renounce the attitude that you are entitled to everything:* stop demanding that everything be due to you. Your attitude should always be.

- It's up to me to get what I want.
- Good things come to those who work hard.
- I adapt easily and quickly to changes.
- I keep going even when the going gets tough.

15. *Visualize:* when things don't go your way, keep a positive attitude by visualizing yourself succeeding and achieving your goals.

16. *Stop complaining:* complaining about everything and anything does not encourage a positive attitude. When you complain, you say negative things about a person, place, or event, without offering a solution to resolve the situation. Instead of complaining, do this:

- Remove yourself from the situation.
- Change your perspective on the situation.
- Suggest a possible solution.
- Accept that you can't do anything to change the situation and that complaining about it only promotes negativity.

Complaining constantly leads to a bad attitude. So, stop complaining. Instead, start looking for solutions or accepting what cannot be changed.

17. *Watch your sayings:* use positive words when talking to yourself. Positive self-talk can boost your willpower and help lift your spirits when you need to complete a difficult task. Plus, it can calm you down when you're worried or anxious.

18. *Use the power of humor:* people who know how to laugh at themselves and at life's nonsense have a terrific attitude. Your sense of humor is a powerful tool, and you can use it to improve your mood and emotional state at any time.

When something goes wrong, ask yourself: what's funny about it?
Such a perspective will have a positive effect on your attitude.

19. *Use gratitude to improve your attitude:* when you focus on what's wrong in your life, what you don't have, or what you lack, adjust your attitude by feeling grateful.

    An attitude of gratitude benefits all aspects of your life: being grateful improves your health, mood, relationships, job satisfaction, and more.

    If you need an attitude change, just think of all the things to be grateful for.

20. *Develop an attitude of curiosity:* the best way to approach any situation is to be open to what you can learn from it by being curious.

    Curiosity gives you a present moment orientation that is similar to mindfulness. Being curious about a situation allows you to experience it more fully. Additionally, curiosity will help you approach uncertainty in your daily life with a positive attitude.

21. *Look for people with a positive attitude:* positive attitude is contagious when you feel as if like you need an attitude boost, find people with a good attitude, and find an excuse to hang out with them. Their positive attitudes can only rub off on you and you can face the world with renewed optimism.

Your attitude towards life determines life's attitude towards you. The tips above will help you always maintain a positive attitude. Live a better life, by always adopting a positive attitude.

A NEGATIVE ATTITUDE

Sometimes bad things happen without anyone being at fault. Sure, some misfortunes can be someone else's fault, but that's not always the case.

If you tend to find fault elsewhere whenever you encounter difficulties, it may be helpful to take a closer look at your role in what happened.

Suppose your partner, has relationship behaviors that affect both of you.

You decide that she or he will not change, and you break your partnership. You feel good about the breakup because their refusal to change, has held you back from moving forward to success. Trustworthy people around you agree that you did the right thing.

However, if you don't take the time to explore how you might have contributed to some of the problems in this relationship, you are sabotaging your chance to learn and grow from the experience.

Bruce Lee.
(1940 – 1973)
Hong Kong and American martial artist, martial arts instructor, actor, director, screenwriter, producer, and philosopher.

Do not allow negative thoughts to enter your mind for they are weeds that strangle confidence.

Let's explore the pitfalls and possible situations you may encounter:

1. *You choose to leave when things aren't going well:* there's nothing wrong with moving on from situations that don't meet your needs.

    This may sometimes be the best option. But it's usually wise to take a step back and ask yourself if you've really put in the effort first.

    Maybe you don't seem to be holding down a job for very long. You left a job because your supervisor treated you unfairly. You were laid off from another job due to overstaffing. Or you quit a job because of toxic co-workers, etc.

    These are valid reasons, but such widespread situations might raise something more.

    Doubts about your own ability to succeed or hold a stable job could cause you to do things that disrupt your performance or prevent you from thriving at work. You may fear conflict or criticism.

It's hard, but overcoming challenges and problems help you grow. When you give up before you've tried hard, you may not learn to make different choices in the future.

2. *You put off until the following day:* Have you ever found yourself stalled or stuck in the face of an important task?

   You are far from the only one in this case.

   You've prepped, done all your research, and sat down to get started, only to find you just can't get started. Your motivation is completely gone.

   So, you avoid the task of cleaning out the fridge, organizing your junk drawer or starting a movie marathon.

   Putting off a task or event can happen for no apparent reason, but it usually has one or more underlying causes, such as you feel overwhelmed with what you need to do, you have trouble managing your time, you doubt your abilities or skills.

3. *You seek to argue:* you can subtly sabotage yourself to damage your relationships in many ways when you seek the argument unnecessarily.

   Maybe you're always up for arguing, even over things that don't really matter, like who picked the last restaurant you went to.

   Or you do things to provoke reactions, like leaving a mess in the kitchen or deliberately forgetting important dates.

   On the other hand, you could easily get offended or take things personally whether they are directed at you or not.

   Or maybe you find it hard to talk about your feelings, especially when you're upset. Thus, you resort to grumbling or even mischievous aggression instead of more effective methods of communication.

4. *You meet people who are not suitable for you:* self-sabotaging behaviors often appear in relationships. Meeting people who don't tick all your boxes is a common type of relationship self-sabotage.

   You could:

   • Keep dating the same type of person even if your relationship continues to end badly.

- Try to make things work with a partner who has very different goals for the future.
- Staying in a relationship that leads nowhere.

You may be monogamous, but you continue to develop attractions for non-monogamous people. You try non-monogamy more than once but end up getting frustrated and hurt each time.

Or, you want kids, but your partner doesn't. But you remain in the relationship secretly hoping that your partner will change their mind.

By continually repeating the same aspirations, you prevent yourself from finding someone who is a better match in the long term, whether in your private life, at work and in society.

5. *You have difficulty expressing your needs:* if you find it difficult to speak for yourself, you may find it difficult to meet all of your needs.

   It can happen in family situations, among friends, at work, in romantic relationships, in everyday interactions.

   - Imagine standing in line at the supermarket with a sandwich when someone with a cart full of groceries cuts in front of you.
   - You're in a rush to get back to work, but you can't bring yourself to say anything.
   - You let them go and found yourself late for a meeting you really couldn't afford to miss.

6. *You belittle yourself:* people often set much higher standards for themselves than they do for others. When you don't meet these standards, you can give yourself some pretty harsh feedback.

   - I can't do anything right!
   - I won't make it so why should I care?
   - I really failed!
   - I'm horrible at this!

   Whether you criticize yourself in front of others or have a habit of speaking negatively about yourself, the same can happen because your words can eventually be taken as the truth.

   Believing these reviews can foster a destructive attitude and prevent you from wanting to try again. In the long run, you might give up before you even start.

What are the causes?

Self-sabotaging behaviors are often the cause, as they are deeply ingrained and difficult to recognize. Once you identify them, notice how hard it is to accept them.

However, remember that by recognizing these behaviors, you will have taken the first step towards changing your attitude.

Also, remember that you don't have to do this alone. Friends and loved ones and trained therapists can all offer support.

THE BENEFITS OF A GOOD ATTITUDE

Are you more of a glass half empty or half full type?

Studies have shown that both can impact your physical and mental health, and thinking positive is the best of both.

Optimistic people with a good attitude have a lower level of risk of dying from several leading causes of death, including heart disease, stroke, cancer, infection, and respiratory disease.

Other proven benefits of positive thinking include, better quality of life, higher energy levels, better psychological and physical health, faster recovery from injury or illness, fewer colds, lower depression, better stress management and coping skills and longer lifespan.

Positive thinking isn't magic, and it won't make all your problems go away. This will make problems more manageable and help you approach difficulties in a more positive and productive way.

Below, you will find a series of tips to get you started with positive thinking:

1. *How to think positively:* positive thinking can be achieved through a few different techniques that have been shown to be effective, such as autosuggestion and positive imagery.

   Here are some tips to get you started that can help train your brain to think positively.

   - *Concentrate on the good things:* difficult situations and obstacles are part of life. When faced with it, focus on the good things, no matter how small or seemingly insignificant.

- *Practice recognition:* Practicing gratitude has been shown to reduce stress, improve self-esteem and promote resilience, even in very difficult times.

  Think of people, times, or things that bring you comfort or happiness, and try to express your gratitude at least once a day.

  It could be thanking a co-worker for helping with a project, a loved one for washing the dishes, or your dog for the unconditional love they give you.

- *Hang out with positive people:* negativity and positivity have proven to be contagious. Consider the people you spend time with.

  Have you noticed how one person in a bad mood can knock almost everyone in a room down?
  A positive person has the opposite effect on others.

  Being around positive people has been shown to improve self-esteem and increase your chances of achieving your goals.

  Surround yourself with people who can uplift you and help you see the bright side of things.

- *Practice a positive inner dialogue:* we tend to be the hardest on ourselves and our own worst critics. Over time, this can cause you to form a negative opinion, of yourself that can be hard to shake.

  To stop this, you will need to pay attention to the voice in your head and respond with positive messages, also known as positive self-talk.

- *Identify your negative points:* Take a good look at the different areas of your life and identify those in which you tend to be the most negative. Not sure?

  Ask a trusted friend or colleague. Chances are they'll be able to offer some insight.

  A colleague may notice that you tend to be negative at work. Your spouse may notice that you become particularly negative while driving. It is suggested that you tackle one area at a time.

- *Start each day on a positive note:* create a ritual where you start each day with something uplifting and positive.

For example, tell yourself it's going to be a great day, listen to a positive tune, or share some positivity by giving a compliment or doing something nice for someone.

- *How to think positively when everything is going wrong:* trying to be positive when you're grieving or experiencing other serious distress can seem impossible. During these times, it is important to relieve yourself of the pressure to find a consoling or hopeful perspective.

Positive thinking is not about burying all your negative thoughts or emotions or avoiding difficult feelings. The lowest moments in our lives are often the ones that motivate us to move on and make positive changes.

When you're going through a time like this, try to see yourself as a good friend in need of comfort and sound advice.

What would you tell her or him?

You'll likely acknowledge her or his feelings and remind her or him that she or he has every right to feel sad or angry about her or his situation, then offer your support by gently reminding her or him that things will get better.

2. *The side effects of negative thoughts:* Negative thinking and the many feelings that can accompany it, such as pessimism, stress, and anger, can cause several physical symptoms and increase your risk of disease and a longer lifespan.

Stress and other negative emotions trigger several processes in our body, including the release of stress hormones and certain immune functions.

Long periods of stress increase inflammation in your body which is implicated in several serious illnesses. Some of the symptoms of stress include headaches, body aches, nausea, chronic fatigue, and difficulty sleeping.

On the other hand, cynicism, stress, anger, and hostility have been linked to an increased risk of heart disease, heart attack, stroke, and dementia.

3. *When to see a doctor:* if you feel overwhelmed by negative thoughts and have trouble controlling your emotions, see a doctor.

You may benefit from medical help, such as positive psychology or therapy. Persistent negative thoughts may be caused by an underlying psychiatric condition that requires treatment.

One thing to remember, don't expect to undo years of pessimism and negative thinking overnight, but with a little practice you can learn to approach things with a more positive outlook.

POSITIVE THINKING AND OPTIMISM

Self-talk is your internal dialogue. It is influenced by your subconscious mind and reveals your thoughts, beliefs, questions, and ideas.

Autosuggestion can be both negative and positive. It can be encouraging, or it can be distressing.

Much of your self-talk depends on your personality. If you are optimistic, your self-talk may be more optimistic and positive. The reverse is generally true if you tend to be pessimistic.

Positive thinking and optimism can be effective stress management tools. Indeed, having a more positive outlook on life can provide you with some health benefits.

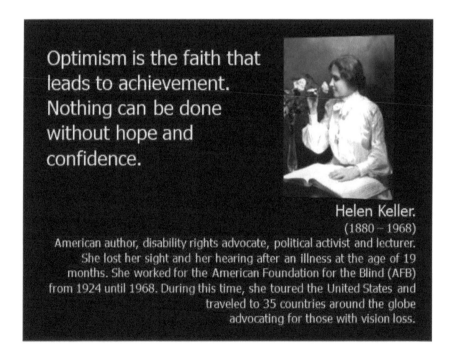

Optimism is the faith that leads to achievement. Nothing can be done without hope and confidence.

Helen Keller.
(1880 – 1968)
American author, disability rights advocate, political activist and lecturer. She lost her sight and her hearing after an illness at the age of 19 months. She worked for the American Foundation for the Blind (AFB) from 1924 until 1968. During this time, she toured the United States and traveled to 35 countries around the globe advocating for those with vision loss.

Generally, optimists have a better quality of life.

Also, if you think your self-talk is too negative, or if you want to emphasize a positive self-talk, you can learn how to modify that self-talk. It can help you be a more positive person and it can improve your health.

1. *Why is it good for you?*

   Autosuggestion can improve your performance and general well-being. For example, positive self-talk can help athletes improve performance and endurance.

   Additionally, positive self-talk and a more optimistic outlook may have other health benefits, including increased vitality, greater life satisfaction, improved immune function, reduced pain, better cardiovascular health, better physical well-being, reduced risk of death, less stress and distress.

   Additionally, people with positive self-talk may have mental abilities that allow them, to problem solve, think differently, and be more effective in dealing with difficulties or challenges. Also, it can reduce the harmful effects of stress and anxiety.

2. *How does it work?*

   Before you learn to practice self-talk further, you must first identify negative thoughts.

   This type of thinking and self-talk generally falls into four categories:

   - *Personalization:* You blame yourself for everything.
   - *Exaggeration:* You focus on the negative aspects of a situation, ignoring all the positive aspects.
   - *Catastrophe:* You expect the worst and rarely let logic or reason convince you otherwise.
   - *Polarize:* You see the world in black and white, or good and bad. There is nothing in between and no common ground in processing and classifying life events.

   When you begin to recognize your negative thought patterns, you can work to turn them into positive thoughts. This task requires practice and time and does not develop overnight. The good news is that it can be done.

3. *Transform negative self-talk into positive self-talk:* the following examples show when and how you can turn negative self-talk into positive self-talk. Again, this takes practice.

   Recognizing some of your own negative self-talk in these examples can help you develop skills to reverse thinking when it occurs.

   - *Negative:* I will disappoint everyone if I change my mind.
     Positive: I have the power to change my mind. Others will understand.

- *Negative:* I failed and embarrassed myself.
  Positive: I'm proud of myself for trying. It took courage.
- *Negative:* I am overweight and out of shape. That does not bother me.
  Positive: I am capable and strong, and I want to be healthier.
- *Negative:* I let everyone on my team down when I didn't score.
  Positive: Sport is a team event. We win and lose together.
- *Negative:* I have never done this before and I will be bad at it.
  Positive: It's a wonderful opportunity to learn from others and grow.
- *Negative:* There is simply no way it will work.
  Positive: I can and will give everything to make it work.

4. *How to use self-talk on a daily basis?*
    Positive self-talk takes practice if it's not already a natural instinct for you. If you are generally more pessimistic, you can learn to modify your inner dialogue to be more encouraging and uplifting.

    However, forming a new habit takes time and effort. Over time, your thoughts may change. Positive self-talk can become your norm.

    The following tips may help you:

- *Identify the pitfalls of negative self-talk:* certain scenarios can increase your self-doubt and lead to more negative self-talk. Work-related events, for example, can be particularly challenging. Pinpointing when you encounter the most negative self-talk can help you anticipate and prepare.

- *Check your feelings:* stop during events or bad days and assess your self-talk. Is it becoming negative? How can you operate a U-turn?

- *Use humor:* laughter can help relieve stress and tension. When you need a boost for positive self-talk, find ways to laugh, like watching funny animal videos or a comedian.

- *Surround yourself with positive people:* whether you notice it or not, you can identify the gaze and emotions of the people around you, this includes negative people and positive people, so choose positive people when you can.

- *Make positive affirmations to yourself:* sometimes seeing positive words and phrases or inspiring images can be enough to redirect your thoughts. Post little reminders in your office, home, and anywhere you spend a lot of time.

5. *When should I seek help?*

Positive self-talk can help you improve your outlook on life. It can also have lasting positive health effects, including improved well-being and improved quality of life. However, self-talk is a lifelong habit.

In the event that you find that you are not successful on your own, talk to a therapist. Mental health experts can help you identify sources of negative self-talk and learn how to flip the switch.

Remember if you tend to have negative self-talk and lean towards pessimism, you can learn how to change that habit. It takes time and practice, but you can develop positive and uplifting self-talk. In fact, your success is a matter of attitude.

Recommended reading and references

We suggest that you consult the works identified below in order to learn more about the particularities contained in this chapter.

ELGIN, Suzette Haden. Ph.D. HOW TO DISAGREE WITHOUT BEING DISAGREEABLE. MJF Books. ISBN-10: 1-567731-739-1.

GREENE, Robert. THE 48 LAWS OF POWER.
Penguin Books. ISBN: 978-01-14-028019-7

SHOOK, L. Robert. IMAGES DE GAGNANTS.
Éditions; un monde différent. ISBN 2-90000-62-4.

SIMMONS, Harry. HOW TO TALK YOUR WAY TO SUCCESS.
Prentice-Hall. 1954 – 43526.

SMITH, Hyrum W. THE 10 NATURAL LAWS OF SUCCESSFUL TIME AND LIFE MANAGEMENT. Warner Books. ISBN 0-446-51741-0.

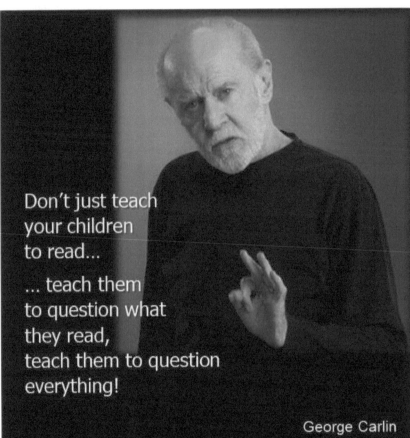

Don't just teach
your children
to read...

... teach them
to question what
they read,
teach them to question
everything!

George Carlin
(1937 – 2008)
American stand-up comedian, actor, author, and social critic.
Regarded as one of the most important and influential
stand-up comedians of all time.

TAKING CHARGE OF YOUR LIFE

Do you find yourself missing out on opportunities?
Do you often feel dissatisfied?
Have you ever wondered what you could accomplish if you learned to take charge of your life?

The answer to living the way you want, rather than being reduced to a mere spectator, is to take matters into your own hands. Although this task may seem daunting at first, there are ways in which people can control their own destiny and take control. Don't sit in the back, be the driver of your life!

SELF-CONFIDENCE

Confidence is feeling sure of yourself and your abilities, not in an arrogant way, but in a realistic and convinced way. Confidence is not about feeling superior to others, but about a sense of inner tranquility that you are capable.

Confident people feel safe rather than threatened. They know they can rely on their skills and strengths to handle whatever comes their way. They feel ready for daily challenges like testing, performances, and competitions. Confident people believe in accomplishment, rather than inability.

Self-confidence is defined as a feeling of confidence in one's abilities, qualities, and judgment. Self-confidence is important for your health and psychological well-being. Having a level of self-confidence can help you succeed in your personal and professional life.

Having self-confidence can bring many benefits, at home, at work, and in your relationships.

Here's a look at some of the positive effects self-confidence can have on your life.

1. *Better performance:* rather than wasting time and energy worrying about not being good enough, you can put your energy into your endeavors. So, ultimately, you'll get better results when you feel confident.

2. *Healthy relationships:* having self-confidence not only impacts how you feel about yourself, not only it also helps you better understand and love others. It also gives you the strength to walk away if you don't get what you deserve.

3. *Try new things:* when you believe in yourself, you are more willing to try new things. Whether you're applying for a promotion or signing up for a cooking class, it's much easier to put yourself out there when you're confident in yourself and your abilities.

4. *Resilience:* believing in yourself can improve your resilience or your ability to bounce back from the challenges or adversities you face in life.

Fortunately, there are things you can do to boost your self-confidence. Whether you lack confidence in a specific area or have trouble feeling confident about anything, the following strategies can help:

1. *Does confidence matter?*
    Confidence helps us feel ready for life's experiences. When we're confident, we're more likely to move forward with people and opportunities, not walk away from them. And if things don't work out at first, confidence helps us to persevere.

    It is the reverse when confidence is low. People with low self-confidence may be less likely to try new things or reach new people. If they fail the first time, they may be less likely to try again.

    A lack of confidence can prevent people from reaching their full potential.

2. *Believe in yourself:* has anyone ever mentioned to you that you are smart, funny, kind, artistic, a good student, a good athlete, a good worker?
    When people praise us or recognize our skills and abilities, it can boost our self-confidence, as long as we believe in it too.

    If you've ever doubted the good things people say about you, that's the opposite of self-confidence.

    To really feel confident, you have to really believe that you can do it.

    The best way to acquire this belief is to use your skills and talents, by learning and practicing.

    Confidence helps us move forward to discover and develop our abilities.

    When we see what we are capable of and are proud of our accomplishments, confidence becomes more and more present.

3. *Be more confident:* everyone can work to gain confidence. Here are some tips to try.

a. *Build a confident mindset:* when your inner voice tells you, I can't, be sure to remind it that it can.

   Or you could also say, I know I can learn or perform a task if only I think about it positively.

b. *Compare yourself nicely:* it is natural to compare yourself to others. It's a way of understanding each other and developing the qualities we admire.

   But if comparisons often leave you feeling bad about yourself, that's a sign that you should further boost your confidence and self-esteem.

c. *Get rid of the doubt:* when we doubt our abilities, we feel inferior, unworthy, or unprepared. It can cause us to avoid people and situations that you might enjoy and grow from.

d. *Take small risks:* join a school committee, volunteer to help with a project or rummage sale, participate in a team or talent show. The more you try, the safer you will feel to dare more.

e. *Challenge yourself:* do something that is just beyond your normal comfort zone: choose something that you would like to do if only you had more confidence in yourself. Give yourself a little nudge and do it. Once done, choose something else to try and keep repeating this same process. Confidence increases with each forward.

f. *Know your talents and help them shine:* we are taught to work hard to improve our weaknesses. However, don't let a weakness stop you from improving even further in the areas you are good at.

g. *Do your homework. Prepare yourselves. Why ?*
   If you have a good understanding of a case or a way of proceeding, you will feel more confident when faced with situations in the workplace or life events in general.

   The best defense against anxiety related to new experiences and the stress of life is to do meaningful work, strike poses and above all stay informed, because knowing is one of the important elements of good anxiety management.

h. *Dare to be yourself:* let others see you for who you are. Insecurities are easier to overcome when you don't feel as if you must hide them.

Accept your quirks instead of trying to look like someone else or act in a way that isn't true to you. It takes courage and confidence to be true.

The more authentic you are, the more confident you become. Confidence builds self-esteem.

4. *The highs and lows of confidence:* whether you are an employee or a boss, life is full of ups and downs.

Some days you will ride the crest of a wave and everything you touch will turn to gold. Other times, the stress and strain of calling the decisions you need to make, will weigh heavily.

It is important for your success to consider that you live in the community with your colleagues and the boss. It does not stop only in the workplace, but also in family and during social activities.

What will you do when you have a bad patch?
What will be your reaction to personal disappointment?
When will a difficult customer, employee, or boss cause difficulty?
Or, when you will lose a contract with a competitor?

The most effective weapon you will use in these difficult times is your own self-confidence.

5. *How do you maintain faith when doubt sets in?*
Self-confidence is something we all need to nurture. None of us are born with an ironclad belief in ourselves.

Luckily, it's something you can farm. Follow the following five incentives to stay confident, which will give you an edge over many people.

a. *Seek a mentorship:* it is always nice to know that we are independent. However, if you want to cultivate your self-confidence, it is reassuring to have someone as a sounding board for big decisions.

Mentoring fills this gap. A mentor should be someone who has experience in the world you want.

A person who can point out pitfalls, so you can avoid them. Knowing that you have this experience to turn to, if you need it, will allow you to move forward with confidence.

b. *Learn from your failures:* every person, no matter how dedicated or prodigiously talented, will face setbacks on the road to success.

How you react to these setbacks will define you and those around you.

In life, you just have to remember whether you win or lose, you never lose, because above all you will learn!

c. *Embrace the discomfort:* either way, you're going to have to tackle the problems you've never encountered before.

This feeling of discomfort is perfectly normal, and it should not bother you.

Meeting challenges successfully will demonstrate your ability to handle whatever life throws at you.

Each milestone you reach proves that you can do it and that success is within your reach.

The more you tackle discomfort head-on, the less you will fear new challenges. Make discomfort an ally.

d. *Embrace the word « no »:* if your default answer to social and professional questions is « yes, » you are opening yourself up to stretching too much.

Our natural inclination is to keep people happy. This feeling can be amplified when trying to build relationships and take the first hesitant steps.

Saying « yes » first and thinking about it later, is likely to overwhelm you and even wear you out as you try to cover more ground than you can handle.

The failures you suffer because you are too eager to please can contribute to eroding your self-confidence.

Respect your own time, sanity, and resources by learning to say "no" when appropriate.

e. *Celebrate every victory:* it's important to take the time to recognize your victories, no matter how small. Whether it's the completion of a job, a contract, or even some good news, give yourself a little celebration to validate your hard work.

Celebrating has the powerful effect of creating a positive feeling that you associate with your achievement. The more victories you savor, the more motivation you will have to keep working hard.

THE LEVEL OF CONFIDENCE

Even in people who seem most confident, the level of confidence improves or decreases depending on the level of combativeness they exert.

If something shakes your confidence, show a good disposition. Don't criticize yourself. Learn from what happened, think about what you could have done differently, and remember that for the next time.

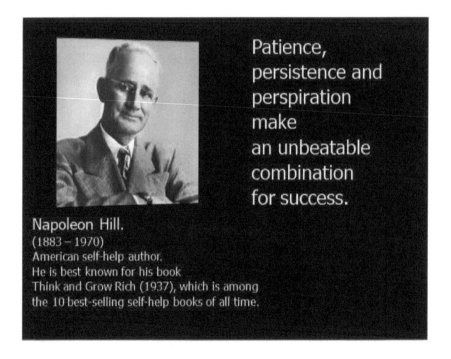

Patience, persistence and perspiration make an unbeatable combination for success.

Napoleon Hill.
(1883 – 1970)
American self-help author.
He is best known for his book
Think and Grow Rich (1937), which is among
the 10 best-selling self-help books of all time.

Talk about what happened with someone you trust. But above all, self-confidence comes through remembering your strengths and the things you have accomplished.

Above all, it's about getting back into the game as quickly as possible!

You might think that really mentally strong people never want to give up, but the truth is that perseverance is usually about keeping going even when you have strong intentions to suspend or even quit.

1. *The strength to carry on:* Here are some tips for those who are tempted to quit, but want to find the strength to keep going:

    a. *Make sure your goals are worth your persistence:* sometimes you really should quit.

        However, make sure it's not one of those unthinking moments. You might be determined to make a mistake.

        This reasoning in addition to the challenge you give yourself, to also consider the possible collateral damage to your health, your relationships, and your integrity that this action will produce when stopping.

    b. *Remember past persistence:* Remembering past times when you refused to give up, can help you be more persistent now. These could be moments of fear, stubbornness, inspiration, clarity, determination, commitment, or a mixture of these.

        Re-energize yourself to draw from within you the resources necessary to continue.

    c. *Take a step forward:* don't get caught thinking too much about the future. Often there is something you can do to make small progress.

    d. *Set your pace:* once you're back in the action, you don't want to find yourself in a new slump a week or a month later, so avoid frantic activities that will only exhaust you once again.

        As the old saying goes, slow and steady often wins the race.

    e. *Carry on, even when in doubt:* putting one foot in front of the other and believing that your efforts will be rewarded are the most fundamental aspect of perseverance.

        However, sometimes this is impossible, in practice at least. Sometimes you are well and truly stuck. For example, perhaps you have contracted an illness or are your ambitions awaiting someone else's move?

Nevertheless, just because real progress isn't possible right now doesn't mean there isn't anything you can do to maintain momentum and morale.

Remember that strong self-confidence will help you identify other possibilities that will surface. To persevere is to continue to seek, evaluate, plan, and improve to better face new potential challenges.

2. *Stop comparing yourself to others:* whether you're comparing your looks to your friends on Facebook or comparing your salary to your friends' earnings, comparisons aren't healthy.

   If you feel envious of someone else's life, remember your own strengths and achievements. When you notice that you are making comparisons, remind yourself that it is not helpful. Everyone is on their own course and life is not a competition.

   Surround yourself with positive people and pay attention, to how your friends make you feel.

   Do your friends lift you or bring you down?
   Are they constantly judging you or accepting you for who you are?

   The people you spend time with influence your thoughts and attitudes about yourself more than you realize. If you feel bad about yourself after dating a particular person, it might be time to say goodbye.

   Stop comparing your appearance, take care of your body instead. It's hard to feel good about yourself if you're mistreating your body. On the other hand, if you take care of yourself, you know you're doing something positive for your mind and body, and you'll naturally feel more confident.

   Be kind to yourself by treating yourself with kindness when you make a mistake, fail, or experience a setback. It is a way of connecting with yourself that allows you to become more emotionally flexible and better manage difficult emotions, in order to improve your interaction with yourself and others.

3. *Confront Your Fears:* stop putting off things like asking someone out on a date or applying for a promotion until you feel more confident. The best way to build your self-confidence is to face your fears.

   Practice facing some of your fears that stem from a lack of self-confidence. If you're afraid of embarrassing yourself or think you're going to screw it up, try it anyway. Tell yourself it's just an experiment and see what happens.

You may learn that being a little anxious or making a few mistakes isn't as bad as you thought. And each time you move forward, you gain confidence, which will ultimately save you from taking risks that could lead to major negative consequences.

When you face your fears and try hard things, you will gain confidence. A little fear is normal.

In fact, fear helps you instinctively protect yourself from harm. Your fear can help you recognize when you're about to do something dangerous, and it could help you make a more confident choice.

However, you might fear things that aren't actually dangerous, like public speaking. Your fear of public speaking can keep you from advancing in your career or participating in traditions like giving a toast at your best friend's wedding.

For example, if you want to go on vacation to Europe, but your fear of flying, has you thinking, you might feel like your fear is holding you back from living your dream.

If you find that your fear is holding you back or creating bigger problems in your life, facing your fear can help you learn how to better confront fear and overcome it.

4. *Assess the risks:* Facing your fears involves assessing the risks, developing an action plan, and making sure you don't completely avoid your fears.

    However, you may first need to decide if you need to deal with a particular fear if it is not part of your daily life.

    Sometimes fear comes simply, from not knowing much about what you fear. For example, you might fear aircraft because you seem to have heard of many in-flight incidents that have resulted in injury or death.

    However, if you look at the statistics, you might learn that the odds of a US commercial airline crash are 1 in 7 million, compared to 1 in 600 due to smoking.

    You can also learn more about the causes of these shocks and jolts during turbulence on board an aircraft. It's simply the movement of the air that influences the aircraft and, if you're properly strapped in, it poses a very little threat to you.

Of course, less tangible fears, like fear of public speaking, don't necessarily have statistics to help you learn more about the risks you perceive.

But you can read about other people's successful public speaking initiatives, or learn more about successful public speaking strategies, to help you feel more confident.

Keep in mind that just because something scares you, doesn't mean it's actually risky. Educate yourself on the facts and the risks you really face doing the things that scare you.

5. *Create an action plan:* the best way to overcome a fear is to face it, but it's important to do so in a healthy way that helps you overcome the fear rather than in a way that traumatizes you.

   If you are having difficulty, a mental health professional can gradually guide you through the situations you fear, making sure to work on the thought patterns that are blocking you first.

   The key to facing your fears is to design an action plan and develop a hierarchy of fear made up of small steps.

6. *Maintain your confidence:* in the workplace as in private life, there are people who always seem to be above the situation.

   For example, there are spirited employees who are always ready to share their ideas or take on new tasks. Their positive attitude manages to convince those around them that they are an asset. The feeling they embrace that many struggles, to find, is self-confidence.

   On the other hand, some people are consumed by doubt and fear, unable to take the necessary risks or to express their opinions. Always remember that self-confidence is as much a skill as it is a way of putting a situation into perspective.

It should be remembered that to be successful at work and in your personal life activities, it is important, to avoid, believes that kill confidence and to manage, sometimes with great restraint, difficult personalities.

Here are five pitfalls to trust that you can work around:

a. *The perfectionism:* high performers often persuade themselves to achieve ridiculous and unrealistic standards and sometimes get discouraged when they don't meet them.

Remember that everyone has different strengths and weaknesses.

Whenever you fail to complete a project, ask yourself if you gave it your all. If so, you know that you are human and accept that you cannot do everything perfectly.

Once assessed, you need to stop the negative mental reflections and just tell yourself that you gave your best and that your action or work is good.

b.   *The micromanager:* being micromanaged can make a person feel as if they're not up to the job. Otherwise, why would the boss penalize you and tell you exactly how to complete a task?

In most cases, you're probably doing nothing wrong. Here, it should be noted that fear is generally underlying behavior control.

Your boss's micromanagement probably has more to do with what that person thinks of themselves and has nothing to do with you. If, you are really confident in yourself, no one can bring you down.

A micromanager can make you feel some insecurities but remember how far you've come and especially where you want to go.

c.   *Disengagement from work:* one of the most common reasons for feeling detached from your job, and therefore lacking in self-confidence, is doing a job that doesn't use your skills.

Everyone has talents and abilities, and if you're not using them in your job, you might want to consider other opportunities.

Another option is to maintain an optimistic and encouraging attitude towards your job performance. If you feel indifferent, try a different perspective or approach.

Maybe you've fallen into a rut or a routine that's wearing you down. Take a different approach that will better support your passions.

What can you do differently that could make your job more enjoyable? Do not hesitate to discuss it with a trusted person and then your employer.

d.   *The fear of failure:* everyone experiences fear and some even more than others. It is crucial, however, to face the fear head-on.

Fear can be so paralyzing that it holds people back in ways they don't even realize and puts them at a disadvantage. For example, someone who is afraid to speak up in meetings might be seen as someone who doesn't add much value.

Or the fear of being yourself, trying to imitate, for example, the boss never learns to truly own what is unique about you. Sure, you want to do it right, but your fear of failing, shouldn't stop you from trying something new.

Or a project may not go as planned and you make mistakes. As long as you learn from these experiences, you haven't really failed.

e. *Uncooperative or critical colleagues:* working with rude, arrogant, or unpleasant co-workers can reduce your job satisfaction, especially if their negativity is directed at you.

Knowing that you are professional, it is better not to take these behaviors too personally, but rather to make an effort to solve the problems with your colleague.

Clean up your side of the street by asking yourself the following question, are you doing anything to contribute to this negative situation?
If so, take appropriate action.

On the other hand, if it is a situation beyond your control, be sure to write down the incident and then seek help from a superior, in order to regain a positive work atmosphere.

7. *Balance of work and private life:* the challenge of balancing work and private life is arguably one of the biggest struggles facing modern men and women.

It can be incredibly difficult to experience a sense of balance and self-worth as we juggle careers, personal responsibilities, family time, self-care, recreational activities, social times, community service, etc.

We all know that in order to achieve career goals and also to be active and present with the family, the need to rationalize one's life is paramount.

To do this, you need to eliminate non-essential activities like mindlessly scrolling through social media or checking email a million times a day, and above all, be mindful of the time wasters of each day.

The important thing is to determine where we spend our time and where we expend our energy if we are to achieve the desired successes.

It requires a sharp focus on your priorities and a ruthless elimination of many time-consuming non-essential activities.

People who lead fulfilling lives have distinctive habits, while most people find it very difficult to be satisfied both at work and in personal life.

Successful and thriving people know it's not impossible.

Voici quelques astuces en ce sens :

a. *Have a clear idea of what you want:* successful and thriving people know exactly what they want to accomplish. They know what is important to them and set very clear goals to achieve in their career and personal life.

   These people don't have vague aspirations. Instead, they set very specific goals that align with their priorities, and they dedicate their time and effort to achieving those goals.

b. *Define success on your terms:* successful and thriving people define success in their own way. They understand that they can only be satisfied if they achieve the success that really matters to them.

   Although they recognize the value of hard work, their definition of a successful life is often more general than simply achieving financial results.

c. *Defend your position:* successful and thriving people understand the importance of saying, « no .» They set boundaries so they can focus their lives and work on what matters most.

   They avoid falling prey to enticing goals that don't align with their true purpose, priorities, and passions.

d. *Be highly productive:* successful and thriving people know how to get things done. They know that to have « everything » and balance their career and personal life, they must avoid wasting time. When they aspire to do something, they achieve it.

e. *Be strategic with time:* successful and thriving people are in full possession of their time. They strategically match their work to their ideal lifestyle.

As a result, their hard-earned success doesn't seem overwhelming. Try to perceive time differently and you will begin to make every second count.

f. *Make decisions with confidence:* successful and thriving people make decisions with force. They make choices that correspond, to whom they are and what they really want. They bravely refuse opportunities that don't align with their values.

g. *Know your priorities:* successful and thriving people have a clear vision of their priorities. They work hard but avoid the « succeed at all costs » mentality.

    Although they achieve great results in their careers, they also perform well in the other life activities that matter to them.

h. *Do not be jealous of others:* successful and fulfilled people congratulate and praise the achievements of others. They don't feel threatened by the success of others. Instead, they are happy to create their own version of success and they greatly enjoy their lifestyle.

i. *Be disciplined:* successful and thriving people know that they are responsible for creating a better life. They realize that ultimately, they are in control of what they do with their lives, and they accept that power.

    They see the vision of what they want to be and stick to their plan.

j. *Learn to delegate:* successful and thriving people declutter. They delegate tasks at work and in their personal lives.

    As a result, they can enjoy more freedom of time and do more of what they love.

k. *Be grateful, but not complacent:* successful and thriving people appreciate what they have.

    However, they also strive to accomplish more of what really matters. They do it because they know they will use their success to have a positive impact on the world.

CRITICAL THINKING

No matter where you live, what industry interests you, or what experience you've already had, we've all seen firsthand the importance of critical thinking.

In fact, the lack of such skills can truly make or break a person's career, as the consequences of their inability to process and analyze information effectively can be massive.

The ability to think critically is more important today than it has ever been. It's all on the line if we don't all learn to think more critically.

If people can't think critically, they not only reduce their chances of moving up the ladder in their respective industries, not only they also become easily susceptible to things like fraud and manipulation.

With that in mind, you're probably wondering what you can do to make sure you're not one of those people.

Developing your critical thinking is something that requires the most concentrated work.

It may be best, to begin by exploring the definition of critical thinking and the skills it includes.

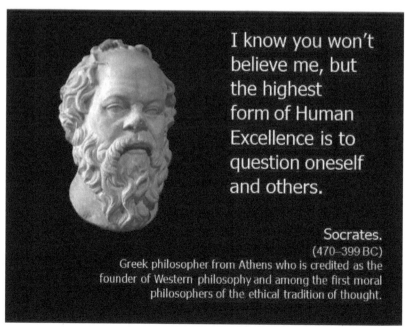

I know you won't believe me, but the highest form of Human Excellence is to question oneself and others.

Socrates.
(470–399 BC)
Greek philosopher from Athens who is credited as the founder of Western philosophy and among the first moral philosophers of the ethical tradition of thought.

Once you've done that, you can then venture on to the all-important question: how can I improve?

I will point out to you that this is not an easy task. So below you can break down the basics of critical thinking, to hone your skills and become a better critical thinker.

What is critical thinking?

Even if you want to be a better critical thinker, it's hard to improve what you can't define. Critical thinking is the analysis of a problem or situation and related facts, data, or evidence. Ideally, critical thinking should be conducted objectively, that is, without being influenced by feelings, opinions, or biases. It focuses only on factual information.

Critical thinking is a skill that allows you to make logical, informed decisions as well as you can. For example, a child who has not yet developed such skills may believe that the tooth fairy left money under his pillow based on stories, his parents told him. A critical mind, however, can quickly conclude that the existence of such a thing is unlikely, even if there are a few dollars under their pillow.

Although there is no universal standard for the skills included in the critical thinking process, below you will find a basic critical thinking process.

1. *Identification:* the first step in the critical thinking process is to identify the situation or problem and the factors that may influence it.

   Once you have a clear picture of the situation and the people, groups, or factors that can be influenced, you can then begin to dig deeper into a problem and its potential solutions.

   For example, a new situation, question, or scenario, pause to take a mental inventory of the state of affairs by asking yourself the following questions:

   - Who does what ?
   - What seems to be the reason for this?
   - What are the end results and how might they change?

2. *Conduct research:* when comparing arguments on an issue, independent research ability is essential. The arguments are persuasive. This means that the facts and figures presented in their favor could lack context or come from dubious sources.

The best way to combat this is through independent verification, to find the source of the information and assess it.

For example, it can be helpful to develop a sense of doubt about unsourced claims. Does the person making the argument, indicate where they got this information from?

If you ask or try to find it yourself and there is no clear answer, this should be seen as a red flag. It is also important to know that not all sources are equally valid. So, take the time to learn the difference between the different sources, in order to have a clearer picture.

3. *Identify biases:* this skill can be extremely difficult, as even the smartest among us may not recognize bias. Strong critical thinkers do their best to objectively evaluate information.

   Think of yourself as a judge in that you want to weigh the claims of both sides of an argument, but you'll also need to keep in mind any biases each side may have.

   It is equally important, and arguably more difficult, to learn to put aside your biases that may cloud your judgment. Have the courage to debate and discuss your own thoughts and assumptions. This is essential for learning to see things from different angles.

   You should be aware that there are biases. When evaluating information or an argument, ask yourself the following questions:

   • Who does this benefit?
   • Does the source of this information seem to have an agenda?
   • Does the source overlook, ignore or does she leave out information that does not support their beliefs or claims?
   • Does this source use unnecessary language to influence the public's perception of a fact?

4. *The deduction:* the ability to infer and draw conclusions based on the information presented to you is another important skill for mastering critical thinking.

   Information is not always accompanied by a summary that explains what it means. You will often need to evaluate the information provided and draw conclusions based on raw data.

   The ability to infer allows you to extrapolate and discover potential outcomes when evaluating a scenario.

It is also important to note that not all deductions will be correct.

For example, if you read that a person weighs 260 pounds, you can assume that they are overweight or unhealthy. However, other data points like height and body composition can alter this conclusion.

An inference is an educated guess, and your ability to infer correctly can be honed by making a conscious effort to gather as much information as possible before jumping to conclusions.

When you are faced with a new scenario or situation to assess, first try to look for clues, things like titles, pictures, and prominent statistics, and then make it a point to ask yourself what you think is going on.

5. *The determination of relevance:* one of the hardest parts of thinking critically during a difficult scenario is figuring out what information is most important to consider.

    In many scenarios you will be presented with information that may seem important, but it may just be a minor data point to consider.

    The best way to better determine relevance is to establish a clear direction in what you are trying to understand.

    Are you in charge of finding a solution?
    Should we identify a trend?

    If you determine your end goal, you can use it to inform your judgment of what is relevant.

    However, even with a clear objective, it can be difficult to determine what information is really relevant.

    One strategy to combat this is to make a physical list of data points ranked in order of relevance.

    When you parse it this way, you'll likely end up with a list that includes some obviously relevant information at the top of your list, in addition to some points at the bottom that you can probably ignore.

    From there, you can focus on the less clear topics that reside in the middle of your list for further evaluation.

6. *Curiosity:* it's incredibly easy to sit back and take anything presented to you for cash, but it can also be a recipe for disaster when faced with a storyline that requires critical thinking.

    It might seem like an inquisitive mind is just something you're born with, practice stimulating that curiosity in a productive way.

    All it takes is a conscious effort to ask open-ended questions about the things you see in your day-to-day life, and then you can invest time in following up on those questions.

    Being able to ask open-ended questions is an important skill to develop and even more so to be able to probe deeper.

Remember, thinking critically is vital for anyone looking to achieve career success and a successful life. Your ability to objectively analyze and evaluate complex topics and situations will always come in handy.

EDUCATION

The value of education is emphasized to us from an early age. It is most important to become more educated because we live in the age of knowledge.

Everything is at our fingertips, and we must take responsibility and train ourselves so that we can improve for the better. The more we know, the more we can help ourselves and the people around us.

The basic education received in primary, secondary and university schools inculcates basic knowledge, theoretical knowledge, which must be used to help us accumulate even more expertise once in the labor market.

This education received, makes it possible to possess a wealth of theoretical intellectual information. However, it must be avoided that the student on receiving his diploma can state that he has the « competence » to place himself on the path to success.

Here, the meaning of the word in the field of work should not be confused:

a. *Recognized competence:* being, the legally recognized ability of an authority to deal with a question, to judge it, to perform an act, according to determined methods.

    For example, a doctor who has obtained an official certificate to practice medicine.

b. *Competence accompanied by experience:* being, a thorough knowledge, a recognized experience in a field, which gives the quality to someone to judge, to decide.

    For example, an employee who demonstrates great skill acquired in the field. The skill of a plumber, electrician, carpenter, teacher, accountant, etc.

Therefore, the newly graduated student must acquire « experience » for a certain period of time, which may even be several years, for example, doctors and engineers.

Knowledge, know-how, expertise, skill, experience, aptitude, and professionalism are the qualifiers of the « competence » designation.

Education is most important for success and should be continued throughout life. A person may think that he no longer has to study or get information, but for this person failure will creep in.

There is the school system, but there is also autodidacticism. A person who learns by himself, who teaches himself without the help of a teacher or an educational establishment.

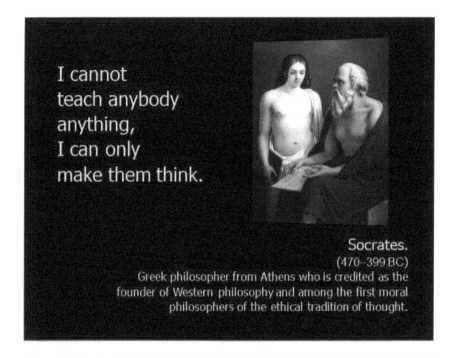

I cannot
teach anybody
anything,
I can only
make them think.

Socrates.
(470–399 BC)
Greek philosopher from Athens who is credited as the founder of Western philosophy and among the first moral philosophers of the ethical tradition of thought.

A self-taught person may aim to learn a little about everything, or they may work hard to master just one subject. Either way, it's the act of taking your learning under your control. It is this drive to push yourself that ultimately leads to personal and financial success.

Successful people never stop learning. The people who hurt an organization, the most, are the people who think they have arrived because they stop growing, innovation, and improving.

Successful people read books, learn new skills, study academic or business journals, learn from their peers, or strive for change through innovation. They all share a passion for wanting to learn new skills and discover new ideas.

Life itself is a long learning experience, and the modern world is moving and changing at a breakneck pace. Change comes through innovation and creativity.

Individuals and organizations that remain indifferent and do not embrace change run the risk of being overtaken by either a competitor or someone who is continually updating.

Take personal development seriously, because trying to learn and grow, will help you and your organization in the long run. Your journey will only be successful if you dedicate yourself to continuous development.

Also, if you've hit a plateau and have no desire to learn anything new, it's time to do some soul-searching to figure out why.

Just as physical exercise develops your muscles, when you learn, your brain develops with mental training to develop new neurons which, in turn, develop greater connectivity to manage information.

Therefore, successful people keep an open mind to new things because they know that no matter how proficient they are, there is always more to discover.

People who understand the goal of continuous development elicit an uncommon tenacity in everyone around them. So ask yourself:

What can I improve?
What should I change?

Simple, if you do nothing or repeat or always do the same thing, you stay the same and staying the same means going back.

1. *Nurture your mind:* feeding your mind with new knowledge and information is essential for creativity. An idea arises when you use your accumulated knowledge and combine it with new information.

    The simple formula (Knowledge + Information = Idea) shows that it is impossible to create an idea out of nothing. For example, knowledge of glass, the ability of lenses to split light, and knowledge of how the eye works led to the invention of eyeglasses.

    All ideas emerge when a person combines their accumulated knowledge with new information. This is why it is so important to gather knowledge, which is varied. Simple, you need knowledge to expand your mind.

2. *How to learn daily:* the following little habits are very useful when you want to become an accomplished autodidact:

    a. *Always look for new elements:* if you come across a word or reference you don't understand, look it up. This is, for example, using a dictionary or an encyclopedia on the Internet. Make it a routine to learn a new word and reference every day.

        There are also other resources like:

        1) *Blogs:* some of the smartest and most inspiring people regularly post their best work and ideas on their blogs for the world to see.

        2) *Online courses:* the reality was that college courses were only offered to people who could afford to attend college. These days, you can take these courses online, and many of them are free.

        3) *Conferences and specialized videos:* the best minds in the world regularly present their best ideas for talks and seminars that are readily available in formats ranging from a few minutes to several hours.

        4) *Audiobooks and podcasts:* this resource is also a good way to learn new things.

        However, when using these means to further your education, be sure to validate the sources you use.

        The Internet is an extraordinary source of information; however, there is a lot of misinformation and even impostors who exploit people's credulity by posing as specialists, scientists, educational organizations who do not have accreditation, etc.

b. *Reserve 15 minutes:* ideally at the same time each day. No matter how pressed for time you can always find 15 minutes. Make it the time you dedicate to your education every day.

c. *Help your brain to retain:* write down the points of information, then repeat them loudly, as this experienced way of absorption will help your brain to archive information more quickly.

Another tip, which is to review the information written down once a week, will not only allow you to put the information into perspective, not only you will retain it more.

3. *Make time to travel:* travel exposes us to different cultures and ancient traditions and through these authentic encounters we learn to accept and celebrate our similarities and differences.

Travel teaches us about humanity and allows us to appreciate, understand and respect different points of view and ways of life.

HOW TO SELL YOURSELF

One of the most valuable skills, a person can have, is knowing how to sell anything. Having sales knowledge helps you take advantage of many opportunities for entrepreneurs and business owners as well as anyone who aspires to success.

Most people don't realize how important selling is unless your salary depends on it!

I often hear « It's not for me, » « You must have a knack for selling » or « I just can't sell, » but that couldn't be further from the truth.

Remember that salespeople are not the only ones who sell something, and especially good salespeople are made, not born, and no one succeeds in life without knowing how to sell.

Think of the last time you convinced your kids to finish their vegetables or convinced your parents to let you borrow the car for the weekend. Believe it or not, you are selling something!

For people who are starting a business or the person who wants to climb the ladder of their organization or society, knowing how to « sell » will make all the difference in their quest for success.

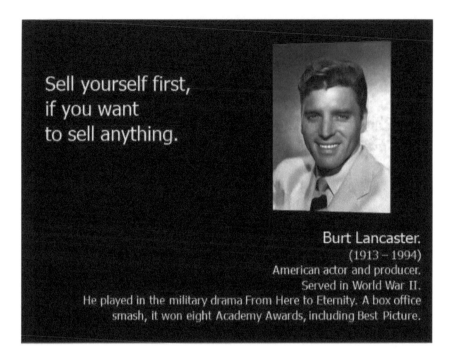

Sell yourself first,
if you want
to sell anything.

Burt Lancaster.
(1913 – 1994)
American actor and producer.
Served in World War II.
He played in the military drama From Here to Eternity. A box office
smash, it won eight Academy Awards, including Best Picture.

Don't worry too much, because you're not alone in not knowing how to sell.

Did you know that over eighty percent of « salespeople » have ever taken the time to develop sales skills?

There is, of course, the little guide or the method to follow when hiring, but nothing more elaborate, and you are automatically a salesperson.

There is much more, before considering being « competent » or « expert. »

You can learn some simple techniques that can be applied to any situation, whether you're selling a product or service over the phone, face-to-face, or even in an interview to advance your career.

Doing this, no matter what you're selling, is easier than most people think. Achieving this is simply a matter of keeping the following five points in mind.

Depending on the degree of expertise desired, you will need to research, understand, deepen and experiment on the ground at each point, because the sale is a science of the most complex.

1. *The first thing you sell is yourself:* forget the product or service. If the person you're selling to, doesn't like you, they won't listen to you. Make sure you know the product well and present yourself well. Be the seller you would buy something from.

2. *Listen more than you talk:* bad sellers cannot realize how amazing, their product is. They can't stop talking about it!

   But good salespeople listen, to what their customers are saying. They pay attention to customer needs from the start and present themselves accordingly.

3. *Know whom to sell to:* if you're selling a product or service that costs $50,000, don't try to sell it to the person whose budget is $2,000. A common mistake salespeople make is trying to sell to everyone.

   Make sure what you're selling meets the needs of your potential customers and is realistic for them. You have a good chance of getting this sale!

4. *Understand what makes the other party tick:* why should people care about what you sell?
   How does your product or service bring them value?

   Pay attention to what drives your potential client to book your appointment in the first place and address it in your presentation.

5. *Keep it simple:* don't overcomplicate your presentation just because you want to look more competent. The mark of true knowledge in anything is how well you can explain to the average person. Keep your pitch simple and under thirty seconds, while going gradually.

   The key to successful selling is to think about the person you are selling to. Approach their needs and think about how they will feel after your presentation and the meeting. There is no « natural born salesperson. » Believe me, anyone can learn to be good at selling.

Take the time to find out more, for example, there is an easy-to-read book on the subject. « You don't need to be a shark: creating your own success » by Robert Herjavec.

TAKE CHARGE OF YOURSELF

Self-determination is a combination of skills, knowledge, and believes that enable a person to engage in autonomous, self-regulated, and goal-directed behavior.

An understanding of one's strengths and limitations as well as belief in oneself are essential factors for self-determination.

By acting on these skills and attitudes, individuals have a greater ability to take control of their lives and assume the role of successful adults.

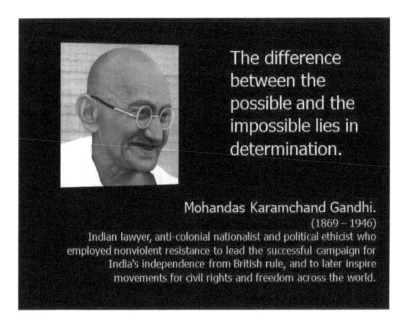

The difference between the possible and the impossible lies in determination.

Mohandas Karamchand Gandhi.
(1869 – 1946)
Indian lawyer, anti-colonial nationalist and political ethicist who employed nonviolent resistance to lead the successful campaign for India's independence from British rule, and to later inspire movements for civil rights and freedom across the world.

To take control of your life, you must learn and then successfully apply several self-determination skills, such as setting goals, understanding your abilities and disabilities, problem solving, and social autonomy.

The assessment of these skills in various contexts, the personal process of learning and its use are at the heart of self-determination.

1. *Define your own success:* people define success in different ways.

    a. *Success is defined:* by whom we are, what we believe in and what we think it means to be successful. For some it's money, for others it can be relationships, family, work, religion, or education. For most, success is about achieving a personal dream. Success is working towards goals regardless of any disabilities you may have. For example, a blind student.

b. *Success is having the ability to self-determine:* self-determination is the ability to decide what I want to do with my life and then act on it.

c. *A successful life:* it is a life where I can be actively engaged in creative activities that contribute to the lives of others. Success is a kind of by-product and NOT an end in itself!

d. *Be able to do things independently:* a successful life is being able to do things independently for yourself, and not always having someone to do things for you. It's about achieving your goals on your own terms and at your own pace.

2. *Set yourself personal, academic and career goals: successful people set goals and maintain high expectations through.*

a. *A combination of people and events:* for example, when a loved one pushed you to improve your academic skills. Remember that success builds on itself.

b. *High standards:* when you agree to do well and maintain high standards.

c. *Never mention that you cannot:* find a loved one or mentor who will help you maintain high expectations of yourself. People who will teach you never to say « I can't » to anything you try.

d. *Be confident in your abilities:* find someone like a teacher or manager who will make you confident in your ability to learn, which will help you maintain high expectations.

e. *Unique talents:* it is important to realize that everyone has their own journey in life with unique talents. However, knowing what talents you have, you should strive to be your best self.

f. *Set goals:* set personal, academic, and professional goals, knowing where your limits lie.

If someone tells you that you can't do something and you've never tried it before, that makes you even more determined to prove them wrong. If you fail, at least you tried. That is what matters.

g. *High expectations:* one of the biggest reasons people don't set high expectations is fear of failure.

Start by setting achievable goals that aren't long-term. Develop achievable one-week goals that lead to success. Build on every success and make every goal a little higher.

Consider them a representative high jump. However, don't set the bar too high in the beginning, or you might just be running into failure.

3. *Understand your abilities and incapacity:* play to your strengths. People with disabilities who see themselves as successful generally accept their disabilities as an aspect of their personality.

They do not define themselves by their disabilities, recognize that they are not responsible for their disabilities and know that they are not inherently disabled. They recognize their responsibility for their own happiness and future.

4. *Develop strategies to achieve your goals:* successful people use creative strategies to achieve their goals. They consider options and make informed decisions.

Successful planning requires you to know your rights and responsibilities, your strengths, and challenges, set goals, work towards those goals, and use the tools and resources available to you.

Remember that your life should not be defined by the assumptions of others.

5. *Use technology as an empowerment tool:* being technologically competent has become an avenue to academic and professional success. Computers are one of the most powerful tools at your disposal.

Technology, including computers, adaptive technology, and the Internet, can help you maximize independence, productivity, and participation.

Without a doubt, it can lead to high levels of success, personally, socially, academically, and professionally.

6. *Work hard. Persevere. Be flexible:* knowing and valuing yourself, setting goals and planning helps build important foundations, but action is needed to achieve your dreams.

To take control of your life, it is necessary to choose and act appropriately. Take matters into your own hands. Go forward. Work harder to achieve the same level of success as your peers.

7. *Develop a network of mutual aid:* do not be afraid to call on family, friends, teachers, colleagues, and managers in your organization to help you grow.

8. *Train your mind:* train your mind to see the good in everything. Being positive is a choice. Happiness and quality of life depend on the quality of your thoughts.

CONTINUOUS IMPROVEMENT

Continuous improvement is a journey of personal growth where you make consistent progress over the long term.

They are not random improvements.

Making continuous improvements is the key to being there for others and the path to success in your life.

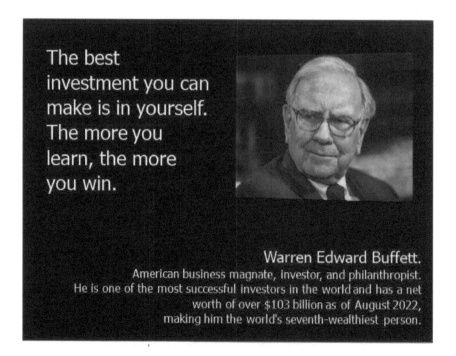

The best investment you can make is in yourself. The more you learn, the more you win.

Warren Edward Buffett.
American business magnate, investor, and philanthropist. He is one of the most successful investors in the world and has a net worth of over $103 billion as of August 2022, making him the world's seventh-wealthiest person.

Not only will self-improvement help you perform at your best by taking steps to improve yourself, but your overall well-being will also be improved.

People who prioritize self-improvement tend to have higher self-esteem and are also more resilient.

Here are some points to help you with continuous improvement, in order to take charge of your life:

1. *Humility:* at the heart of humility is a desire to serve and a dedication to helping others become great. Do not confuse humility with weakness.

    In fact, it takes great strength of will and character to put the needs of others before your own, to admit mistakes, to be vulnerable, transparent, and fallible in front of your peers.

2. *Happiness: this is* a choice, not a result. Nothing will make you happy unless you decide to be happy. Your happiness will not come to you. It can only come from you.

3. *Smile:* be the reason someone smiles today.

4. *Be positive:* a negative mind will never give you a positive life. Be so positive that negativity doesn't want to approach you.

    Ships do not sink because of the water around them. Ships sink because of the water entering them. Don't let what's going on around you get inside you and weigh you down. Positive thoughts keep you afloat, so don't let someone's negative energy and behavior weigh you down.

    Remember to surround yourself with positive people who motivate, inspire, and uplift you, who will push you towards excellence. And stay away from people who try to downplay your ambitions, especially in these unprecedented times. Simple, be so positive that negative people won't want to be around you.

5. *Be confident:* believing in yourself is the first secret of success. It doesn't matter how you feel, get up, get dressed, show up and never give up. Also, remember that you are so busy doubting yourself while so many others are intimidated by your potential. Believe in yourself!

6. *Believe in yourself:* you are braver than you think, more talented than you think, and capable of more than you imagine. You are someone and make sure your actions and behaviors are driven by your internal desires to

become the best version of yourself, not external expectations set by anyone.

7. *Have dreams:* surround yourself with people who have dreams, desires, and ambition; they will help you push and achieve yours.

8. *Your comfort zone:* the hardest part is getting out of your comfort zone. But you have to let go of the life you're used to and take the risk of living the life you dream of.

    You can't grow as a person unless you take on new challenges, face your fears, overcome something difficult, or do something you've never done before.

    Also, to become a great person, you need to be comfortable with things going wrong sometimes because things won't go your way all the time.

    Therefore, to become one of the greatest, you have to feel comfortable with being uncomfortable to continue growing. In many cases, the best things in life often lie outside of your comfort zone.

9. *Control:* you can't control everything. Sometimes you just need to relax and trust that things will work out. Let go and let life unfold.

10. *Character:* you can judge a person's character by how they treat people who can't do anything for them. The moment you think you have the right to put others down because you are better than them is when you prove you have no power.

    People tend to make others feel what they experience themselves whether big or small. How a person labels, judges, and values the people around them give us insight into their personality and even their self-esteem.

11. *How to address:* I talk to everyone, the same way, whether he's the garbage collector or the president of the university. (Albert Einstein)

    Too many people think that having a position of authority is their God-given right. They feel superior to those they employ or to the so-called lower levels of the organization.

    Surely you have already noticed a certain level of arrogance manifesting itself in people in positions of power who seek to tear people down instead of uplifting them.

Smart people don't hit people with demeaning comments and never intentionally try to put people in an embarrassing or demeaning position. Instead, they show genuine personal and professional interest by asking, « How are you? » or « How's your family? » while listening and expressing real concern for the situation.

Remember that you can change a person's life, every day by how you address them. So never pass up an opportunity to encourage others, never pass up an opportunity to inspire someone.

12. *Mistakes:* if you only do things, you've already mastered, you will rarely, if ever, make mistakes. However, it will lead you to a most boring life.

A person who has never made a mistake has never tried anything new. (Albert Einstein)

It's when we try something new that we make the most mistakes. However, it is impossible to live without failing at something unless you live with such caution that you might as well not have lived at all, in which case you fail by default.

13. *Fix errors:* Although many errors are minor and do not cause much ripple in the world, some errors hurt others and should be addressed quickly and in full. Here is a process for dealing with any errors whether professional or personal:

a. *Acknowledge the error:* don't add to the mistake already made by ignoring it in the hope that it will go away.

Whether you missed a customer order or forgot your spouse's birthday, ignoring the failure won't make it seem less important, it will just make you look unintelligent.

Be honest. Acknowledge directly and briefly, but honestly, that you lacked judgment. State specifically what you did and mention how much you regret the action.

b. *Accept your responsibilities:* the automatic response of human nature is to jump into a self-defense mode. At no time, is this response stronger, than when we are forced to acknowledge our own shortcomings.

Resist the urge to find someone to blame, even if it's justified. There are always extenuating circumstances, and most of us don't intend to be wrong.

But not all good intentions change the fact that you made a mistake.

Don't point fingers or use circumstances to come up with an excuse, it only makes it seem as if you care more about getting out of trouble than actually fixing the problem you've caused, even unintentionally.

c. *Apologize:* those three little words « I'm sorry » should be heard by the person who bears the brunt of your mistake. « Please forgive me » is fine too.

This demonstrates that you understand that this person has a choice whether or not to forgive the mistake. She recognizes that you need to be forgiven. And that puts the blame on the offended person, forcing them to either accept the apology, and therefore move on, or choose to ignore or deny your apology and leave you with nothing else to do.

Nobody wants to be the bad guy and refuse to accept an apology.

However, if you don't acknowledge your wrongdoing and ask to be forgiven directly by the person who was hurt, the person who was hurt will not have to make that choice to forgive and move on.

d. *Offer a convenient way to redeem the error:* in some rare cases there is really nothing you can do to compensate for what has been done. Maybe you accidentally hit a neighbor's dog with your car and killed it?

Offering to buy a new puppy isn't going to fix the situation, so don't get bogged down any further. However, in most cases, you can think of a way to redeem yourself.

If you have broken, lost or otherwise damaged property, you must offer to pay for the damage.

If you have hurt someone close in your life, you might offer to go and seek help together, such as from a medical professional. If you don't know what to give, just ask, « What can I do to make it up to you? »

e. *Give the other time to think and respond:* the deeper the wound, the more difficult it is for a person to forget about it.

Don't force an immediate response. People need time to reflect, process, and let go of feelings of being hurt and offended.

Acknowledge your responsibilities in person and apologize, then offer a way to make amends. For example, you might say something like,

« I'll give you time to think about it. » Offer another specific time to talk, so you don't forget to continue the reconciliation process.

f.   *Listen and respond:* during the initial conversation and during the follow-up, take the time to let the other person speak.

Sometimes what people need most is to share how hurt they were or the repercussions of the mistake that was made.

This part of the exchange isn't fun to listen to, but it helps people sort through the feelings and get to the bottom of it, which is where you both need to get to correct the error and move on.

g.   *Do what you said you would do:* most importantly, if you offered a way to make up for the error and it were accepted, act quickly.

If you don't do what you said, you'll only bring up the error again in an even more unpleasant way, and it'll be nearly impossible for you to be taken seriously when you try to apologize again.

However, situations must always be put into perspective. Remember the famous philosopher and Scotch drinker Ron White's suggestion: « You can't change fools. »

The people who insist that they never make the same mistake twice, are the people who always make the same mistake twice. And, in fact, they never stop making the same mistake.

14. *Trust the process:* sometimes our lives have to be completely turned upside down, changed and rearranged to relocate us to where we are meant to be. Sometimes when things seem to be falling apart, they fall into place.

The best thing you can do is not to think, wonder, or obsess. Just breathe and trust that everything will be fine.

15. *Breathe:* you have already experienced, you have been so frightened, uncomfortable, and anxious and you have survived. Breathe and know that you can survive this too.

I know this is all unbearable right now, breathe, keep breathing, this too will pass, I promise. Everything will be fine for you.

16. *The competition:* I am not in competition with anyone. I have no desire to play the game of being better than anyone. I'm just trying to be better than the person I was yesterday.

    You can spend your whole life competing with others, trying to prove you're somebody while feeling like a nobody. However, you don't have to prove your worth to anyone.

    You were created for a purpose. Your life has meaning and when you develop the confidence to follow your heart and your dreams, you are now in competition with yourself to become the best version of yourself. Nobody else!

    Sometimes you may doubt yourself, feel fear, but the truth is that you are more powerful than you think.

    However, you will need to reprogram yourself to get rid of your fears and doubts, in order to reconfirm your self-esteem and self-confidence.

17. *Support others:* when you see something beautiful in someone, tell them. It may take a second to say, but for them it could last a lifetime.

18. *Appreciate:* spend the day appreciating every little thing that happens to you, and you'll end the day feeling deeply grateful for your life.

    When we take the time to let people know we appreciate them, it encourages them to keep doing even more. This is precisely why gratitude is the ultimate gift that keeps on giving.

    Remember that a simple « thank you » makes the recipient feel important and valued, which boosts their self-esteem and helps improve their self-image.

19. *Always be polite:* politeness is the practical application of good manners or etiquette so as not to offend others. It is a culturally defined phenomenon, and so what is considered polite in one culture can sometimes be quite rude or simply eccentric in another cultural context.

    To be polite is to be aware of the feelings of others and to respect them. We don't always notice politeness, but we usually notice rudeness or inconsiderate behavior.

    Many of the points raised may seem obvious, in most cases they are common sense, but too often social mores are overlooked or forgotten.

Take the time to read the following points and think about how being polite and following social etiquette can improve your relationships with others.

Always use common sense and try to behave in the most appropriate way possible, taking into account any cultural differences:

a. *Say hello :* greet people appropriately, make eye contact and smile naturally, shake hands or hug when appropriate, but say hello, especially to colleagues and other people you see every day.

b. *Be approachable:* don't push people away just because you're having a bad day. Make time to chat: maybe talk about the weather, ask about the other person's family, or talk about something that's making headlines.

    Make an effort to strike up a light conversation, show some interest, but don't overdo it. Stay friendly and positive and pick up on the other person's verbal and non-verbal cues.

c. *Try remembering:* things about the other person and make appropriate comments. Use her spouse's name, date of birth, any significant events that have happened or are about to happen in her life. Always be aware of other people's problems and difficult life events.

d. *Always use « please » and « thank you »:* be sure to thank people for their input and always include « please » when asking for something. If someone offers you something, use « Yes, please or NO, thank you. »

e. *Use suitable language:* be respectful of gender, race, religion, political opinions, and other potentially controversial or difficult topics. Do not make derogatory or potentially provocative comments.

f. *Learn to listen attentively:* pay attention to others while they are talking, don't get distracted in the middle of a conversation, and don't interrupt.

g. *Be assertive:* when this is the case, I respect the right of others to be assertive as well.

h. *Respect other people's time:* try to be precise and to the point in your explanations without seeming rushed.

i. *Praise others for their accomplishments:* congratulations should come across as genuine, it can be difficult if you feel jealous or angry.

j. *At work:* be polite and helpful with subordinates, co-workers, bosses, visitors and customers. Respect and recognize the positions, roles and obligations of others.

Recommended reading and references

We suggest that you consult the works identified below in order to learn more about the particularities contained in this chapter.

BLANCHARD, Kenneth & JOHNSON, Spencer. THE ONE MINUTE MANAGER. Berkley Books. ISBN 0-425-09847-8.

BENNIS, W. & NANUS, B. LEADERS: THE STRATEGIES FOR TAKING CHARGE. Harper Press. ISBN 0-06-015246-X.

BLIWAS, Ron. THE C STUDENT'S GUIDE TO SUCCESS. MJF Books. ISBN: 13:978-1-56731-952-1

DAVENPORT, Thomas H. & PRUSAK, Laurence. WORKING KNOWLEDGE. Havard Press. ISBN 1-57851-301-4.

GEORGE, Bill & All. FINDING YOUR TRUE NORTH. Jossey-Bass publisher. ISBN 928-0-470-26136-1.

HOPKINS, Tom. HOW TO MASTER THE ART OF SELLING: How to Persuade Others Positively. Champions Press. ISBN 0-938636-03-0.

RYE, E. David. 1,001 WAYS TO INSPIRE. Your Organization, Your Team and Yourself. Castle Books. ISBN: 0-7858-2094-9

MICHAELSON, Steven. SUN TZU FOR EXECUTION. How to use the Art of War to get results. Adams Media. ISBN: 13:978-159869-052-1

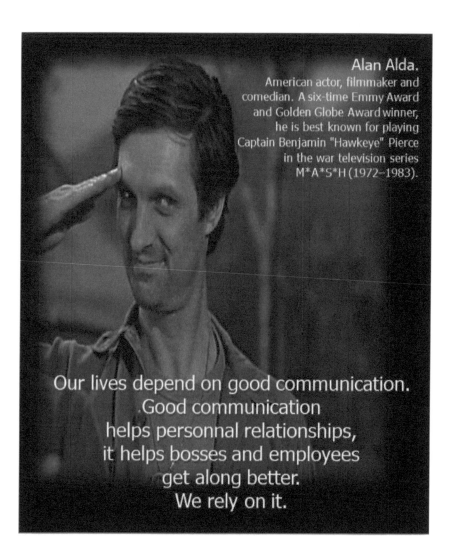

Alan Alda.
American actor, filmmaker and comedian. A six-time Emmy Award and Golden Globe Award winner, he is best known for playing Captain Benjamin "Hawkeye" Pierce in the war television series M*A*S*H (1972–1983).

Our lives depend on good communication.
Good communication
helps personnal relationships,
it helps bosses and employees
get along better.
We rely on it.

FACILITATE POSITIVE EXCHANGES

Whether you are an employee, a boss, a teacher, a politician, a parent, or a military leader, you must at one time, or another promote positive exchanges around you.

To do so, you must develop a temperament above all, which listens, inspires, motivates, influences, and persuades. In fact, a person who favors the exchanges around him.

For many people, it is easy to yell orders, rush and even browbeat people to create an environment of fear in order to get things done. However, they are not actually success-seeking people.

People who promote exchanges for their part, set an example, they show appreciation and don't let their position of authority, make them feel as if they are better than anyone else.

Realize that you will not become a successful person overnight!

You will have very difficult days and sometimes you may even have doubts about your ability to trade and even lead. Don't be too hard on yourself, as this is a natural part of the process.

Never lose hope, keep your beliefs, and pursue your personal development, because each progressive improvement brings you a little closer to success.

Your success, like that of others, depends on the interpersonal learning of the progressive mastery of listening, inspiration, motivation, influence and persuasion.

LISTEN TO

Listening is an essential aspect of success. Speak in a way that others like to listen to you. Listen in a way that others enjoy talking to you.

When you take the time to listen to someone, you really take the time to listen well, because it shows that you value the person, which is the ultimate form of respect.

If you seem bored or if you interrupt the person while they're talking, you show that you don't really care what the person has to say.

You have certainly noticed in your daily life that many people do not listen, they can hear, but they do not listen. To become an effective person, you sometimes have to shut your mouth and really listen to those who approach you.

You should never be too busy to listen, as it is the ultimate form of respect anyone can give to another human being.

Do not listen with the intention of responding, but with a willingness to understand. It shows that you value your interviewees by actively listening to their concerns, comments, or suggestions.

A little trick is to take a few notes, which will promote relationships and, moreover, will allow you not to forget in order to address the resolution of a situation and thus reinforce with your interlocutors the level of confidence that they grant you.

However, when listening, try to discern what is not being said. People may provide you with information that comes from hearsay or sources that support a particular agenda.

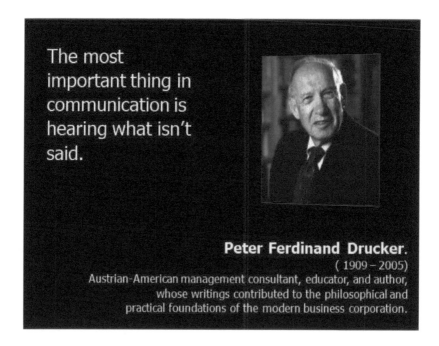

The most important thing in communication is hearing what isn't said.

Peter Ferdinand Drucker.
(1909 – 2005)
Austrian-American management consultant, educator, and author, whose writings contributed to the philosophical and practical foundations of the modern business corporation.

For example, we only have to look at the press and social media to easily see the distortions in relation to economic, political and social issues.

INSPIRE

Has anyone ever inspired you to change your life in a meaningful way that made you healthier, happier, or more fulfilled?

If so, you have a good understanding of the difference positive inspiration can make in a person's life.

Inspiration is powerful, but it's actually not so easy to harness it to help you in your quest for success.

Knowing more about the issue will help you avoid needlessly torpedoing people of good faith and will help you avoid being singled out as disruptive.

If you want to be a positive influence who can inspire your loved ones to become better versions of themselves, please consider the following tips:

1. *Care:* if you can't show someone you really care, do you think you can inspire them?

    The answer is a resounding « No »

    Show that you care, for example, with a simple « how are you today? » Without forgetting that small gestures of kindness go a long way.

2. *Be enthusiastic:* reflect your enthusiasm for the people you are in contact with every day, and I am sure that your sincere smiles, your positive energy, and your attention to them will be increased tenfold.

3. *Gain trust:* if someone you know and love tells you a secret, it stays between you and them. Trust takes a long time to develop, but it can vanish overnight.

    So don't get involved in workplace gossip or unnecessary drama on social media. Keep your distance and comment only to influence positively.

    This way, people will find that they can interact with you and will not hesitate to talk to you and even support you.

    If it's not positive, don't say it: it's easy to criticize people, but that doesn't mean it's the right thing to do.

4. *Think it over:* how do you react if someone insults your intelligence, makes fun of your outfit, or criticizes your performance?

Whether the criticism is true or not, I bet you get angry. No one likes to be criticized, so if you don't have anything positive to say, don't.

5. *Value people:* little compliments have a way of brightening up any day, no matter what melancholy shadows may be hanging over your head. You have surely noticed in the past, when you gave a small compliment to someone, their face would light up.

6. *Hang in there:* It's easy to let the stresses of life shake our foundation of inner strength as human beings, but if you want to inspire those around you, learn to hold your own against the odds.

    Stand firm if you want to show the people around you that even the worst circumstances can be overcome with positive thinking, continuous improvement, and a never-desperate attitude.

7. *Admit your flaws:* while it's important not to flinch when life throws a curveball at us, it's equally important to recognize the fact that we are all human beings and therefore all of us are inherently flawed.

    We all have at least one obvious weakness. So accept your flaws to humanize yourself, so that people can understand you more deeply.

    Show me a person who claims to be beyond reproach, and I'll show you a liar.

8. *Do active listening:* Anyone can hear the words that others say, but few people can actively listen and understand those words to fully grasp their meaning.

    Make eye contact if someone is talking to you about a particular situation or problem, then following the information received and analyzed, ask follow-up questions to show them that you care about what he's going through.

9. *Be ambitious:* aim high and never give up if you want to inspire people so they too can achieve whatever they set out to do.

10. *Provide constructive criticism:* first, constructive criticism should only be given if requested. Also, if it isn't positive, don't say it.

    If you criticize someone for their flaws without any rational input being communicated to them, you're just going to upset them. Provide constructive criticism.

11. *Treat everyone equally:* we are all equal human beings, regardless of gender, race, religion, political affiliation, or any other factor.

    Love and care for people without regard to those irrelevant factors which have no influence on the quality of a person.

    Treat others as they wish to be treated, regardless of their background to inspire trust.

12. *Walk confidently:* keep your head up and eyes forward so you can say; « Hello » or « how are you? » to everyone you meet. Walk with a friendly gait that reflects confidence.

13. *Keep Calm:* how people react to insults or criticism speaks volumes about their ability to inspire others.

    If you respond to hate with more hate, how are you better than the person who triggered the confrontation?

    No matter how inappropriate or harsh an insult was, it's best to stay calm, because getting upset, won't make you feel better, and it certainly won't inspire the people around you.

    Ignore insults as if they didn't happen, and those who witness your unwavering nature may be inspired to do the same.

    If it is a serious insult, keep calm. There will always be a good time to try to discuss it or bring in a referee to put the situation into perspective.

14. *Share your inspirations:* what are the books that have influenced you, the most?
    What are the sources of inspiration that guide the most important decisions of your life?
    How did you become the happy, healthy, positive person you are today?

    Share the influences that shaped you, so others can benefit too.

15. *Acknowledge the contributions of others:* no matter how great you are, you are only one person, so make sure other people have contributed to your success or not, before praising it.

    Acknowledge contributions publicly, if possible, to show people you're humble and thoughtful enough to give credit where it's due.

16. *Keep your promises:* if you've volunteered for a social cause or job or been invited to a movie, you should keep your word, even if other factors influence you not to keep your word.

    It's easy to let go of our responsibilities when a better opportunity presents itself, but it's an infallible way to destroy the trust you've worked hard to get, so be wise to keep your word no matter what.

17. *Stay true to yourself:* many of us have a variety of Me's « Moi » that emerge depending on the social situation at home, work, and friends that all require a different song and dance. This is what I call the « Moi » experience of Miss Piggy, the Muppet character.

    For example, setting up a different scenario for each group of people you meet is very exhausting and definitely not a good way to inspire people around.

    Embrace your true « Moi. » People will understand where you come from and will accept you more without you having to develop scenarios of circumstances, without forgetting the excuses you will have to make, when you are exposed.

18. *Explore other possibilities:* Anyone who thinks they have all the answers is kidding themselves, so don't hesitate to question your beliefs regularly. You always have to keep in mind that there is always another side to a coin.

    Talk to people who think differently from you to find out what motivates them. Chances are you won't change your mind if you truly believe something with confidence.

    However, it is important to explore other possibilities that could validate or invalidate your strategy.

    This discussion should reinforce your point of view or open your eyes to an angle that you have overlooked.

    Additionally, you will also develop trust in people who think differently than you, who otherwise might have been afraid to approach you.

19. *Don't go overboard:* if you win an argument, there's no need to brag about it. « I told you so » will make you look arrogant and rightly discourage people from approaching you about important situations.

20. *Leave people free to act:* Don't just give people step-by-step advice, but rather give them the freedom to figure it out for themselves. Nobody likes micromanagers!

   If asked for help, provide a rough instruction to get a person moving in the right direction, but intentionally leave something to the imagination so they have the freedom to fill in the blanks.

   When a person discovers that they are able to figure things out on their own, they discover that they are more powerful than they ever thought possible. She or he will understand where she or he comes from and because of this, she or he will understand you better.

MOTIVATE

One of the oldest questions known to mankind is « Why do people do what they do? »

This question is often closely followed by « How can I get them to do what I want them to do? »

When you need to do something and the task is too big for you, you need to ask other people for help.

But motivating others to do what you think is important is one of the greatest challenges of leadership.

It is well known that humans are driven by autonomy, mastery and determination.

People want to be in control of their actions, to be recognized for what they've done, to learn new things, and to feel that what they're doing matters.

So how can you give them that?

1. *Explain to them:* explain exactly what you need when and why.

   Explaining the big picture lets others see how important their contributions will be and provides the context needed to make better decisions about how to complete tasks.

2. *Involve them:* ask them what it will take to get involved. Everyone is different, and what may be very motivating for one person may be difficult for another. Find out what motivates them and tailor your expectations accordingly.

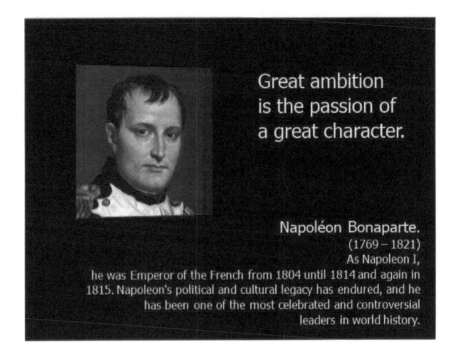

Great ambition
is the passion of
a great character.

Napoléon Bonaparte.
(1769 – 1821)
As Napoleon I,
he was Emperor of the French from 1804 until 1814 and again in
1815. Napoleon's political and cultural legacy has endured, and he
has been one of the most celebrated and controversial
leaders in world history.

3. *Trust them:* give them the autonomy to decide how the work will be done, within a parameter. Give them the ability to decide, but make sure they know you're available for any questions.

4. *Inspire them:* explain why you asked them, as opposed to someone else. List their knowledge, skills and experiences that prepare them well for the job.

    People will often live up to expectations, so set high expectations for yourself and let them know you expect success.

5. *Value them:* thank them sincerely. Congratulate publicly and share positive comments with their peers, bosses, or social networks.

6. *Reward them:* provide tangible proof of your gratitude. Send a handwritten note thanking them for the extra effort on a great project.

    Certificates, gift cards, plaques, public recognition, another worthwhile project, and more responsibility are all ways to reward people.

Even if you only have a small budget, there are things you can do to show your gratitude.

7. *Challenge them:* start a friendly competition between teams or departments, ideally a competition in which everyone can win or learn something.

   Keep the competition between teams, not between individuals, to prevent it from becoming too contentious.

8. *Celebrate them:* celebrate success as a team but recognize everyone's contribution. If it's a big project, break it down into smaller goals that can be celebrated.

9. *Inform them:* even after their contribution is complete, let them know how the project went.

   Especially if they aren't part of the project from start to finish, make sure they know their input was important to its ultimate success.

The main thing, if you want to accomplish great things, you need the cooperation of others.

Motivating others will help you realize your vision, your mission for your success and that of those around you.

INFLUENCE

Everything we do depend on our ability to connect with others and build deep relationships.

You cannot sell a house or buy one, progress in most careers, sell a product, present a story, teach a class, etc. without establishing healthy relationships.

Successful people get better results from their teams, not by brute force, but by appealing to their sensitivity to communicate.

By using a series of tactics, they can influence others toward excellence, toward productivity, and toward success.

Most of us have had or we have in our life a person who influences us positively.

And in turn, we owe it to ourselves to positively influence the people around us, in order to foster our success while helping the people around us in their own pursuit of success.

However, if you don't know such a person, chances are you know a gifted person in your surroundings who can help you in your quest.

During your research remember that a person who really knows how to influence does not sound like nails on a blackboard, but like beautiful music to your ears.

So, how do you influence people in a positive way?

1. *Be authentic:* to positively influence people, be authentic. Rather than being a carbon copy of someone else's authentic version, find out what makes you unique. Discover your unique perspective on an issue, then respect and honor it.

2. *Listen:* to positively influence others, you must listen to what is being said and what is not being said. Therein lies the explanation of what people need to feel validated, supported and seen.

   If a person feels invisible and unnoticed by others, they are less likely to be positively influenced. Listening responds to a person's primary need for validation and acceptance.

3. *Become an expert:* most people are predisposed to listen to, and even respect, authority. If you want to positively influence others, become an authority in the area where you seek to lead others.

   Research and read everything you can about the subject at hand, then look for opportunities to put your education into practice.

   Also, you can discuss on opinions. However, it is unwise to discuss expert facts or untested assumptions.

4. *Use narratives:* I never cease to be amazed at the effectiveness of a story told at the right time.

   If you want to influence people, learn to tell stories. Your stories should relate to the issue or concept you are discussing.

   It should be an analogy or metaphor explaining your topic in layman's terms and with vivid detail to influence and make it all happen right.

5. *Lead by example:* to influence people in a positive way, we must lead by example, lead with intention, and execute with excellence.

6. *Identify people who do well:* a powerful way to positively influence people is to find people who do well.

   Instead of looking for problems, look for successes. Look for the often overlooked, but of critical important things that your peers, subordinates, and bosses do that make work more efficient and enjoyable.

   Once you find these good people, name, and write down their contributions.

7. *Be praiseworthy:* find ways to celebrate the unique qualities and skills of the people around you.

   Be able to assess what people quickly and accurately are doing right, then let them know.

   Make the qualities and skills of each individual known to other members of the group or community.

8. *Be nice instead of always being « right »:* for people who lack self-confidence or those who prioritize the opinions of others, being « right » is important to them. The validation that comes with being perceived as being « right » feeds their ego.

   However, in our quest to be « right, » we can hurt others. Once we have hurt someone by being disagreeable, it is much more difficult to get someone to listen for the purpose of influencing them.

   In order to influence, it is better not to use intimidation, but to promote kindness, rather than to insist on being « right. »

   You can be nice and stand firm. For example, many people think they need others to validate their experience.

   If someone doesn't see the situation, you've been through the way you see it, you get upset. Here it's all about just telling yourself that your experience is your experience and moving on.

9. *Understand logical, emotional and cooperation needs:* the best way to influence others is to appeal to their logical, emotional, and cooperative needs.

- Their logical need corresponds to their rational and educational need.
- Their emotional need is information that touches them in a deeply personal way.
- The cooperative need is to understand the level of cooperation that different individuals need and then offer it appropriately.

The trick with this system is to understand that different people need different things. For some people, a strong emotional appeal will outweigh logical explanations. For others, having the opportunity to collaborate will outweigh the emotional connection.

Remember that if you know your audience, you will know what they need to be positively influenced. If you have limited information about the people you are trying to influence, you will be ineffective.

10. *Your sphere of influence:* If you want to positively influence others, act from your sphere of influence. Leave the rest to others.

Gone are the days when being a jack-of-all-trades is celebrated, as most people these days appreciate more people who understand the target medium and respond with expertise and experience to what people want.

As a final thought, influencing people is all about centering your humanity.

If you want to positively influence others, focus on how you communicate and improve the relationship with yourself first.

It's hard to influence others if you're still trying to figure out how you communicate with yourself.

TO PERSUADE

You might want a raise from your employer, a partnership with a new business that has opened, or maybe just an extra dip for your chicken fingers without paying an extra 50-cent fee.

However, you don't want to turn this into an argument that will escalate.

To do this, let's look at the definition of the words, argue and persuade.

An argument explains what someone believes, while persuasion attempts to change someone else's opinion. Arguments typically examine both sides of an issue and then form a final opinion based on the evidence.

Persuasion is more one-sided because you want others to believe that your idea is the best.

You can get a lot in life just by convincing someone else to give it to you, but they won't give it to you without a good reason.

Your greatest tool for getting what you want is through the psychology of persuasion.

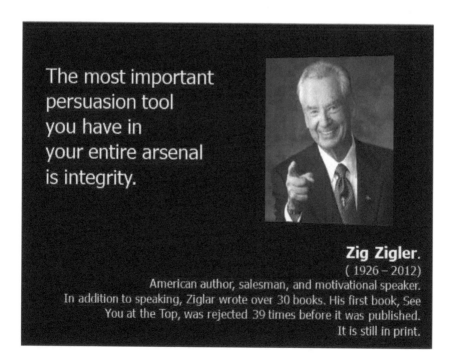

The most important persuasion tool you have in your entire arsenal is integrity.

Zig Zigler.
(1926 – 2012)
American author, salesman, and motivational speaker.
In addition to speaking, Ziglar wrote over 30 books. His first book, See You at the Top, was rejected 39 times before it was published.
It is still in print.

Here are some tricks you can use to get what you want:

1. *Be confident:* your first step is to stay confident and project throughout your call. The surer you are of yourself, the more convincing your arguments will be and the more powerful you will appear.

   Self-confidence is easy to fake and hard to tell apart, so don't be afraid if you don't feel confident, just act confident, and that will probably be enough.

   Trust subtly implies that you are already convinced that you are going to get what you want, which subtly influences the other party to give it to you.

   Just be careful not to overdo your display of confidence, or you run the risk of arrogantly pushing people away.

2. *Present a logical argument:* people are easily persuaded by logic. However, it should always be kept in mind that persuasion is the process of convincing an adversary to change their beliefs or behavior through moral or logical arguments rather than force.

   When a person is persuaded to do something, they do it because they have come to believe that it is the right thing to do.

   For example, suppose you persuade your co-worker to take on one of the toughest parts of an assignment you're working on together.

   Initially, your colleague might resist, but you can use a logical argument to explain that he is better equipped to handle this section, which means that the mission will be carried out faster and more efficiently, making you both look good and helping the company in its approach.

3. *Make it seem beneficial to the other party:* one of the most effective means of persuasion is to make your request seem valid to the other party. It can be tricky, but under the right circumstances, it can be just fine.

   For example, let's say you're trying to convince a friend to help you move house. Obviously, there's a lot of work involved in moving, and your friend may not be so willing to accept.

   Instead of talking about all the furniture you need to move, talk about the fun you'll have exchanging pleasantries and discussing sports and buying pizza and a good beer to celebrate the day.

4. *Choose your words carefully:* some words have inherently greater value than others, and some words have more positive associations than others.

    Take the time to choose the words that will positively vibrate the discussion. In the process, you will become a better communicator, which will make you seem smarter and more thoughtful, and therefore more reliable.

5. *Use flattery:* you know that a good percentage of the population will see you coming quickly if you are too direct or obvious. Instead of outright corrupting your subject with frivolous flattery, use subtle phrasing and supportive and above all proportionate remarks to flatter your interlocutor.

6. *Be patient, but persistent:* you can't always convince you are subject to give you what you want on the first try. If you can't, don't resort to pleading or arguing. Instead, let go of the situation, pull yourself together, and try again later.

Your persuasive messages will stay in the person's subconscious, and the next time you bring up the argument, you'll have a chance to sound more reasonable and persuasive. Don't give up on your goal but allow plenty of time between attempts.

Remember that persuasion is a skill that can be perfected and improved over time.

You probably won't be successful, the first time you practice the tips above, but the more often you use them, the more skilled and, natural you will be in performing them.

Be careful not to manipulate or intimidate people. Rather, your goal should be to help them see things in a different light.

CONVINCE

Some consider George C. Parker the most convincing American who ever lived.

At the beginning of the twentieth century, once or twice a week for several years, Mr. Parker convinced people that he owned the Brooklyn Bridge.

After convincing them, he sold it to them.

Its buyers usually found out about the scam when the police stopped them for setting up toll barriers on « their » bridge.

Although Mr. Parker is certainly not a good role model when it comes to honesty, there is no doubt that he knew how to get others to share his point of view.

Once you know exactly how to convince someone, in the right way and above all honestly, you will be a better communicator, politician, salesman, entrepreneur, professional.

Here are ways to cleverly convince someone without being dishonest:

1. *Give them the opportunity to explain themselves:* when was the last time someone convinced you by verbally attacking you?
   Probably never.

   Even though you're submissive on the surface, in your head you're still clinging to your beliefs. In fact, you are irritated and resentful of the other person.

2. *The reverse approach is much more efficient:* listen respectfully to the other person. In fact, let them come first. As soon as you decide you want to convince them, say, « I'd like your opinion on X, could you please share with me? »

   Here are some alternatives:

   • I know you will have well thought out opinions on Y, are you open to discussing it?

- Sounds like a topic close to your heart. It would be nice to hear your reasoning.
- Could you please guide me through your thought process?
- Let's talk about Z, please tell me what you think.

Simple, ask them to share their thoughts.

3. *Match their reasoning:* It turns out that « fighting fire with fire » is a clever persuasion technique. The experiences of many prove that it is much more effective to use the same type of reasoning as the person you are trying to persuade than to use a different one.

So, if the other person is logical, use logic as well. If, on the other hand, they make decisions based on their emotions, influence them with an emotional argument. Pay attention to the words used by the other person.

a. *Logical Reasoning Words:* analyze, calculate, conclude, constrain, determine, discover, find, gauge, hypothesize, predict, reveal, I think, validate, verify.

b. *Emotional Reasoning Words:* believe, feel, guess, imagine, intuitive, assume, I suspect.

Simple, it is a question of associating with their type of reasoning. If they're emotional, appeal to their emotions, and if they rely on logic, be logical.

4. *Compliment their thought process:* The next time someone mentions something to you that you agree with, replies, « Looks like you've thought about it. »

Most of the time, people who are led to believe that they have given a situation a lot of thought has a better attitude and feel more secure than those who are led to believe that they have given the same situation little thought.

In other words, if you make people believe that they've spent some time developing a belief, they're much more likely to stick with it.

Here are some alternatives to complement their thought process:

- You make excellent points.
- You have certainly given me much to think about.
- I am impressed with your reasoning.

- I wish more people had your ability to consider both sides of the subject.

Simple, it's about getting them to let their guard down with a sincere compliment.

5. *Present the counter-argument:* not only should you be prepared to deal with the other person's counter-arguments, but you might even consider making the counter-arguments for them.

   From experience, two-sided arguments are more convincing than one-sided arguments. The key is to refute the counter-argument after raising it otherwise this approach doesn't work.

   For example, consider a software sales situation where you might say to the prospect, « Our accounting software does not allow users to give customers their own accounts. I know this is a feature that you are interested in. »

   Playing cards on the table immediately makes you more credible. But you don't want to leave any potential issues unaddressed, so follow up with, « We've chosen to offer automatic, recurring billing instead, so once you've set it up, you'll never have to worry about payments. Additionally, customers can view their invoices in their email without having to log into a whole new platform. »

   Because you've earned the prospect's trust, this explanation will have more impact than if you had waited for them to bring up the issue.

   Simple, it's about presenting a counter-argument without putting the person on the defensive.

6. *Be clear and direct:* the strength of your argument will not matter if your interlocutor cannot understand it. And that's true whether you're talking about a complex psychological theory or how a product works.

   It can be tempting to fill your explanations with five-dollar words, jargon, and industry buzzwords, but you'll only confuse the person you're trying to convince.

   Simple, it is a question of subtly questioning your interlocutor, in order to know his level of expertise on the subject treated. When you're not sure, pretend you're talking to someone who's just starting out.

This strategy will help you choose clear and understandable language and examples.

Now that you know these smart ways to convince, don't forget to touch the heart and mind of the person you're talking to, it should be a little easier. But be sure to use your powers for good, not evil, in other words, don't sell any bridges.

MARS AND VENUS

Thirty years ago, the book « Men are from Mars and Women are from Venus » was published. This hugely popular book by author John Gray contains many suggestions for improving relationships between men and women by understanding the communication style and emotional needs of the opposite sex.

As the title suggests, the book affirms the idea that men and women are as different as beings from other planets, and that learning the code of conduct of the opposite sex is of essential value even if individuals do not necessarily conform to stereotypical behavior.

Communications and relationships are based on understanding each other. As much in your life as a couple, at work and in society, you have to be careful about how to understand the differences between men and women, because your success depends on it.

To help us understand the possible differences and similarities, it is worth reviewing some facts from Dr. Gray's research.

1. *Enjoy the difference:* it is important to remember that men and women have mutually different natures. Men and women need to appreciate these differences and stop expecting the other to act the same or feel the same.

2. *The differences:* men love to have their abilities recognized and appreciated and hate to have them looked down upon or ignored. Women love having their feelings acknowledged and appreciated, and hate having them looked down upon or ignored.

   Men don't place much importance on feelings, as they believe they can lead to extremely passionate and extremely unstable behavior. Women do not place great importance on abilities, because in their opinion, they can lead to coldly impartial and aggressive behavior.

   Men like to work alone and exercise their abilities by solving problems quickly and alone. Women like to cooperate and exercise their feelings through interactive communication with each other.
   Men value solutions and find unsolicited help undermines their efforts to solve problems on their own. Women value assistance and view unsolicited solutions as undermining their efforts to proceed interactively.

   Men want their solutions to be appreciated. Women want their assistance to be appreciated.

3. *Dealing with problems:* men like their abilities to be recognized and appreciated and hate to have them looked down upon or ignored. Women like to have their feelings.

    When faced with difficult issues, men become non-communicative, so they can find the best way to help themselves, while women become communicative, so that others can find the best way to help them.

    Men like to demonstrate their abilities by allowing them to solve problems without interference. Women like to show their feelings by being allowed to relate issues without interference.

    When men communicate, they like to cut to the chase and generally only want to listen if they determine there is something in the conversation to discuss. Women like to talk for fun and are happy to listen unconditionally.

    A man's instinct is to take care of himself, even if it means sacrificing others. A woman's instinct is to care for others, even if that means sacrificing herself.

    In a relationship, a man must learn to take care of his partner rather than sacrificing his needs in favor of hers, and a woman must learn to be cared for by her partner rather than sacrificing her own needs in favor of hers, to so that everyone's needs are met.

    If successful, both wins, unlike their instinctive behaviors where one person benefits from another's loss.

    It takes work, because if either partner feels that their relationship efforts aren't succeeding in pleasing their partner, they may feel hurt and decide to revert to their instinctual behavior.

    Unfortunately, this then causes the other partner to do the same and the relationship inevitably falls apart.

    In a relationship, a man needs to feel that his attentions are needed and a woman needs to feel that her needs are taken care of.

    To achieve this, a man must express his desire to have his needs met and his dignity to receive his care, and a woman must express her desire for his care and her dignity to have his needs met.

    Both must remember to appreciate, accept, and forgive the other, and avoid blaming them when they fail.

4.   *Information exchange:* men speak in very objective terms for the purpose of conveying information. The women use their artistic sense and a theatrical vocabulary to fully express and tell their feelings.

Men like to sort through their thoughts before communicating with them and tend to become aloof and uncommunicative when pondering their concerns. At this time, a woman needs reassurance that her partner still considers her worthy of care.

Women like to sort out their thoughts when communicating with them and tend to pour out a litany of general grievances when they relate their concerns.

Currently, a man needs reassurance that his partner still deems him worthy of taking care of things.

Both should try to avoid feeling personally blamed when their partner is facing problems.

5.   *The elastic effect:* men periodically rush to safety when they suddenly fear their self-sufficiency is threatened. At such times, they can become totally unapproachable, demanding the right to be on their own and not express their feelings.

But, if they receive support by giving them space for a little while, they will soon feel better and return to their usual state of self-love.

It can be difficult for women to deal with the suddenness and speed with which men rush for cover and then bounce back.

When men withdraw into themselves, they can help their partners, not worry too much or take it personally by providing a brief assurance that they will return in due course.

Women should resist the temptation to try to bring their partner back prematurely or to criticize him for this natural behavior.

Men like to sort through their thoughts before communicating with them and tend to become aloof and uncommunicative when pondering their concerns.

At this time, a woman needs reassurance that her partner still considers her worthy of care.

Women like to sort out their thoughts when communicating with them and tend to pour out a litany of general grievances when they relate their concerns.

Currently, a man needs reassurance that his partner still deems him worthy of taking care of things. Both should try to avoid feeling personally blamed when their partner is facing problems.

When a man is troubled, he doesn't want his partner to worry about him, but likes to be told that the problem is easily within his abilities to be rectified due to an implied vote of confidence in his abilities.

When a woman is troubled, she likes her partner to express concern for her, but doesn't want to be told the problem is easy to solve because of the implied dismissal of her concerns about it.

A solution must be sought once his feelings have been fully listened to, a solution that is too quick justifies his abilities, but devalues his worries, a problem that is too persistent justifies his worries, but devalues his abilities.

Men feel validated and gratified when left on their own to sort things out and feel undermined by sympathy or unsolicited help.

Women feel valued and gratified when they are offered unsolicited sympathy or help and feel undermined when they are left on their own to sort things out.

6. *A mutual understanding:* women periodically sink into depression when they feel it is time to cleanse and resolve themselves emotionally.

   At that point, they may become completely negative in their outlook, dwelling on all the issues that are bothering them, including long-standing ones that will usually have been raised and dealt with before, and if they cannot find real issues to focus on, so they find something else to worry about.

   They suspend their normal offering nature, demanding the right to express their feelings and not be left on their own, and if supported and given enough time to express and release their negative feelings, they will begin to feel happier again and regain their self-esteem.

   The slowness with which they sink into depression and later recover can be difficult for men to deal with.

At times when women are sinking into themselves, they can help their partners, not worry too much or take it personally by providing a brief reassurance that it is not their partner's fault.

Men should resist the temptation to try to prematurely straighten their partner out or criticize her for this natural behavior.

Men claim the right to be free from time to time. Women ask for the right to be heard from time to time. When a man feels free, he finds it easier to support a woman's need to be heard. When a woman feels heard, she finds it easier to respond to a man's need to be free.

If a man's periodic need to be free coincides with a woman's periodic need to be heard, the best solution is for the woman to be content to be heard by her friends instead.

7. *Emotional needs:* men and women need to remember that the emotional needs of the opposite sex are not the same as their own. Providing our partners with the wrong kind of emotional need will not be very desired.

    Deep inside every man is a knight in shining armor looking for a damsel in distress who will love and cover him, of trust, consent, appreciation, admiration, approval, and encouragement.

    Deep within every woman is a damsel in distress looking for a knight in shining armor who will love her and shower her with kindness, understanding, respect, devotion, validation, and comfort.

    Men should listen carefully to women to understand their needs, avoiding becoming angry or defensive.

    Women should have faith in men's abilities and do their best to meet their needs, avoiding trying to change or control them.

8. *Arguments:* communication between partners should be loving and respectful. Verbal attacks, on the other hand, are very destructive. It's often not so much what is said that causes the damage, but the tone of voice and the body language that accompanies it.

    Arguments thrive on the fact that men don't pay enough attention to women's feelings and that women critically disapprove of men.

    Either can be the initial trigger, as a man's inattention can cause a woman to get upset and express disapproval, and a woman's disapproval can cause a man to become defensive and stop listening to her feelings.

When men make mistakes, they get frustrated and angry, and it's best to leave them alone until they calm down. For men, an apology is an admission of guilt.

Women see apologies as an expression of compassion. This difference in perception is why men are generally much less willing to apologize than women.

When engaged in an argument, men use strong, aggressive words to ensure they win the argument, and women are frequently forced to back down when faced with an utterly determined and implacable opponent.

The men then feel as if they've won the argument, but it's an empty victory, because their female partners haven't changed their minds, they just evade the arguments, in order to avoid that the conflict continues to worsen.

Sometimes people would rather avoid arguments than engage in them. Men tend to do this by withdrawing into themselves and refusing to talk.

Often women claim that the disagreement has been forgotten. The resulting peace is cold, as the problems continue to fester unresolved.

To prevent communication from degenerating into arguments, men should try to listen without becoming defensive, and women should try to express their feelings without criticizing their partners.

9. *Give and appreciate:* men feel loved if their efforts to give are appreciated. Women feel loved based on what they receive. For women, loving someone means knowing and meeting their needs without waiting to be asked, and therefore a loved one should never have to claim anything, because their needs must be anticipated.

    Thus, women give unconditionally and proactively seek out ways to help others, while men only give when they feel their efforts will be fairly appreciated and rewarded, and often do not know, how or what to give without specifically asked.

    Men often quickly suspend donations when they feel satisfied that they have done something. Women can only suspend donations when they feel unhappy that their partner is not doing anything.

    Men value results. For women, it's the thought that counts. Therefore, men appreciate big things much more than women, who feel more appreciated by receiving lots of small gifts instead. A woman may consider a bouquet of flowers as much proof of love as an entire month of hard work paying the bills.

If men and women don't consider these different perspectives, they risk not giving their partners what they really want.

When this happens, the man will tend to withhold offerings, as he feels he is not getting enough reward for what he has given, but the woman will continue to give unconditionally even though she feels she is giving more and has started to feel unloved, unappreciated, and bitter.

Men should try to identify various small ways to give to their partner without expecting to be asked first and should avoid the mistake of assuming their partner is happy to give and not asking for anything in return.

Women need to be careful not to give their partners the wrong impression of being happy when they're not, and if they start feeling resentful, they need to gently reduce their giving, learn to ask for things in return, and make sure to continue to express a lot of appreciation for the efforts of their partners, in order to encourage them to give more.

If men give and women appreciate, both end up being happy.

10. *Communicate difficult emotions:* unresolved negative feelings can cause us to act in ways we really don't want to or manifest in all sorts of compulsive or addictive behaviors.

    By acting as loving parents to our own inner child, we finally allow our pent-up feelings to fully express themselves and be released.

    To ease pain and win love, men often seek success obsessively and women often seek perfection obsessively.

    Men can use anger, ego, or forgetfulness, such as immersing themselves in their work, to avoid vulnerable feelings of pain or fear. Women may become depressed or confused to avoid aggressive feelings of anger. Constructive communication is a learned skill, and many of us must first unlearn the paradigm of negative communication and repression of feelings that we experienced as children.

    Communication works best if it presents the full picture, so that the root of the problem is revealed rather than just the symptoms.

Writing down our feelings is a great way to express our negative emotions such as anger, pain, fear, and regret in a controlled way, rather than letting them explode against our partners in the heat of the moment.

Once this is done, we can reconnect with our romantic feelings, and we are then in a much better shape to explain to our partners how we feel and what they can do to help us feel better.

It is important to communicate such feelings in a loving atmosphere because we may need to feel loved safely while communicating such intimate and revealing feelings.

For their part, our partners may need the same if some of these feelings are painful to hear or can be taken personally. Sometimes it's worth discussing it with friends or advisors first.

11. *How to request assistance:* men like to do things that are appreciated and hate to do things that are required. Criticizing him or giving him excessive instructions will make him feel more like a slave than a loved and trusted partner.

   Men like to prove their worth through the things they do, but they usually wait to be asked. Generally, men take a long time to learn how to offer their services unsolicited.

   Women should avoid asking a man for help in a way that doesn't sound like a clear request or carries an implied criticism that he should have done it already.

   Questions that begin with the words « Could you » or « Can you » are often interpreted by men as questioning their abilities, and so they respond more positively to the same questions if they instead start with; « Would you like » or « Do you want. »

   The difference may seem small, but it can seem as different as the man who says « No, I can't » or « No, I won't » in response to the request.

   It's best to give a man the freedom to do things in a way and at a time that suits him.

   If a man is busy doing something and a woman needs his help with something else, she should feel free to ask him for help, but be prepared for him to ask to defer her or even to refuse it.

If requests always call for positive responses, they are indeed requests and men will feel the difference.

If a man complains about a request, he's really thinking about it, and the best approach is to just wait for him to make a decision without saying anything more while aiming to accept the outcome gracefully.

12. *A question of maturity:* in relationships, unresolved negative feelings can arise without warning, and we suddenly become upset, sensitive, or distant. When this happens to our partners, we must encourage them to overcome this situation, accepting that it may take time and that they may need outside support as well as ourselves while doing our best to control any impatience or resentment we might feel toward them during these times.

Love necessarily changes over time. The pristine happiness we feel when we first fall in love doesn't last forever, and over time our personal flaws and negative baggage inevitably become exposed. But if we remain faithful through the ups and downs of each other's lives, then our initial happiness gradually transforms into a mature form of love that can become stronger and more complete over the years.

13. *Life Changing Factors:* be responsible for your actions, otherwise you are a victim. We react differently to external stress.Men detach themselves and analyze calmly. Women experience strong emotions when evaluating support. Men misinterpret women's emotions as needing resolution.

Most couples get stuck in a pattern where she gives more and he gives less, then she resents him, so he gives even less because he's not appreciated.

Remember that the world is constantly changing. It is also important to understand that you must take into account the society around you, not only from a gender point of view, but also from a racist, spiritual, political, economic, etc. side, in order to gauge your interactions.

There is also the genetic history that comes into account. Women these days are much more eager for career challenges and are looking more for a certain level of independence. Traditionally male occupations are now filled by energetic women who wish to be in control of their destiny.

However, man is a man and woman is a woman and the genetics of several thousand years quickly comes to the surface among other things under the emotions.

Today, what it means to be a man, or a woman is more nuanced and complex than ever. Men and women are moving beyond stereotypes and embracing their true selves, which has important implications for relationships today. As the roles of men and women evolve, the mastery of the relations of the two genders must also evolve.

Recommended reading and references
We suggest that you consult the works identified below in order to learn more about the particularities contained in this chapter.

BLANCHARD, Ken et al. KNOW CAN DO!
Audio renaissance. ISBN-10-1-4272-0251-6.

BURSK, CLARK & HIDY. Harvard Business School. THE WORLD OF BUSINESS: Selected Library of the Literature of Business from the Accounting Code of Hammurabi to the 20th century. Simon & Schuster. Library of Congress catalog card number: 62-14278

BRIAN, Denis. A LIFE: PULITZER. Wiley & Sons. ISBN 0-471-33200-3.

CAMUS, William. COMMENT S'ACCOMMODER DES FEMMES.
Presse de la cité, Paris, 1971.

CARTER, Lee Hartley. PERSUASSION. Convincing Others When Facts Don't Seem to Matter. Tarcher Perigee. ISBN: 978-0-14-313347-6

CLEMMER Jim, FIRING ON ALL CYLINDERS.
Macmillan of Canada. ISBN 0-7715-9133-0.

GÉRARD, H. & WUNSH, G. COMPRENDRE LA DÉMOGRAPHIE : Méthode d'analyse et problèmes de population. Marabout, Université, 1973, Paris.

GRAY John, Ph.D. MEN ARE FROM MARS, WOMEN ARE FROM VENUS: A Practical Guide for Improving Communication and Getting What You Want in Your Relationships. Harper. ISBN 1-55994-878-7.

KRAUSE, G. Donald. THE ART OF WAR FOR EXECUTIVES.
Penguin Books. ISBN 0-399-53150-5.

MACKAY, Harvey. SWIM WITH THE SHARKS WITHOUT BEING EATEN ALIVE.
Ballantine Books. ISBN 0-8041-0426-3.

RYE, David E.1001 WAYS TO INSPIRE YOUR ORGANIZATION, YOUR TEAM AND YOURSELF. Castle's Books. ISBN 0-7858-2094-9.

SCHARMER, Otto C. THEORY U: Leading from the Future as it Emerges, the Social Technology of Presencing. BK Publishers. ISBN 1-57675-763-3.

LIEBERMAN, David J. YOU CAN READ ANYONE: Never be fooled, lied to, or Taken Advantage of Again. Audi Coach. ISBN 1-59659-153-6.

PATTERSON, Kerry & all. INFLUENCER. Mc Graw Hill. ISBN: 13:978-0-07-148499-2

Commitment
is what
transform
a promise
into reality.

Abraham Lincoln.
16th president of the United States
(1809 -1865)
Lincoln led the nation through the American Civil War and succeeded
in preserving the Union, abolishing slavery, bolstering the federal
government, and modernizing the U.S. economy.

COMMIT TO SUCCESS

Generally, when we talk about commitment, we refer to a strong sense, of will and focus in order to fulfill a promise, an obligation, a responsibility, a contract.

In a context of commitment to success, the commitment to succeed must be accompanied by a declaration of intent or an action plan.

Very often we use this word about the statements we can make about the seriousness of our relationships.
For example, « I'm in a committed relationship » or « I'm totally committed to this relationship. »

We take it for granted that the word or phrase has the same meaning for all of us. However, this is not always the case, because often people, according to the principles of morality, does not always respect their commitments for all sorts of valid and invalid reasons.

With respect to relational commitments, they are usually statements regarding proposed behavior or outcomes.
For example, « I'm committed to you » suggests that maybe I'm not looking for another relationship or that I'm going to be monogamous.

The institution of marriage is most identified with the pledge of commitment. It is a commitment of legal and social moral vows to justify our commitment to fidelity and an enduring love.

However, statistics reveal that even when we formalize our commitments through marriage, there is as much chance of failure as of success. After all, more than half of marriages experience infidelity and we all know the divorce rate.

So, if our most honored commitments are not kept, we should try to understand why this is so. The problem is that we make promises about behaviors and results, but ignore the process needed to achieve those goals.

Imagine a student committing to earning « A's » without devoting himself to his studies. The commitment simply becomes a lip service without the sincere devotion to fulfillment.

In relationships, the outcome people refer to, are things like continued love, happiness, and faithfulness. It is foolish to think of achieving such results if there is not some level of focus on the process necessary to achieve lofty goals.

Ordinarily, you will hear troubled couples mentioning that they unfortunately don't have time to talk about their problems because life seems to be moving too fast for them.

And as unfortunate as it may seem, too often many couples don't spend enough time together privately. They don't remember their last date. They say life has become too busy.

Here, it is easy to imagine the rate of failure caused by emotional detachments, extramarital affairs, or subsequent divorces. Otherwise, an atmosphere of mediocrity and indifference surrounding the relationship.

Now, what is a result?

A « result » is just a snapshot of life. In an instant, we take that snapshot and call it a result. In truth, it is only a moment taken from the flow of our life experience.

You can choose to look at the behavior or the singular decision that we call the outcome, or you can look at the process of life and know if you are fully committed to that process.

What we need to examine is the flow of experiences and the quality of how we choose to live. The result is simply the by-product of this process flow.

If we learn to engage fully in the process, then the results will be what they should be. But, if we just commit to the outcome and ignore the process, we sabotage both.

Committing to success is a series of cumulative results, that improve your life and that of those around you.

COMMITMENT TO WORK

Work engagement is defined as the level of enthusiasm of an employee, volunteer or boss towards the tasks assigned to them in a workplace.

It is the sense of responsibility that a person, has towards the goals, vision, and mission of the organization with which he is associated.

High levels of employee satisfaction in an organization are linked to a commitment to work and to one's organization.

This results in superior performance, which in turn results in increased profitability, productivity, employee retention and overall improved working atmosphere.

However, most great things in this world are achieved through persistence, hard work, and dedication. All of these qualities are not just manifested in one day.

A person develops these qualities over the years. The same goes for organizations, if an organization expects its employees to perform exceptionally well, it will need to provide a work environment that will help increase engagement at work.

How to improve your engagement at work?

Improving work engagement cannot be done in a single day. It takes time to bring higher levels of engagement to the workplace.

All commitment generates compromises, and it is obviously much easier to remain yourself by doing nothing.

Ethan Hawke.
American actor, writer and director.
He has been nominated for four Academy Awards.
Hawke has directed three feature films, three off-Broadway plays and a documentary. He has also written three novels and one graphic novel.

Below you will find tips for making effective and immediate changes to achieve the desired success. It is important that both the employee and the boss participate actively and above all in a positive way.

1. *Build a strong team:* teamwork works wonders. Organizations should develop a culture where teamwork should be important. Achieving goals together makes difficult tasks easier to accomplish.

   Teamwork depends on the ability of employees to interact and work in tandem with the boss, so they can function as a group.

2. *Let the team know what you expect of them:* hard-working employees are an asset to an organization. Most employees want to be part of the success story of the organization with which they are associated.

   Therefore, it is important to clearly communicate the goals, vision and mission to employees. This way, employees will know what the organization expects of them.

   Clarity of thoughts is important during the tenure. With clarity comes the determination to work and achieve excellence.

3. *Foster a culture of transparency:* the organization must be transparent. Let employees participate freely in discussions, important decisions related to employees and the contribution they can make to the organization.

   When an organization informs its employees, they feel valued and trusted. This increases their sense of belonging and, therefore, their commitment to work.

4. *Foster, open, free communication:* open and free communication within an organization facilitates an environment of trust. The open door policy is one way to promote free communication. Additionally, an organization can use employee satisfaction surveys, polls, etc. to provide feedback to the organization.

   When receiving this feedback, organizations should keep an open mind to interpret and then respond logically to employee expectations with the goal of improving the work culture, without criticizing the employees who provided the feedback.

   Take advantage of these comments. Once employees know their suggestions or feedback is appreciated work engagement will increase.

5. *Establish a strong work ethic:* work ethic includes not only how an employee feels about their job or career, but also how seriously they take their job responsibilities.

It involves a positive attitude and behavior, respect for colleagues, effective communication, and interaction in the workplace. The work ethic shows who and how a person is.

Historically, successful organizations have worked tirelessly to introduce, improve, and promote work ethics, honesty, integrity, and accountability.

These key factors contribute to establishing and improving a work ethic with the aim of increasing the chances of success.

When employees demonstrate such values in an organization, they are tempted to stay and commit to the organization.

6. *Develop a culture of trust:* trust is an essential factor that brings exceptional results in any relationship.

   Trust is not just a plaque on the door, a welcome sign telling employees: « Here, we offer trust. » Both the boss and the employee must do everything possible to create an environment of mutual trust.

   It involves a lot of effort from senior management and the organization as a whole to introduce and promote this culture in the organization. Trust is earned by putting a consistent effort into everyday actions.

   When an organization promotes such a culture, it attracts employees who will have a real impact on the organization in all the right ways and thus increase work engagement.

7. *Make use of innovation:* let your employees be innovative by coming up with ideas, strategies, means of communication, etc.

   Innovators are engaged collaborators. These employees are always looking for better ways to perform even the most mundane tasks.

   These employees should be valued by organizations and encourage them to come up with better ideas and reward their achievements and innovations.

8. *Help your employees to develop:* an organization that helps its employees grow professionally and personally and respond to their logical aspirations in a positive way is much more likely to be in a position to have people working for the organization for long periods of time.

An organization can support its employees by providing learning opportunities, cross-training, and any other interactive method that supports their overall development. Such gestures help organizations to retain their employees while engaging them more in their work.

9. *Offer incentives:* organizations need to reward employees who perform exceptionally well. Each person has different things that motivate them. Incentives linked to follow up and results make employees feel important.

   It is important for organizations to recognize the hard work of employees to achieve the desired result. Incentives should be awarded based on objective criteria.

10. *Celebrate success:* employees need to feel validated and valued by the organization. The leader must show that he cares for them.

    Employees do not leave an organization if they know their opinions matter, if they are treated fairly, if their achievements are recognized and if they feel part of an organization.

    Celebrate success with your employees, tell them they made a difference, encourage them to do better. The slightest gesture will lead them to improve with each passing day. This will lead to better engagement at work.

11. *The difference between involvement and commitment:* involvement and commitment are different, although there is some overlap.

    The employees involved are engaged and it shows through their actions and work ethic. They will be more attentive, productive, responsible, and energetic in their work.

    Although the two terms are often used interchangeably, there are obvious differences. For example, we may claim to be committed, but we do not demonstrate through our work that we are.

12. *The benefits of commitment to work:* a team of dedicated employees is an organization's dream come true.

    A team, of engaged employees is the best solution for the long-term future of an organization or any business.

    The leaders within the organization as well as the positivism of the employees are responsible for building this culture.

Here are the advantages of having a team that is committed to work:

- *Increased productivity:* engaged employees need a leader to guide them. They don't need someone who has to be constantly behind them to get things done. Such organizational commitment results in increased workplace productivity.

   A compliant team will create their own tasks and ensure they are implemented. They will show up on time to get the job done and even go the extra mile.

- *The goal is reached:* a complacent team will only do what is asked of them, a committed team will do that and more to achieve their targets and objectives.

   An engaged team understands the goals and their individual role in achieving those goals. They are driven and set higher goals than what is expected of them.

   For a committed team, goals aren't just a number, a date, or a target. It is for them a vision, an adventure!

- *Spread the « joie de vivre» at work:* in simple terms, an engaged team promotes enthusiasm and joie de vivre in the workplace.

   Engagement brings ownership and more creativity in tasks. A committed team thrives on new and innovative ideas, and it's fun to implement such ideas again and again.

Engagement at work brings added value through active participation in company-related discussions.

Engaged employees contribute great ideas and are always happy to help others visualize those ideas.

An organization needs commitment and dedication from its employees to achieve its goals.

STRATEGIC SUCCESS

Traditionally, the military uses the word « strategy. » Strategy refers to the "deployment" of troops. It expresses the positioning of the troops before the enemy is engaged.

Today, this word is used in several sectors and types of activities. To facilitate the context of the use of the word, it is a question of substituting « resources » for troops.

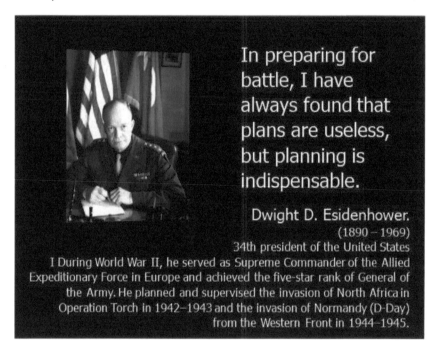

In preparing for battle, I have always found that plans are useless, but planning is indispensable.

Dwight D. Esidenhower.
(1890 – 1969)
34th president of the United States
I During World War II, he served as Supreme Commander of the Allied Expeditionary Force in Europe and achieved the five-star rank of General of the Army. He planned and supervised the invasion of North Africa in Operation Torch in 1942–1943 and the invasion of Normandy (D-Day) from the Western Front in 1944–1945.

A strategy is an action that managers take to achieve business or organizational goals.

A strategy can also be defined as a general direction set for the business and its various components to achieve a desired state in the future.

1. *The strategy is derived from a detailed strategic planning process*: a strategy consists of integrating the organizational activities and using and allocating the necessary resources within the organizational environment, in order to achieve the objectives.

   When planning a strategy, it is essential to consider that decisions are not made in a vacuum and that any action taken, is likely to provoke a reaction from the people concerned, competitors, customers, employees, suppliers, and society at large.

A strategy can also be defined as the knowledge of goals, the uncertainty of events, and the need to consider the likely or actual behavior of others.

A strategy is an organization's decision plan that sets out its objectives, policies, and key elements for achieving the objectives.

In addition, it defines the business or goals to be pursued, the type of economic and human organization it wants to be and the contribution it expects, to make, to its shareholders, customers, and society as a whole.

A strategy is meaningful because it is not possible to predict the future. Without perfect foresight, organizations must be prepared to deal with the uncertain events that constitute the environment in which they operate.

A strategy deals with long-term developments rather than routine operations, that is, it deals with the likelihood of innovations or new products, new production methods, new markets to be developed or social policies in the future.

2. *How to elaborate a strategy?*
Many leaders find it difficult to adopt a strategy. They know well that it is important to have strategies, in order to logically present the decision-making in their organizations.

They understand that they cannot observe and control everything in their organizations, contrary to what many of them would like.

They sincerely want to develop good strategies and they understand the theory. But when it comes to detailing the strategy, they quickly get bogged down.

It's unfortunate, but it's not that surprising. This is a direct consequence of the confusion over what an « organizational strategy » is and is not.

An organizational strategy is a set of guiding principles that, when communicated and adopted in the organization, generate a desired decision-making model.

A strategy is therefore about how people in the organization should make decisions and allocate resources in order to achieve key objectives.

A good strategy provides a clear roadmap, made up of a set of guiding principles or rules, that defines what actions employees should or should not take and what they should prioritize or not to achieve the desired goals.

So, a strategy is just one piece of the overall strategic direction that leaders need to set for their organization.

A strategy is not a mission, unlike what the leaders of the organization want it to accomplish. The missions are developed into specific objectives and performance measures.

A strategy is also not the value network that includes the network of relationships with suppliers, customers, employees, and investors within which the business creates and captures economic value.

Finally, a strategy is not a vision, which is an inspiring portrait, of what pursuing and achieving the organization's mission and goals will look like.

Vision is part of the incentives of what leaders do to motivate members of the organization to engage in above-average efforts and mission is about what will be accomplished.

The value web is about the people with whom value will be created and captured.

A strategy addresses how resources should be allocated to accomplish the mission within the context of the network value. And a vision that includes incentives, explains why members of the organization must feel motivated to perform at a high level.

Together; mission, networks, strategy, and vision define the strategic direction of an organization.

They provide, the WHAT, WHO, HOW and WHY needed to powerfully align action during complex structuring.

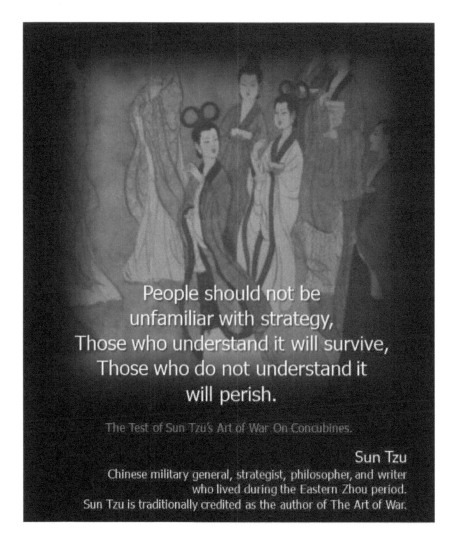

People should not be
unfamiliar with strategy,
Those who understand it will survive,
Those who do not understand it
will perish.

The Test of Sun Tzu's Art of War On Concubines.

Sun Tzu
Chinese military general, strategist, philosopher, and writer
who lived during the Eastern Zhou period.
Sun Tzu is traditionally credited as the author of The Art of War.

Simple, you cannot develop a strategy for your business or organization without first thinking about the mission and goals.

Similarly, one cannot develop a coherent strategy by isolating oneself from decisions concerning the network of partners with which the organization will create and capture economic and social value and even in some cases both in parallel or sequentially.

By focusing on the four elements and sequencing them correctly, the strategy building process can be demystified.

3. *Which strategy to choose?*
    A strategy is the collective term for all the steps that a business or organization takes to achieve its goals and achieve its mission and vision.

    This involves understanding what the business or organization does, what it needs and what it needs to do to achieve those goals.

    This information helps in making decisions about resource allocation and helps in setting priorities.

    When everyone in the organization understands the strategy, it creates a framework for the team to keep working in the same direction.

    Strategic decisions will guide your business or organization in the direction you are working towards.

    However, with so many ways to do it, it's important to keep your vision in mind.

    Here are some guiding questions to ask yourself and your team along the way:

    - Who are we?
    - How to stand out?
    - Where do we want to go in the future?

    Once you have an overview of your goals, refine your questions to focus on the most immediate goals that will help you achieve them.

    Make sure you stay realistic by keeping your action plan within the limits of your available resources, your user base, and the specific needs of your market.

Here are some business strategies to consider:

a. *Structuralist:* By adopting a structuralist strategy, you will build your business, political, or social operations around current market conditions and use industry structure to your advantage.

    For example, in a business this may mean that you order products or supplies using established processes from your suppliers, or that you take into account generally recognized barriers.

b. *Growth:* if you choose a growth strategy, it means that you focus on introducing new products or features or expanding into new markets.

    To do this, you will seek, for example, a competitive advantage by offering a unique experience that your potential customers will not find anywhere else. Or you will find a new clientele through market research or professional networking.

    This is when you need to consider a growth strategy for your business.

c. *Competitive price:* becoming a cost leader is one way to set yourself apart by offering a competitive price for your product or service.

    If you have a unique strategy to reduce costs without sacrificing quality, use it to stand out in your industry.

    There are many benefits to being a cost leader, including.

    • Leaders can charge the lowest amount for a product and still be profitable.

    • Leaders can withstand recessions better than their competitors because they are experienced in attracting consumers with budgets in mind.

    • Leaders can be more flexible. Since their costs are low, they can reduce prices more often to attract a larger customer base.

    Note that a cost containment strategy carries several risks. If a competitor can cut costs more frequently, it could take away your customers.

d. *Differentiation:* with a truly unique product or service that you can offer to potential customers, you can stand out in the market. Differentiation allows a business to take a creative approach and charge high prices for products or services.

Strategies to drive brand differentiation include emotional response, innovation, creative presentation, unique experience, and pricing.

Product differentiation is important because it can lead to a competitive advantage in the market.

If differentiation were not an option for small businesses, large businesses would still dominate, as they have the opportunity to set the most attractive price.

e. *Inflate prices:* Price inflation strategies involve charging a high price for your product or service upfront to cover upfront costs such as production, manufacturing, and marketing.

Usually, this approach makes sense for a company introducing something that has never been done before and is worth a premium price.

The advantages of a pricing policy are the ability to make a product attractive to customers, while covering costs.

The downsides of pricing strategies that aren't appealing enough to customers won't provide, the revenue, you need to operate successfully.

f. *Acquisition:* acquisition strategies are a way to drive growth through the purchase of another business. This is different from an organic growth strategy, where the focus is on growing internal products or services.

Here are some reasons to pursue the acquisition of another company:

- Obtain quality personnel or additional skills, knowledge of your industry and sector or other business information.

- Access funds or valuable assets for new development.

- Attract a larger customer base, increase your market share and reduce competition.

- Diversification of products or services.

- Reduced costs and overhead through shared budgets.

Above all, remember that acquiring a business can be extremely complex. Make sure you have legal, finance, organizational and marketing professionals on your team.

g. *To concentrate:* the idea behind targeted approaches is that you can choose the segment of the market you want to target through one of the strategies already covered.

If you see an opportunity to be a leader in a specific area, focus and focus your efforts on pursuing it.

Sometimes it can pay off more than trying to capture the entire market with a targeted strategy.

When deciding on a new business strategy, your first step should be to review your business plan.

You will learn about your strengths, weaknesses, competitive challenges, and resource allocation.

This information can help you craft the most effective business strategy for your unique business.

THE OBJECTIVE

There are many people who feel as if they are adrift in the world. They work hard, but they don't seem to be achieving anything worthwhile.

One of the main reasons they feel this way is that they haven't spent enough time thinking about what they want out of life because they haven't set formal goals.

After all, would you embark on a great journey without really knowing where your destination is?
Probably not!

Goal setting is a powerful process for thinking about your ideal future and for motivating yourself to turn your vision of that future into reality.

The goal-setting process helps you choose where you want to go in life. By knowing precisely what you want to accomplish, you know where to focus your efforts. You'll also quickly spot the distractions that can so easily lead you astray.

Why set objectives?

Top athletes, successful business, and successful people in all walks of life all set goals.

Goal setting gives you long-term vision and short-term motivation. It focuses on knowledge acquisition and helps you organize your time and resources, so you can get the most out of your life.

By setting yourself specific, clearly defined goals, you can measure to take pride in achieving those goals, and you'll see progress in what might have seemed like a long, pointless period.

You will also increase your self-confidence, as you will recognize your own abilities and skills to achieve the goals you have set for yourself.

Start by setting personal goals. To do this, you should set your goals at different levels:

- First, you create your « big picture » of what you want to do with your life or in, say, the next 10 years by identifying the large-scale goals you want to achieve.

- Then you break them down into smaller and smaller goals that you need to achieve in order to achieve your lifetime goals.

- Finally, once you have your plan, you start working on it to achieve those goals.

Therefore, it's about starting the goal-setting process by looking at your life goals.

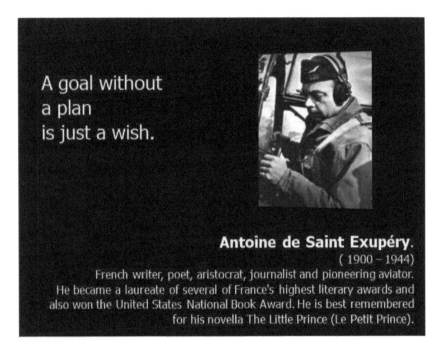

A goal without
a plan
is just a wish.

Antoine de Saint Exupéry.
(1900 – 1944)
French writer, poet, aristocrat, journalist and pioneering aviator.
He became a laureate of several of France's highest literary awards and
also won the United States National Book Award. He is best remembered
for his novella The Little Prince (Le Petit Prince).

Then, to start setting your goals, look at the things you can do in, say, the next five years, then next year, next month, next week, and today.

1. *Set lifelong goals:* the first step in setting personal goals is to consider what you want to accomplish in your lifetime or at least, far into the future.

   Lifetime goal setting gives you the big picture perspective that shapes all other aspects of your decision-making.

   To give broad and balanced coverage of all the important areas of your life, try setting goals in some of the following categories or other categories unique to you where they are important to you:

   - *Career:* what level do you want to reach in your career, or what do you want to reach?

- *Financial:* how much do you want to earn, at what stage? What is the link with your career goals?

- *Education:* is there any knowledge you would like to acquire in particular? What information and skills will you need to achieve all of your goals?

- *Family:* do you want to be a parent? If so, how are you going to be a good parent? How do you want to be seen by a partner or your extended family members?

- *Artistic:* do you want to achieve artistic goals?

- *Attitude:* is part of your mindset holding you back? Is there any part of your behavior that bothers you? If so, set a goal to improve your behavior or find a solution to the problem.

- *Physical:* are there any sporting goals you want to achieve, or do you want good health into old age? What steps do you want to take to achieve this?

- *Pleasure:* how do you want to have fun? You have to make sure that part of your life is for you!

- *Public service:* do you want to make the world a better place? If so, how?

Spend some time thinking about these things, then select one or more goals from each category, that best reflects, what you want to do.

Then consider scaling back again, so you have a few really important goals to focus on.

In doing so, make sure that the goals you set, are the ones you really want to achieve, not the ones your parents, family, or employers might want.

If you have a partner, you probably want to think about what they want, but also be sure to stay true to yourself!

2. *Set smaller goals:* Once you've set your lifetime goals, make a five-year plan of smaller goals that you must complete if you want to achieve your lifetime plan.

Then, create a one-year plan, a six-month plan, and a one-month plan of progressively smaller goals that you need to achieve in order to arrive at your life goals. Each of the levels must be based on the previous plan and in an overall vision.

Next, create a daily « to-do » list that you should do today to achieve your life goals.

At an early stage, you are more modest goals might be to read books and gather information about achieving your higher-level goals. This will help you improve the quality and realism of your goal setting.

Finally, review your plans and make sure they fit the way you want to live your life.

3. *Stay the course:* once you've decided on your first set of goals, continue the process by reviewing and updating your « to-do » list daily.

   Periodically review long-range plans and modify them to reflect your changing priorities and experience. A good way to do this is to schedule regular exams and record them in a diary for future reference.

4. *Intelligent goals:* the following general guidelines will help you set effective and achievable goals:

   - *State each goal as a positive statement:* express your goals in a positive way, for example, « Do this skill well » is a much better goal than « Don't make that stupid mistake. »

   - *Be precise:* set specific goals, including dates, times, and amounts, so you can measure achievement. If you do, you will know exactly when you have reached the goal and can derive complete satisfaction from it.

   - *Set priorities:* when you have multiple goals, give each one a priority. This helps you avoid feeling overwhelmed by too many goals and helps direct your attention to the most important ones.

   - *Write down the objectives:* this crystallizes them and gives them more strength.

   - *Keep operational objectives by elements:* keep reasonable goals that you are working towards one or a series of items that you know are achievable. If a goal is too big, it may seem as if you're not making progress towards it. Keeping goals small and incremental gives more opportunities for rewards.

- *Set performance goals, not outcome goals:* you need to be sure to set goals over which you have as much control as possible. It can be quite disheartening not to achieve a personal goal for reasons beyond your control. For example, in the business world, these reasons can be an unfavorable business environment or unexpected effects of government policy. In sports, the reasons can include poor judgment, bad weather, injury, or just plain bad luck. Remember to base your goals on personal performance, so you can stay in control of achieving your goals and get satisfaction from them.

- *Set realistic goals:* it is important to set goals that you can achieve. For example, all kinds of people such as employers, parents, media, or society may set unrealistic goals for you. They will often do this without knowing your own desires and ambitions. However, it's also possible to set goals that are too difficult because you might not appreciate the obstacles in your way or not understand how much skill you need to develop to achieve a particular level of performance.

5. *Achieve the goals:* when you have achieved a goal, take the time to enjoy the satisfaction of having done so. Let the implications of reaching the goal sink in and observe the progress you have made towards other goals. If the goal was important, reward yourself accordingly. All of this helps you build the self-confidence you deserve. With the experience of achieving this goal, review the rest of your planned goals:

- If you reached the goal too easily, make your next goal a little more difficult.

- If the goal took a long time and maybe at times daunting to complete, make the next goal a little easier.

- If you learned something that would cause you to change other goals, do it.

- If you noticed a deficit in your skills despite achieving the goal, decide if you want to set goals to address it.

It's important to remember that it doesn't matter that much about not hitting the intended target, as long as you put it into perspective and learn from the experience.

Essentially, goal setting is an important method for:

- Decide what you want to accomplish in your life.
- Separate what is important from what is irrelevant, or a distraction.
- Motivate oneself.
- Build self-confidence, based on achieving goals.

First define your life goals. Next, make a five-year plan of smaller goals that you must achieve if you want to achieve your lifetime plan. Continue the process by regularly reviewing and updating your goals. And don't forget to take the time to enjoy the satisfaction of achieving your goals when you do. If you have not already set goals, do so now.

As you incorporate a sense of commitment, strategy and purpose into your life, your career will accelerate, and you will wonder how you would have managed to achieve any success without it!

Recommended reading and references
We suggest that you consult the works identified below in order to learn more about the particularities contained in this chapter.

BLANCHARD, Ken & BOWLES, Sheldon. BIG BUCKS! How to Make Serious Money for Both You and Your Company. Morrow, Harper Collins, ISBN 0-688-17035-8.

BOUCHARD, Jacques. LES 36 CORDES SENSIBLES DES QUÉBÉCOIS. Éditions Héritage. ISBN 0-7773-3944-7.

BOUCHARD, Jacques. L'AUTRE PUBLICITÉ : La publicité sociétale. Éditions Héritages. ISBN 0-7773-5478-0.

BRICKER, D. & WRIGHT, J. WHAT CANADIANS THINK ABOUT ALMOST EVERYTHING. Seal Books. ISBN 0-7704-3008-2.

DEL, Michael. DIRECT FROM DELL: Strategies That Revolutionized an Industry. Harper. ISBN 0-694-52023-3.

Kotter, P., John. THE HEART OF CHANGE. Harvard Press. ISBN: 1-57851-254-9

Kotter, P., John. LEADING CHANGE. Harvard Press. ISBN: 13:978-0-87584-747-4

COHEN, Dan. S. THE HEART OF CHANGE FIELD GUIDE. Harvard Press. ISBN: 1-59139-775-8

The true sign
of **intelligence**
is not
knowledge,
but **imagination.**

Albert Einstein.
(1879 -1955)
German-born theoretical physicist,
widely acknowledged to be one of the greatest and
most influential physicists of all time.
Einstein is best known for developing the theory of relativity.

INTELLECTUAL CAPACITY

Intellectual capacity is your ability to think, learn, plan, and perform work with discipline. It is thanks to your brain that you can develop this capacity which will allow you to do more in less time and with less energy.

A big part of developing your intellectual capacity is believing that you can do it. High performers are always looking for opportunities to learn more and improve.

They recognize that mistakes are not just part of life, but an opportunity to learn. They understand that failing at something today is a necessary step to mastering situations in the future.

To improve, we need to understand our weaknesses. Part of this can be done by looking at ourselves honestly, but often we have to look to others. Think about the people in your life who know you well and whom you can trust to be honest with you about your shortcomings.

In some cases, you will receive feedback that will be hard to hear, but part of building capacity involves being open to feedback and using it to grow.

Once you have an idea of what you want to improve, look for resources that will help you. A great strategy is to pick a topic you want to learn more about, research the most respected books on that topic or check it out at a library, and set aside time to read them.

Intellectual capacity is thinking, learning, designing, and implementing rigorously. Intellectual strength develops when a person does things that inspire them to excel.

Intellectual capacity can be demonstrated by constant learning, reading, physical activity, broadening the horizon of thought and imagination.

To do this, you will need to develop different strengths necessary for healthy intellectual growth:

- *The analysis:* it is defined as a wide range of professional skills, including critical thinking, making difficult decisions and solving complex problems. This skill involves receiving new information and mentally internalizing it in a productive way.

- *Problem solving:* involves analyzing and evaluating information to be able to resolve an unfamiliar situation. Analyzing new information by correlating it with several sets, of known information, then synthesizing it to find a potential solution, in order to empirically test the solution is at the heart of problem-solving skills.

- *Verbal comprehension:* refers to the ability to understand the meaning of words read or heard and to understand how words are related to each other. Verbal comprehension can be tested by asking a person to repeat a sentence they have just heard, thus testing their intellectual strength.

- *Reasoning skills:* are critical thinking skills, including information analysis, evaluation, and synthesis. However, reasoning skills include more intriguing skills such as abstract thinking, information processing, creative thinking, and excellent problem-solving abilities.

In short, an intellectual person refers to anyone who engages in critical thinking, reflection, and in-depth research on societal realities and finds an appropriate solution to societal normative problems.

CREATIVITY

Creativity is the act of turning new and imaginative ideas into reality.

Creativity is characterized by the ability to perceive the world in new ways, to find obscure patterns, to make connections between seemingly unrelated phenomena, and to generate solutions.

If you have ideas, but you don't put them into practice, you are imaginative, but not creative.

Creativity is our ability to tap into our « inner » reservoir of resources, knowledge, insight, information, inspiration that populates our minds and that we have accumulated over the years, simply by being present, alive, and awake to the world, in order to combine them in extraordinarily new ways.

Creativity is the process by which something new happens. Creativity requires passion and commitment. It makes us aware of what was previously dark and points in a new direction.

Innovation is the implementation of a new or significantly improved product, service or process that creates value for business, government, or society.

Why are innovation and creativity important?

Once an idea is possible, innovation becomes an easier challenge. Creativity is the step of identifying that something might be possible.

However, innovation is the action of putting things into practice, despite challenges and resistance, rather than simply contemplating.

In business, creativity and innovation contribute to overall growth and success by meeting unique needs in markets, differentiating companies from competitors, and evolving a brand as desires and consumer needs are changing.

Creativity and innovation keep an organization dynamic.

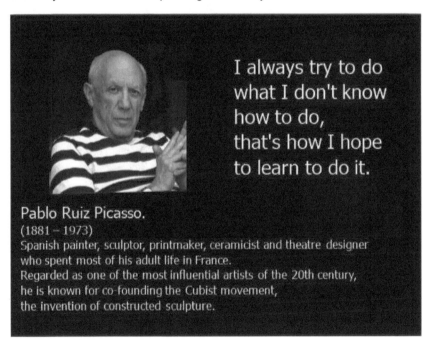

I always try to do what I don't know how to do, that's how I hope to learn to do it.

Pablo Ruiz Picasso.
(1881 – 1973)
Spanish painter, sculptor, printmaker, ceramicist and theatre designer who spent most of his adult life in France.
Regarded as one of the most influential artists of the 20th century, he is known for co-founding the Cubist movement, the invention of constructed sculpture.

Being creative means solving a problem in a new way. It means changing your point of view.

Being creative means taking risks and ignoring doubt and facing fears.

It means breaking away from routine and doing something different for the sake of doing something different.

It means plotting a thousand different routes to reach a destination.

It means challenging yourself every day.

Being creative means looking for inspiration even in the most mundane places. This means that you ask simple questions, without criticizing.

Being creative is knowing how to find the similarities and differences between two completely random ideas. Foremost, being creative means thinking!

A. Develop intellectual habits.

Here are some intellectual habits to foster creativity in your life:

1. *The imagination exercise:* observing children in imaginative play reveals a source of natural creativity. When engaged, in pretend play, children embrace multiple perspectives and playfully manipulate emotions and ideas.

    As an adult, cultivating a childlike sense of play can revolutionize the way we work. Hybrid forms of work and play can provide the most optimal context for learning and creativity, for both children and adults.

    Play and intrinsic joy are intertwined, creating a synergy that naturally leads to greater inspiration, effort, and creative growth.

2. *Passion*: passion often stems from an experience or relationship that has moved us in some way and can be a source of inspiration. It's often emotional fuel that launches us down a creative path, but that's just the beginning.

    People who achieve their long-term creative dreams balance their enthusiasm for the future with realistic strategies to get closer to their goals with the help of inspiration and hard work.

    When someone advises you to « follow your passion, » be careful: besides being one of the most common clichés, it's not very helpful advice. You must seek a passion in harmony with your authentic « self » and compatible with your other activities.

    The passion to prove yourself to others is unlikely to translate into creativity because it relies on you avoiding challenges that would otherwise lead to your growth.

    So, while you should be open to what inspires you, don't blindly follow passion. Make sure it really resonates with you and your skills.

3. *Daydream:* creative people know, despite what their parents and teachers may have told them, that daydreaming is anything but a waste of time.

   Reverie exposed that mind-wandering offers very personal rewards, including creative incubation, self-awareness, future planning, reflection on the meaning of one's experiences, and even compassion.

   As idle as it may seem, the act of mind wandering is often anything but senseless. This can lead to improvements in creative thinking.

   So, the next time you're hard at work on a creative project or task that requires intense focus, try taking a five-minute daydream break every hour.

   Try engaging in a simple activity that will get your mind wandering, like walking, doodling, or cleaning, and see how it affects your ideas and the way you think.

4. *Solitude:* the symbolism « room of one's own » is a basic need for many creative people.

   For example, the work habits of countless artists have demonstrated that solitary thinking time truly nurtures the creative spirit.

   It is important to take time for solitude, to give yourself space to reflect, to establish new relationships and to find meaning.

   Unfortunately, loneliness is vastly undervalued in society, leading many people to avoid spending time alone.

   We tend to view alone time as wasted time or an indication of an antisocial or melancholy personality.

   But the ability to appreciate and productively use our own companionship can stimulate creativity by helping us tap into our thoughts and our own inner world. So, don't avoid it, embrace it!

5. *Intuition:* intuition arises from unconscious or spontaneous information processing and plays an important role in how we think, reason, create and behave socially. Intuition is part of the cerebral system.

   Thus, the brain system helps us assimilate new information into our existing knowledge structures and helps us recognize complex patterns and make unconventional connections that lead to more original ideas and solutions.

This generation of creative ideas, along with a greater role in exploring and playing with these ideas, will determine their possible uses.

6. *Open to experiment:* the willingness to cognitively explore one's inner and outer worlds is the trait of a stronger, more coherent personality that predicts creative success.

   This openness can be intellectual and characterized by a search for truth and a willingness to engage in ideas marked by a desire to explore fantasy and art and to experience this beauty emotionally or affectively, characterized by exploring the depths of human emotion.

   So, whether you want to boost your creativity, try a new creative outlet or an entirely different medium, take a new route home from work, or seek out a new group of people with different interests or values that you could learn from.

   Being open to new experiences can help increase your integrative complexity and ability to recognize new patterns and find connections between seemingly unrelated pieces of information.

7. *Full consciousness:* while the ability to observe the present moment without distraction or judgment is a vital skill for anyone seeking joy and fulfillment in life, it is especially important for creative thinkers.

   Mindfulness as an activity and as a personality trait provides numerous cognitive and psychological benefits such as improved task concentration and sustained attention, empathy and compassion, introspection, self-regulation, memory improved and improved learning, as well as positive affect and emotional well-being. Many of them are central to creativity.

   However, for optimal cognitive flexibility and creativity, it is best to achieve a balance between mindfulness and mind wandering.

   Some forms of mindfulness can actually work against creativity.

   More specifically, those encouraging the letting go of the thought in itself rather than accepting the thoughts more openly.

Interestingly, free meditation, which emphasizes listening to one's subjective experience, has been shown to increase both activation and functional connectivity of the imaginary network.

So, try practicing a non-directive form of meditation and allow the mind to wander constructively while stimulating attention.

8. *Sensitivity:* if we think of creativity as a way of « connecting the dots » in some way, then sensitive people, those with heightened sensitivity to their environment and also heightened sensory experience, such as sound, lighting and perfume, experience a world where there are both more points and more possibilities of connection.

Sensitivity can be both a blessing and a curse leading to greater intensity of experience as well as emotional overwhelm. So, rather than trying to toughen yourself up, you might want to harness your sensitivity through artistic expression.

9. *Transform adversity into advantage:* experiences of loss, struggle, pain, and defeat can be powerful catalysts for personal growth, creativity, and profound transformation.

It is often through suffering that we learn compassion, through loss that we learn to understand, and through overcoming struggles that we discover our strength and beauty.

Adverse events can force us to re-examine our beliefs and life plans, and therein lies their power and creative potential.

After experiencing adversity, the mind actively dismantles old belief systems that no longer hold and create new structures of meaning and identity.

To make sense of difficult experiences, try expressive writing, which research shows can alleviate symptoms of post-traumatic stress and depression, while improving certain cognitive functions, such as working memory, part of short-term memory, which concerns immediate conscious perceptual and linguistic processing.

Interestingly, overwhelmingly positive events, especially those that evoke feelings of admiration, wonder, inspiration, and connection to something bigger than yourself, can also encourage creativity.

Positive emotions strengthen a person's psychological resources, expand attention, inspire new thoughts and behaviors, and stimulate creative thinking.

So, if you're looking for a creative boost, look to all of life's significant moments, good and bad, as potential sources of inspiration and motivation.

10. *Thinking otherwise:* creative people are united by their reluctance to respect ways of thinking and conforming to decorum.

By choosing to do things differently, they accept the possibility of uncertainty and failure, but it is precisely this risk that opens up the possibility of true innovation.

The secret to creative greatness seems to be doing things differently, even when it means failing. Especially during the idea generation phases, trial and error is key to innovation.

Remember, the more ideas creators generate, the more likely they are to produce a masterpiece eventually.

Doing things differently means you'll likely do things wrong or make mistakes, so expect that and don't let caution get in the way of creativity.

Will following all these paths to creativity mean that you will become a creative genius?

Not necessarily. But, when the artist is alive in a person, whatever his type of work, he becomes an inventive, searching, daring and expressive creature.

If we learn to embrace our own messy, creative selves, we give other permission to do the same.

We help create a more welcoming world for the creative spirit and enable us to find a greater connection with others and with ourselves in the process.

B.   Develop your creativity.

If you think you're a creative person, you should know that most people won't necessarily benefit from being creative.

However, true creatives over time develop the ability to use and observe all of their resources, senses, and knowledge to help them succeed.

So, take the time to prepare well because the road will be long.

Two obstacles can hinder your creativity. These are your external and internal barriers.

Things that limit your imagination and inspiration are internal barriers and examples of external obstacles are poor speaking or presentation skills.

Below, you will find tips to increase your creativity:

1.   *Give up depending on others:* start learning to use your own resources. Look around you to identify your resources and what you can get out of them. It will be a bit difficult at first, but over time you will adapt.

This does not mean that you will be alone and risk disobeying your superiors. It just means that you can develop learning ability by learning from others.

This means establishing appropriate interactions and creating your own resources.

2.   *Dream, think and create:* you have to believe that you have an incredible mind, full of thoughts and ideas. You have to express them. Talk to others and see what they say.

Some of your ideas may seem funny or inappropriate, but it doesn't matter. They say a man is only as big as his dreams. So, don't stop dreaming.

3.   *Surround yourself with excellence:* Pablo Picasso said, « Good artists copies, great artists steal. » It means good people learn from the best people and the best people learn from the best.

You cannot develop your creativity when you are surrounded by those who constantly discourage and distract you.

So have real talents around you and learn from them. It's not just about surrounding yourself with talented people, it's also about knowing. Don't limit yourself. Always study and experience a variety of new things. It can propel your creativity forward.

4. *Look for jobs with no added value:* take the time to include in your daily schedule, an hour or more to let your hobbies guide you. It can be gardening, collecting, memorabilia, painting or whatever you like.

   Maybe these things will not benefit you financially, but it will definitely help awaken your creativity.

5. *Combat your fear of failure:* fear that you might make a huge mistake or fail in your efforts to do something new can cripple your creativity.

   You have to remember that mistakes will always be there, they are just part of the creative process.

   Many great minds have struggled with the fear of failure all their lives, but they never gave up and they kept trying until they succeeded.

   Nevertheless, to overcome your fear of failure; analyze all potential outcomes, develop a contingency plan, and think about the worst possible scenario. This will help you regain confidence and start again with confidence.

6. *Expand your comfort zone:* people are often stuck in their comfort zone and afraid to try new things in life. This can be a huge problem because when we keep the same routine, our creativity shuts down.

   We have to change things and allow different adventures to supercharge our creativity.

   You don't have to climb the highest mountain, but you can do simple things, like go visit a nearby town, talk to a stranger, read a book of a genre you've never read.

7. *Avoid stress, enjoy life:* don't get discouraged or stressed by your failures. Take a long drive, hang out with friends and family, or just go to the movies. All of these things will help you get back on track.

   When we're feeling down, our creativity gets stuck inside us and it's hard to think of a new idea in that state of mind. That's why it's important to fight it and just enjoy life.

C. Cultivate a creative life.

We all yearn for a creative life but living one can sometimes feel like a challenge.

However, the thing to remember is that living a creative life is more of a habit than anything else and as with all habits, there are certain rules you can follow to make it easy to stick to them.

If you want to lead a more creative life whether you are a painter, engineer, accountant, carpenter, military man or anyone else, follow the rules below and you will soon find that living a creative life is easier than you never imagined.

1. *Learn to say, no to things that do not enlighten you:* to live a creative life, you need to be specific about what you do.

    By saying no, to the things that don't turn you on and excite you, you'll make room for the things that do it. You can't do everything, so make sure the things you do, are best for you and your creativity.

2. *Let curiosity lead you:* let your curiosity guide your creativity and really take the time to explore.

    Being creative is all about exploring and discovering, so let your imagination run wild and be open to possibilities. You never know what amazing opportunities might come your way.

3. *Anticipate, accept, and embrace your natural imperfections:* nothing is perfect, nor is your creative work. It's easy to fall into the trap of lamenting your blemishes, but they're natural and completely normal.

    Creative work is not supposed to be « perfect. » It's meant to be real and raw, made by a human, not a machine. Embrace the imperfections of your work and you will see yourself blossoming creatively.

4. *Don't compare yourself to others:* a comparison can be a huge pitfall to living a creative life. The problem with comparing yourself is that you are not compared to the original.

    When you compare your work, with all its known inconsistencies and difficulties, to someone else's carefully curated presentation of their work, you are comparing two completely different things. It's just not a fair comparison and you will lose every time.

Remember that your creative work is wonderful and unique, there is no need to compare.

5. *Making space and time for a creative Life:* living a creative life is easy when you have the time and space to make it work.

   Even if you work full time and live in a small apartment, you can still devote some time and space to your creativity. It can be a simple desk in the corner of your living room and a small daily commitment to showing up and creating.

6. *Create a daily habit of creativity and stick to it:* there's incredible power in forming a habit of daily creativity, and it doesn't have to be a huge time commitment either.

   If you only have thirty minutes available per day, start there. Commit to a specific time of day each day and make it your time to create.

   Schedule it like a date and stick to it as part of your daily routine. Forming a daily habit has incredible power to harness your creativity.

7. *Stop being your own worst critic:* despite all the criticism you might receive from others, chances are you are actually your own worst critic.

   Think about how you talk to yourself about your creative work and ask yourself if it's negative or positive.

   If you find it leans to the negative side of the spectrum, end it by affirming more positive thoughts. Your work is good, you have enough time, and you will get there!

8. *Keep learning:* to live a creative life, it is important that you never stop learning. Whatever your creative field, make an effort to learn something new every week.

   It can be as simple as reading the story of a great designer in your field or as in-depth as learning a completely new style or technique.

   Learning keeps your creative mind active and your ideas fresh.

9. *Expose yourself to new experiences:* living a creative life and creating every day means exposing yourself to new experiences.

   Developing an idea during the creative process can sometimes be difficult, especially when you lack experiences to draw on. Living is what fuels your creativity.

   This is where you will draw your inspiration from, and its importance cannot be underestimated.

10. *Keep showing up no matter what:* if you want to live a creative life, you have to keep showing up and creating no matter what.

    We all have tough days when we don't feel inspired, but the most important thing to remember is that inspiration comes from action.

    The more you show up and participate in creative work, the more inspired you will feel.

11. *Get in touch with a creative community:* a creative community is most important to you.

    It will keep you on track, motivated, inspired and give you an amazing support system. If you want to live a creative life, find creative people in your area to connect with.

    They will be there to support and encourage you in your work, while you also encourage them with theirs.

12. *Don't limit yourself to one creative medium:* just because you consider yourself a writer, painter, designer, inventor, or researcher, doesn't mean that's all you should be doing.

    If you feel as if you want to explore a new creative realm, let yourself be.

    Living a creative life is not about relentlessly pursuing a creative way, but about experimenting and finding what works.

13. *Share your creations:* always share your creative achievements with others!

    You've worked hard to get there, and your good work should not go unnoticed. Show off your creative work with pride.

14. *Let your creativity evolve over time:* your creativity must constantly evolve, grow, and change. Don't close in on yourself just because you think your way is all you have to offer.

    The magic of living a creative life is to steer it in the direction of your choosing. Let your creativity evolve, it might surprise you.

15. *Don't forget to have fun:* don't forget to have fun, creativity is meant to be fun!

    Let your imagination run wild, experiment with different avenues, and when the pressure gets too much, create something just for fun. No goals, no pressure, just free creativity!

D. Can creativity be learned?

We are naturally creative and as we grow up we learn not to be. Creativity is a skill that develops and a process that is managed.

Creativity begins with a knowledge base, learning a discipline and mastering a way of thinking. You can learn to be creative, by experimenting, exploring, challenging assumptions, using imagination, and synthesizing information.

Learning, to be creative, is like learning a sport. It takes practice to develop the right muscles and a supportive environment in which to thrive.

Your ability to generate innovative ideas is not just a function of the mind, but also a function of five key behaviors that optimize your brain for discovering:

- *Association*: making connections between questions, problems, or ideas from unrelated fields.
- *Questioning*: Asking questions that challenge common wisdom.
- *Observation*: scrutinizing the behavior of customers, suppliers and competitors to identify new ways of doing things.
- *Network*: meet people with different ideas and perspectives.
- Experiment: Build interactive experiences and provoke unorthodox responses to see what ideas emerge.

Everyone has creative abilities. The more training you have and the more diverse, it is, the greater the creative potential.

In creativity, quantity equals quality. The longer the list of ideas, the higher the quality of the final solution.

Very often, the most qualitative ideas appear at the end of the list.

E. Overcoming the myths about creativity.

The beliefs that only special, talented people are creative and that you must be born that way to have creative abilities are just fantasies.

According to a study by the University of Exeter, the idea that geniuses such as Shakespeare, Picasso and Mozart were « gifted » at birth is a myth.

Researchers examined exceptional performance in the arts, mathematics, and sports, to determine whether the widespread belief that to achieve high levels of ability, a person must possess an innate potential called talent.

The study concluded that excellence is determined by the right circumstances, encouragement, training, motivation and above all practice.

Few of the « gifted » showed early signs before parental encouragement.

No one has achieved high levels of success in their field without devoting thousands of hours to serious training.

For example, Mozart trained for 16 years before producing a recognized masterpiece.

INNOVATION

Creativity and innovation are two related but distinct concepts, and each is necessary for success. Creativity does not lead to inventions and growth, but to innovation.

However, innovation does not happen without creative people. Generating creativity means allowing people to think outside the box and sometimes go against the norm.

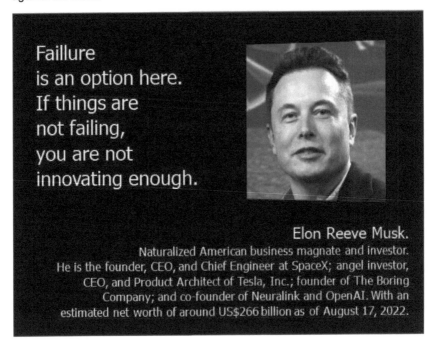

Faillure is an option here. If things are not failing, you are not innovating enough.

Elon Reeve Musk.
Naturalized American business magnate and investor. He is the founder, CEO, and Chief Engineer at SpaceX; angel investor, CEO, and Product Architect of Tesla, Inc.; founder of The Boring Company; and co-founder of Neuralink and OpenAI. With an estimated net worth of around US$266 billion as of August 17, 2022.

If you let bureaucracy stifle creativity, innovation will fall victim, leaving your competitors to push forward with new market share.

1. *What is innovation?*
    Innovation is the implementation or creation of something new to realize value. Innovation most materializes as a tool, physical advantage, or aid that solves a problem or creates an advantage.

    Types of innovation:

    There are several dozen types of innovation framework; here we present the three major categories of innovations that promote the process of creativity and innovation that can partly or wholly be used or adapted to economic sectors, to social and governmental organizations:

- *The economic model:* Focused on internal management, these configuration innovations analyze how an organization operates and generates revenue. These can pose a higher risk, as they sometimes alter fundamental decisions on which organizations are built.

  For example, business model innovations are best pursued when operators identify oversaturated markets, low customer satisfaction, or outdated technology.

- *Products and services:* Whether tangible or intangible, innovations in products, services, or a combination of the two improve existing goods in some way. For example, smart phones, pharmaceuticals, wireless headphones, or new financial services.

- *Commercialization:* marketing innovation creates new markets or increases existing market share. Marketing innovations are positively disruptive new ways for brands to interact with consumers. Not only can market innovation introduce a new way to connect with audiences, not only it can be as simple as promoting an existing product for a different use than originally intended.

An innovation makes a demonstrable, often disruptive, difference in a product, service, industry, and social or governmental organization. This is a fundamentally new and tangible change and departure from the conventional.

2. *Why don't we innovate more?*
   A lot of people who are full of ideas just don't understand how an organization should work to get things done, especially radically new things. Too often there is the strange underlying assumption that creativity automatically leads to true innovation.

   This type of thinking is a particular disease of « brainstorming » proponents, who often treat their approach as some sort of ultimate business liberator.

   The process of forming and linking ideas and innovation are not synonymous. The first type deals with the generation of ideas and the second with their implementation.

   To avoid confusion, it is not essential that the innovation be successfully implemented to be considered an innovation.

The object of innovation is success, but to demand in advance that there be no doubt of its success would negate its chance of ever being tried.

Here, it must be understood that there are many people who are overflowing with ideas, but who simply do not understand how an organization must operate to get things done.

It's not about putting a dozen inexperienced people in a room and conducting a brainstorming session with the goal of producing exciting new ideas for ideas to spring up and come to fruition.

Rather, bring together people who have an open mind, the know-how, the energy, the audacity, and the stamina to implement ideas.

Whatever the objectives of a business, it must make money. For that, we have to move things forward. But having ideas rarely equates to getting things done in a business or organizational sense if they don't become innovations.

Ideas are not implemented in business or in art, science, philosophy, politics, love, war, if there are not bold people and endurance who concretize them.

3. *A form of irresponsibility:* Since business is only an institution that « gets things done, » creativity without action-oriented follow-through is a particularly sterile form of individual behavior. In a way, it's even irresponsible.

   This is because first the creative man who comes up with ideas and does nothing to help them get implemented shirks responsibility for one of the main requirements of business, namely action. Second, by avoiding tracking, it behaves in an organizationally intolerable way or at best, simple negligence.

   The problem that most often emerges from the creative process today is that many of the people who come up with ideas have a particular notion that their work is done once the ideas have been suggested. They think it's up to someone else to work out the details and then implement the proposals.

   Generally, the more creative, the person, the less responsibility they take to act. It is that the generation of ideas and concepts is often their only talent.

She or he rarely has the energy or the persistence, or even the interest, to work out the details that need attention before her or his ideas can be implemented.

Take the time to observe around you that there are certain people with ideas that can constantly sprinkle everyone in the organization, with proposals and memos that are just brief enough to grab attention, intrigue and maintain interest without including responsible suggestions regarding implementation and potential impacts.

In some cases, it must be inferred that they are using pseudo-novel ideas for their disruptive or self-promotional value.

It should be emphasized, however, that something favorable can be said about the relation of irresponsibility to ideation.

Leaders who are generally effective in their role as leaders can often exhibit what might be called controlled momentary irresponsibility, recognizing that this attitude is practically necessary for the free play of the imagination and hold it back just long enough to be more productive.

4. *The discontented:* in most businesses and organizations, you will find people who are actively dissatisfied with the « here and now » and who are full of suggestions on what to do about it. They are also commonly known as corporate or organizational malcontents.

    They tend to constantly complain about the senility of management, its refusal to see the obvious facts of its own massive inertia. They complain about management's refusal to do things that have been suggested to them for years.

    They often complain that management doesn't even want creative ideas because the ideas disrupt the running of the business. They will even insinuate that management, by their inertia, slowly leads to the ruin of the enterprise.

    In short, they speak of the business or organization as a festering sore of deadly conformity, full of rotting vegetables who systematically oppose new ideas against ancient ideologies.

    For your success and the success around you, it is important to identify these individuals, to ensure that one of them does not torpedo you.

    Also, when appropriate, discuss with management rather than confronting them.

Often, management will be able to take the necessary measures such as distributing additional information to reassure everyone.

For the radicals of discontent, more often than not they shoot themselves in the foot with their remarks and if they do not take notice, they find themselves unemployed by their own fault.

5. *Why resistance?*
    One of the reasons the boss so often rejects new ideas is because he's struggling with day-to-day tasks and that he has to manage a constant flow of problems.

    In addition, he receives an endless stream of questions on which to make decisions. He is constantly forced to deal with problems whose solutions are more or less urgent and whose answers are far from clear-cut.

    It may seem wonderful to a subordinate to provide his boss with a bunch of new and brilliant ideas to help him in his job. However, creative advocates need to understand that the pressing facts of the boss's life take precedence.

    It must be remembered that each time an idea is submitted to him, he must take the time to examine it, put it into perspective and then put himself in solution mode if he thinks that the idea submitted could help the success of the organization.

6. *Make ideas viable:* ideas are useless unless used. The proof of their value is their implementation. Otherwise, they remain in limbo.

    To do this, when you suggest an idea, the responsible procedure is to include at least a minimal indication of what it involves, in terms of cost, risk, labor, time, and perhaps even specific people who need to carry it out.

    This is responsible behavior, because it makes it easier for the boss to evaluate the idea and thus pose fewer problems for him. This is how creative thinking is more likely to turn into innovation.

7. *Determining factors:* that doesn't mean that every idea needs careful study before it's mentioned to anyone. Far from there. Needs vary from case to case based on four factors.

    a. *The position or rank of the initiator of the idea in the organization:* the level of a person's « responsibility » to act for an idea to gain a hearing clearly depends on their rank. The big boss can simply ask one of his subordinates to take and develop the idea. This is enough to grant him a meeting and, if necessary, to initiate an implementation.

Similarly, the head of a department can do the same in his area. However, when ideas are flowing in the opposite direction, up rather than down, they are unlikely to flow unless they are supported by minimal guidance regarding the definition of the idea, inherent costs and risks and a certain level of communication from the initiator.

b. *The complexity of the idea:* the more complex the implications of an idea and the more it may require changes and reorganizations within the organization then obviously the more it will be necessary to expand the proposal, in responsible ways to receive the necessary attention.

c. *The nature of the sector:* The amount of supporting detail a subordinate must submit with their idea often depends on the industry involved and the focus of the idea.

For example, one of the reasons why so much emphasis is placed on « creativity » in advertising is that the first requirement for an advertisement is to attract attention.

Thus, « creativity » often revolves around trying to achieve visual or auditory impact, so that advertising stands out from the ever-expanding stream of advertising noise to which the harassed consumer is subjected.

At this point, in the advertising industry, being « creativity » is quite different, on the whole, from what it is, say, in the steel industry. Putting a new logotype on a shirt is « No sooner said than done. » The idea practically goes hand in hand with its implementation.

However, in the steel industry, an idea, for example, to change the price discount structure to encourage users of cold-rolled steel sheets to place larger orders is so fraught with complications and potential problems, that talking about it is not enough to establish such a discount program.

To get a sympathetic first hearing, such an idea must be accompanied by a good deal of factual and logical evidence.

d. *The attitude and occupation of the person to whom the idea is submitted:* everyone knows that some bosses are more receptive than others to new ideas. Even, there are some who are more receptive than others to novelty.

The extent of their known receptivity will in part determine the elaboration of the support that a new suggested idea requires at its initial stage.

However, just as importantly, it is essential to recognize that the greater the pressures of day-to-day operational responsibilities on the boss, the more resistance they are likely to have towards new ideas.

It should always be remembered that the operating burden is on him. The boss's job is to make the current setup work properly and smoothly.

A new idea demands change and change upsets the smooth regularity of the current operation regarding efficiency, on which its professional future depends.

The boss has very good reason to be extremely cautious about a new proposal. The latter needs several good reasons to reduce the risk before considering an idea very carefully.

In addition, the requirements, he will have to consider, will also depend on the attitude of his superiors towards taking risks and making mistakes. For example, in some organizations, some leaders will have a higher level of receptivity to novelty and even sometimes the more out of the ordinary, the better.

Such organizations are rather rare, because usually business leaders are conditioned by the environment, and it is extremely difficult for them to refute the hierarchical order.

However, you will find this wind of innovation when new leaders with different experiences or from other backgrounds are parachuted into the organization.

The latter perceive their contribution more to improve, change and evolve than to maintain habits that are no longer profitable.

In short, a permissive, open, and conducive environment for risk taking, cannot be created simply by the good intentions of senior management.

The reason for this is either that those senior executives who have risen to their senior positions through a lifetime of wise executive behavior are unable to change their habits or that if their habits are changed, their subordinates will not believe that they really mean it. And in many ways, they see a vindication of their skepticism.

e. *The need for rigor:* organization and creativity do not seem to go together, but organization and compliance do.

The defense of a « permissive environment » for creativity in an organization is often a veiled attack on the very idea of the organization. This quickly becomes clear when we recognize this inescapable fact.

One of the collateral goals of an organization is to be inhospitable to a large and constant flow of ideas and creativity.

Whether it is a large corporation or a large labor group, an army or the Salvation Army, a country like the United States or the People's Republic of China, the purpose of organization is to achieve the type and degree of order and conformity necessary to perform a particular job.

To do this, the organization exists to restrict and channel the range of individual actions and behaviors, a predictable and knowable routine. Without organizational routine, there would be chaos and decadence.

The organization exists to create the number and kind of inflexibility necessary to get the most urgent work done efficiently and on time.

Creativity and innovation disrupt this order. Therefore, the organization tends to be inhospitable to creativity and innovation, although without creativity and innovation, it would eventually perish.

This is why small organizations are so often more lively and « Innovative » than large ones. They have virtually no organization precisely because they are one-person businesses and are often run by people who act on impulse.

Organizations are created to bring order. They have policies, procedures and rules that are not directly expressed in a formal way but are well understood.

The work for which, the organization exists, could not be accomplished without these rules, procedures, and policies.

These same rules that produce the so-called conformism that is so cheerfully decried by the organization's critics, and which seems to disrupt life inside the company.

Remember, where there are enough rules, there will also be silly rules, those that can be ruthlessly caricatured.

But some rules, which to some experts seem nonsensical are far from nonsense if they bother to learn about the problems of the company, the government, or any other group for which the particular organization of work is intended to face.

CREATIVITY TO INNOVATION

All of this raises a question that seems frightening. If conformity and rigidity are necessary conditions of organization, and if these help to stifle creativity, and, moreover, if the creative man can indeed be stifled if he has to spell out the details necessary to convert his ideas into efficient innovations, does all this mean that modern organizations have become such incomprehensible monsters that they have to suffer the terrible fate of dinosaurs, too heavy and unwieldy to survive?

Of course, the answer is no. In fact, great organizations have important attributes that facilitate innovation. Their abilities to spread risk over a broad economic base and among the many people involved in implementing the novelty are significant. They facilitate for the individuals involved personally a certain economic insurance, to thus increase the possibility of innovating.

What often misleads people is that making big operational, or policy changes also requires big organizational changes. Yet it is precisely one of the great virtues of a great organization that in the short term at least its course is irreversible, and its organizational structure is, practically, almost impenetrable.

A vast machine exists to do a certain job. This work must continue to receive the utmost attention, no matter how exotically revolutionary a major operational or policy change may be.

The « boat » may need to be shaken, but one of the advantages of a big boat is that it takes a lot to shake it.

Some people or some departments on the boat may feel the pitching more than others and try to avoid the incidents that produce it.

But the built-in stabilizers of the importance of group decision-making can be used as powerful influences to encourage people to risk these incidents.

Finally, the large organization has an organizational alternative to the supposed "conservative" consequences of greatness.

There is evidence that the relatively rigid organization can build into its own structure certain flexibility that would provide an organizational home for the creative, but irresponsible individual.

What may be needed, especially in a large organization, is not so much a suggestion box system as a specialized group whose function is to receive ideas, develop them and follow them as necessary.

This would be done after the group had evaluated each idea and, preferably, had a long discussion with its author. Then, when the idea and the necessary follow-up are passed on to the appropriate executive, they will be more willing to listen.

The important point is to be aware of the need or the possible value of a system that allows creativity to produce more innovation.

Some companies need such measures more than others. And, as we pointed out earlier, the need partly depends on the nature of the industry.

Certainly, it is easier to turn creativity into innovation in the advertising industry than in an operational company with elaborate production processes, long distribution channels and a complex administrative configuration.

The potential for creativity to mature varies enormously with the industry, the climate in the organization, the organizational level of the originator of the idea, and the kinds of day-to-day problems, pressures, and responsibilities of the people to whom he addresses his ideas.

Without clearly appreciating these facts, those who claim that a business will somehow grow and prosper simply by having more creative people worship their own illusions.

GROUP REFLECTION

Group reflection or more commonly known as brainstorming can generate many radical and creative ideas.

How often have you used brainstorming to solve a problem?
Chances are you've used it at least once, even if you didn't realize it. People have long used brainstorming to generate ideas and come up with creative solutions to problems.

However, you must use brainstorming correctly for it to be fully effective.

1. *What is brainstorming?*
   Brainstorming combines a relaxed, informal approach to problem solving with an open mind, to encourage people to come up with thoughts and ideas that may, at first, seem a bit crazy.

   Some of these ideas can be turned into original and creative solutions to a problem, while others can spark even more ideas. This way of working helps unblock people by allowing them to venture outside of their comfort zone.

   Therefore, during brainstorming sessions, people should avoid criticizing or rewarding ideas. Here it is about being open to the possibilities and breaking down incorrect assumptions of the problem itself.

   However, judgment and analysis at this stage should not slow down, idea generation and limit creativity.

   Once the session is completed, it will be a question of evaluating the ideas resulting from the meeting, in order to further explore the solutions using more conventional approaches.

2. *Why use brainstorming?*
   Conventional group problem solving can, often be undermined by unhelpful group behavior.

   And, while it's important to start with a structured, analytical process of problem solving, doing so can lead to a group developing limited and unimaginative ideas.

   In contrast, brainstorming provides a free and open environment that encourages everyone to participate.

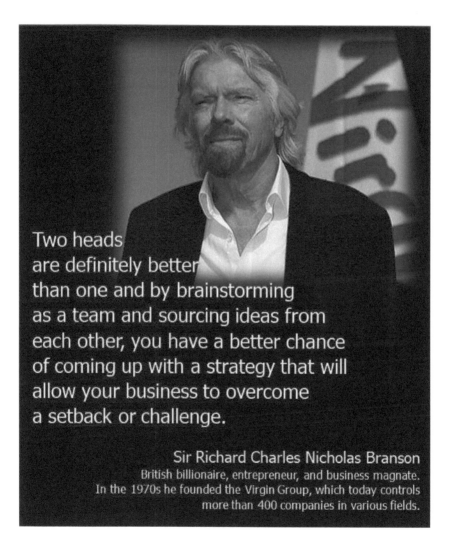

Two heads
are definitely better
than one and by brainstorming
as a team and sourcing ideas from
each other, you have a better chance
of coming up with a strategy that will
allow your business to overcome
a setback or challenge.

Sir Richard Charles Nicholas Branson
British billionaire, entrepreneur, and business magnate.
In the 1970s he founded the Virgin Group, which today controls
more than 400 companies in various fields.

Original ideas are welcomed and developed, and all participants are encouraged to contribute fully, helping them to develop a rich array of creative solutions.

When used during problem solving, brainstorming brings into play the diversity of experiences of team members. This increases the richness of ideas explored, which means you can often come up with better solutions to the problems you face.

It can also help you get buy-in from team members for your chosen solution, after all, they're likely to be more engaged with an approach if they've been involved in its development.

Plus, because brainstorming is fun, it helps the team members' bond as they solve problems in a positive and nurturing environment.

Although brainstorming can be effective, it is important to approach it with an open mind and a non-judgmental spirit. If you don't, people « Shut up, » the number and quality of ideas drop, and morale can suffer.

3. *Instructions for use!*
    You often get better results by combining individual and group brainstorming, which we explain below, and managing the process according to the « rules » below.

    By doing this, you can get people focused on the problem without interruption, you maximize the number of ideas you can generate, and you get that great sense of team cohesion that comes with a well-run brainstorming session!

    To effectively organize a group brainstorming session, follow these steps.

    a. *Prepare the group:* how much information or preparation does your team need to brainstorm solutions to your problem?

        Remember that preparation is important, but frame it enough, so as not to destroy the free nature of a brainstorming session.

        First, choose an appropriate and comfortable meeting space. It can be in the office or virtual. Consider what would work best, for your team. Make sure you have the right resources beforehand.

        You can use virtual brainstorming tools like Miro or LucidSpark, and you'll need pens, and Post-it Notes for an in-person session.

Now consider who will attend the meeting. A brainstorming session bringing together like-minded people will not generate as many creative ideas as a diverse group, so try to include people from a wide range of disciplines and include people who have a variety of thinking styles.

When everyone is reunited, appoint someone to record ideas from the session. This person should not necessarily be the team leader. It is difficult to register and contribute at the same time.

Post notes where everyone can see them, like on flip charts, whiteboards, or use a computer with a data projector.

Make a habit of opening the session with a fun activity to break the ice, especially if people are not used to working together. A relaxed atmosphere is always conducive to a good brainstorming session.

b. *Introduce the problem:* clearly define the problem you want to solve and state the criteria you must meet. Make it clear that the purpose of the meeting is to generate as many ideas as possible.

Give participants a quiet moment at the beginning of the session to generate as many ideas as they can. Then ask them to share or pitch their ideas, while giving everyone a fair chance to contribute.

c. *Guide, the discussion:* once everyone has shared their ideas, start a group discussion to expand on others' ideas and use them to create new ideas. Building on the ideas of others is one of the most valuable aspects of group brainstorming.

Encourage everyone to contribute and develop ideas, including the quieter people, and discourage anyone from criticizing ideas.

As the group facilitator, you should share ideas if you have any, but devote your time and energy to supporting your team and guiding the discussion.

Stick to one conversation at a time and refocus the group if people wander off.

Although you are guiding the discussion, remember to let everyone have fun while brainstorming.

Welcome creativity and encourage your team to come up with as many ideas as possible whether practical or impractical.

Use thought experiments such as provocation through encouragement and engagement or use a random word, image or even sound to open up new lines of thought.

Don't follow one line of thought for too long. Be sure to generate a big quantity of different ideas and explore individual ideas in detail. If a team member needs to « step back » to explore an idea on their own, allow them the freedom to do so.

Also, if the brainstorming session is prolonged, take plenty of breaks, so people can recover to better continue thinking.

4. *Individual brainstorming:* although group brainstorming is often more effective at generating ideas than normal group problem solving, several studies have shown that individual brainstorming produces more ideas and often better ideas than group brainstorming. This can happen because groups aren't always strict about brainstorming rules and bad behavior creeps in.

   Most of the time, however, this happens because people pay so much attention to others that they either don't generate ideas on their own or forget about their ideas while waiting for their turn to speak. This is called. « Idea blocking. »

   When you think for yourself, you don't have to worry about other people's ego or opinions, and you can be freer and more creative. For example, you may find that an idea you would be hesitant to bring up in a group turns into something special when you explore it on your own.

   However, you may not fully develop your ideas when you are alone because you don't have the experience of other group members to draw on.

   Remember that individual brainstorming is most effective when you need to solve a simple problem, generate a list of ideas, or focus on a general problem. Group brainstorming is often more effective in solving complex problems.

5. *The next step - take action!*
   After your individual or collective brainstorming session, you will have plenty of ideas.

   While it may seem difficult to sort through these ideas to find the best ones, analyzing these ideas is the next important step.

This is for you to organize ideas and find common themes by looking at ideas from different angles and thus help you choose options, especially when the differences between options are rather subjective.

Finally, when brainstorming is handled well, it can help you generate radical solutions to problems. It can also encourage people to engage with solutions because they have contributed and played a role in their development.

Also, remember that the best approach combines individual and collective brainstorming and during the process there should be no criticism of ideas and creativity should be encouraged.

Recommended reading and references
We suggest that you consult the works identified below in order to learn more about the particularities contained in this chapter.

ADAM, Scott. SLAPPED TOGETHER. THE DILBERT BUSINESS ANTHOLOGY.
Harper Press. ISBN 0-06-018621-6.

BARKLEY, Bruce T. & SAYLOR, James H. CUSTOMER-DRIVEN PROJECT
MANAGEMENT: Building Quality into Project Process.
McGraw Hill. ISBN 0-07-136982-1.

BRINCKERHOFF, Peter C. MISSION-BASED MANAGEMENT.
Wiley & Sons. ISBN 9-780471-390-138.

DE SCHIETÈRE, J.C. & TURCOTTE, P.R. LA DYNAMIQUE DE LA CRÉATIVITÉ DANS
L'ENTREPRISE : Perspectives et problèmes psychologiques.
Les presses de l'Université de Montréal. ISBN 0-8405 0357-1.

LOGAN, John R. EVOLUTION NOT REVOLUTION: Aligning Technology with Corporate
Strategy to Increase Market Value.
McGraw Hill. ISBN 0-07-138410-3.

MAURER, Rick. CAUGHT IN THE MIDDLE: For Partnership a Leadership Guide in the
Workplace. Productivity Press, Oregon. Library of Congress.

MILLER, J. Gloria & All. A TEAM APPROACH TO MAXIMIZING COMPETITIVE
ADVANTAGE. Wiley Books. ISBN: 0-470-04447-0

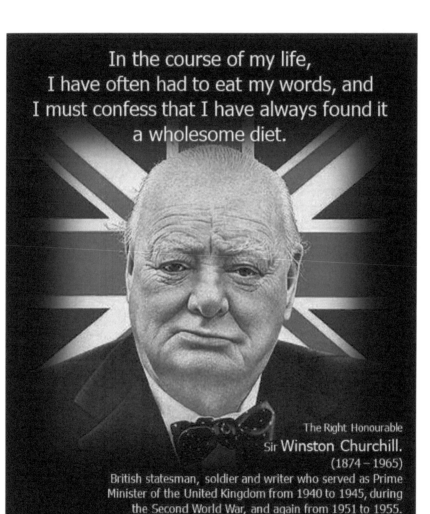

In the course of my life,
I have often had to eat my words, and
I must confess that I have always found it
a wholesome diet.

The Right Honourable
Sir **Winston Churchill.**
(1874 – 1965)
British statesman, soldier and writer who served as Prime
Minister of the United Kingdom from 1940 to 1945, during
the Second World War, and again from 1951 to 1955.

HOW TO UNDERSTAND EACH OTHER

The most important single ingredient in the formula for success is knowing how to get along with people.

One of the most profound experiences we can have in our lives is the connection we have with other human beings. Positive and supportive relationships will help us feel healthier, happier, and more satisfied with our lives.

One of the biggest challenges we face in relationships is that we are all different. We can perceive the world in many ways. The stumbling block we certainly encounter when trying to build relationships is the desire or expectation that people think like us and that way it is so much easier to build a relationship.

We feel more comfortable when we feel that people « understand » us and see our point of view.

Life, however, would be very boring if we were all the same, and although we would find, it was easier initially, the novelty of the similarity would quickly wear off. So, accepting and celebrating that we are all different is a great place to start.

To do this, listening is a crucial skill to build another person's self-esteem, in order to start getting to know them.

This quiet form of flattery makes people feel supported and valued. Listening and understanding what others are communicating to us is the most important part of a successful interaction on both sides.

Active or reflective listening is the most useful and important listening skill. In active listening, we must genuinely wish to understand what the other person is thinking, feeling, and wishing for, or simply, the meaning of the message.

Then, we must validate our understanding of the facts and the feelings expressed before responding with our own new message.

One way to ensure understanding is to reiterate or paraphrase our understanding of the message and return it to the sender for verification.

This process of checking or feedback is what sets active listening apart and makes it effective.

Listening is also about giving people enough time to interact with you. We live in a world where time is of the essence, and we all try to fit in more than one life and for most of us we don't always have the time to give to our loved ones, friends, and co-workers.

Additionally, technology has somewhat eroded our ability to build meaningful relationships.

Being present in your time with people is also important, so that when you're with someone, you're really with someone and not dwelling on the past or the future.

The connection we make with others is the stumbling block of our existence, and devoting time, energy, and effort to developing and building relationships is one of life's most valuable skills.

Communication happens when someone understands you, not just when you talk. One of the greatest dangers of communication is that we can work on the assumption that the other person has understood the message we are trying to convey.

Poor communication can lead to a culture of backstabbing and blame, which in turn can affect our stress levels, especially when we don't understand something, or feel they have been misled. It can also have a positive effect on morale when it works well and motivates individuals to be proactive.

Communicating is also managing mobile technology. Nowadays, almost everyone has a mobile phone, and many people even have two or more.

While they are a lifesaver in an emergency and an effective communication tool, they can also be a complete distraction when people show a lack of mobile phone etiquette.

Learn how to give and receive feedback. Feedback, in my opinion, is the food of progress, and while it may not always be delicious, it can be very good for you.

The ability to provide constructive feedback to others helps them tap into their personal potential and can help forge positive and mutually beneficial relationships.

From your point of view, any feedback you receive is free information that you can choose to include or not. It can help tap into your personal potential and provide you with a different perspective.

Always remember when communicating that people will forget what you did, but people will never forget how you made them feel.

Empathy and understanding connect people. It is a state of perceiving and relating to another person's feelings and needs without blaming them, offering advice, or trying to fix the situation.

Empathy also means "reading" another person's inner state and interpreting it in a way that will help the other person, offer support, and develop mutual trust.

Every relationship can teach us something, and by building positive relationships with others, we will be happier and more fulfilled and feel more supported, united, and connected.

It is important for your success in both business and private life to develop good conditions for everyone to communicate.

Good communication helps us understand people and situations better.

It helps us overcome diversities, build trust, and respect, and create the right conditions to share creative ideas and solve problems, like dealing with drama, manipulators, mindset shift.

COMMUNICATION

Developing strong communication skills is essential to building a successful career and also plays a key role in private life. Using, improving, and showcasing your communication skills can help you succeed.

Although communication itself seems simple, often when we try to establish communication with others, there is always a possibility of misunderstanding which could cause conflicts and frustrations in personal or professional life in relation to others.

In this modern age in which we live, we receive, send, and process a large number of messages every day. But successful communication is much more than sharing information. It is also an understanding of the feelings behind this information.

Successful communication can deepen relationships in our personal or professional lives, helping us to better understand the people and situations that occur daily.

Developing communication skills can help us avoid conflict, compromise, and make better decisions.

For example, employees today expect to be informed about all aspects of the business and not to miss any important information. They expect leaders to regularly communicate their roles and goals. They expect continuous feedback on their work, and they expect to be able to find the information they need in seconds.

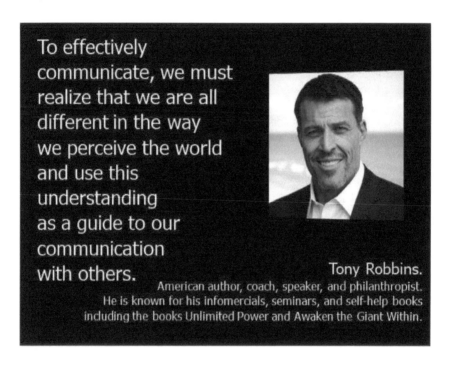

To effectively communicate, we must realize that we are all different in the way we perceive the world and use this understanding as a guide to our communication with others.

Tony Robbins.
American author, coach, speaker, and philanthropist. He is known for his infomercials, seminars, and self-help books including the books Unlimited Power and Awaken the Giant Within.

Leaders who successfully communicate organizational values and goals to their employees have much lower turnover rates.

Although we can develop certain communication skills, communication is more effective when it is spontaneous than when it follows certain quickly applied formulas.

It takes time and effort to develop such skills and become a good communicator.

The more effort and practice, the more spontaneous and instinctive the communication skills will be.

Below you will find some tips for developing the communication skills that are so important to your success.

1. *Active listening:* active listening means paying close attention to the people you are communicating with, by engaging with them, asking questions, and asking to rephrase or clarify.

    Practicing active listening can build respect for others and increase understanding at work and in life in general.

    As you actively listen, focus on the person conversing with you, avoiding distractions such as mobile phones, computers, or other projects, while preparing questions, comments, or ideas to respond in a meaningful way.

2. *The communication method:* using the right medium of communication is an important skill. There are pros and cons to exchanging through emails, letters, phone calls, in-person meetings, or instant messages.

    Communicating is best, when you consider your audience, the information you want to share, and how best to share it.

    There are many methods to communicate clearly to ensure that no communication problems arise.

    For example, with non-verbal communication, you can send wordless messages with your tone of voice, gestures, facial expressions, and other methods.

    Here are some helpful ways to communicate nonverbally:

    a. *Body language:* use positive body language to emphasize important points. Stand up straight and use handshakes to convey confidence and certainty.

        Look at the people you are talking to and avoid rolling your eyes or looking away frequently. Wear formal clothes, like a suit, to look confident and prepared.

    b. *Gestures:* common gestures are waving, pointing, shrugging, and using arms and fingers to indicate.

        You can check your watch to show you're ready to end a conversation and move on to another task, or you can nod to show you understand and agree with what another person is saying.

c. *Facial expressions*: a person's facial expression is the first thing you see when you meet them.

Facial expressions of happiness, anger, fear, sadness, and other emotions are the same across cultures, making them very understandable.

You should smile when appropriate and ensure your expression remains calm and confident.

d. *Paralanguage:* is your tone of voice, volume, and pitch. A different tone can make the same statement sound enthusiastic, hesitant, angry, sad, or sarcastic.

Paying attention to your paralanguage can help people perceive you as relaxed, confident, and authoritative.

You should use a tone of voice that suits your environment. Words can mean different things to different people, and it depends on the tone of voice you use. Yelling or using an inappropriate tone of voice can turn people off.

Avoid mumbling and speak clearly to avoid confusion, save time, and avoid repeating yourself. Don't assume people understand the information given to them if you speak in a way that doesn't allow everyone to hear clearly.

3. *Written communication:* written communication is essential for press releases, brochures, memos, contracts, manuals, etc.

You have to write clearly and precisely to convey the thoughts and ideas to everyone.

You must plan, organize, write, edit, and revise your words and phrases as needed and write with the intended readers in mind.

Where appropriate, use concise headings and subheadings and write simple words in clear, short sentences and paragraphs.

Make sure everything is easy to understand and back up your opinions with as many facts as possible.

Always summarize the main points of your writing at the end and let the reader, know what happens next.

4.   *Visual communication:* visual communication can make it easier to understand verbal communication. Many people retain information better when it is presented to them visually.

For example, a helpful diagram or video can help people put together a piece of furniture better than several pages of written instructions.

5.   *Amiability: Friendly traits like honesty and kindness can help foster trust and understanding when communicating at work or socially.*

Try to communicate with a positive attitude, keep an open mind, and ask questions to help you understand where they are coming from.

Small gestures like asking someone how they're doing, smiling while they're talking, or praising a job well done can help foster productive relationships.

You can practice friendliness by remembering skillful details of past conversations. For example, if a friend tells you that her child's birthday is coming up and you contact her later, you might ask her how the birthday party went.

6.   *Trust:* in the workplace, people are more likely to respond to ideas presented with assertiveness.

There are many ways to appear confident, including making eye contact when talking to someone, sitting up straight with your shoulders open, and preparing yourself so that your thoughts are polite, and you can respond to any questions.

Confident communication is useful not only at work, but also during social activities.

7.   *Share comments:* good communicators are keen to accept critical feedback and provide constructive feedback to others. Comments should answer questions, provide solutions, or help reinforce the project or topic in question.

Providing and accepting feedback is an essential skill in the workplace and in society because it can help you and the people around you make meaningful improvements.

A great way to learn how to give feedback is to take notes on the feedback people give you. When you come across a well-explained comment, take the time to observe and analyze why it was good, why it resonated with you, and how you might apply this new skill in the future.

8. *Volume and transparency:* when you speak, it is important that you be clear and audible. Adjusting your voice so you can be heard in a variety of contexts is a skill, and it's essential for communicating effectively.

    Speaking too loudly can be disrespectful or embarrassing in certain situations. If you are unsure, observe to see how others are communicating.

    Another aspect of verbal communication is changing the pronunciation of a vowel and the tone. This involves how your pitch rises and falls, your tonality, your accent pattern, and the spaces you place between sentences.

    Such details can be effective in communicating emotion and giving your audience insight into how your message should be interpreted whether you realize it or not.

9. *Empathy:* having empathy means not only understanding, but also sharing the emotions of others. This communication skill is important in team and individual situations. In either case, you will need to understand other people's emotions and select an appropriate response.

    For example, if someone is expressing anger or frustration, empathy can help you recognize and neutralize their emotions. At the same time, empathy allows you to assimilate if a person is positive and enthusiastic and thus help you gain support for your ideas and projects.

10. *Respect:* a key aspect of respect is knowing when to initiate communication and respond. Respect above all else is to allow others to speak without interruption. It is considered a necessary communication skill for success.

    Communicating respectfully also means making the best use of your time by staying on topic, asking clear questions, and fully answering any questions you are asked.

11. *The ability to react quickly:* whether you're answering a phone call or an email, quick communications are considered more effective than those that are slow to respond.

    One method is to determine how long your response will take. Is this a request or question you can answer in the next five minutes?

    If so, it might be a good idea to fix it as soon as you can. If it is a more complex request or question, you can always confirm that you have received the message and let the person you are talking to know that you will answer in full a little later and if necessary, with an urgent request, your response time.

THE TRAGEDIANS

We've all had people at work and in society who inject drama into every situation.

They radiate negativity with remarks like:
So-and-so is mad at me!
Did you hear what the boss said to Lise? And
this project is doomed!

Attention-seeking, victim-playing, name calling, and blaming others are all part of a drama seeker's toolkit. They are masters of the blame game.

Drama lovers never believe they are at fault. This is because they are likely overcompensating for intense anxiety or a lack of ability or responsibility.

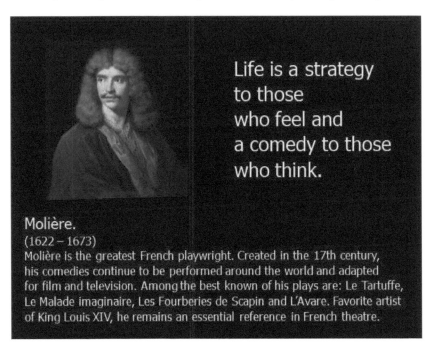

Life is a strategy
to those
who feel and
a comedy to those
who think.

Molière.
(1622 – 1673)
Molière is the greatest French playwright. Created in the 17th century, his comedies continue to be performed around the world and adapted for film and television. Among the best known of his plays are: Le Tartuffe, Le Malade imaginaire, Les Fourberies de Scapin and L'Avare. Favorite artist of King Louis XIV, he remains an essential reference in French theatre.

Luckily, there are proven ways to handle the crazy outbursts of a drama seeker. Here are some tips for navigating in these circumstances:

1. *Break free:* don't look upset; it's exactly what a drama seeker wants. Don't take their accusations personally, as they are meant to get attention and probably have nothing to do with you.

2. *Try to figure out what's behind the drama:* does this person feel underappreciated and therefore want attention?
   Is he or she, afraid that others will find out that she or he lacks a particular skill?

3. *Find out the facts:* Is a project really going off the rails?
   Do dozens of people gossip behind his back?

   Ask the person to calmly describe what they specifically think is wrong with a project or person. If a drama seeker gets upset, keep asking for the facts of the case.

4. *Ask them to come up with a solution:* feel free to suggest options, but never offer to fix a problem for a drama lover. Otherwise, they will harass you as soon as they have a problem, or they have no audience.

5. *Set boundaries:* tell them politely, but firmly, that their stories of unhappiness, angry accusations at others, and passive-aggressive behavior bother you and you won't listen to them anymore.

6. *Distance yourself:* if setting boundaries does not work, tell the drama seeker that you have a project to complete or a meeting to attend.

   Put on headphones and listen to music, do not return replies to their emails, texts, or calls. Here it is all about ignoring and just carrying on with your activities.

7. *Look for nice people:* spend time with good-natured people, as well as friends and family members who are calm and collected.

8. *Don't become a drama seeker:* recognize the moments we all have sometimes when you find yourself playing the victim, looking for minor inconveniences, flying off into baseless talk, or thinking you're within your rights for no good reason. It's just not a way to live!

How do you deal with an unpleasant person?

Interacting with someone who is abrasive, rude, negative, or difficult on a daily basis can test anyone's professionalism.

If you find yourself around an unbearable person, here are some tips to help you deal with the situation.

1. *Act impeccably:* although you cannot control, another person's behavior, you are responsible for your own.

    No matter what tactics an irritating person uses, maintain your sense of decorum without lowering your personal standards. It's not always easy, but you'll show others that you're calm and capable of handling stressful situations.

2. *Observe the dynamics:* make subtle observations about the interpersonal relationships around you.

    - Do several people seem to have a problem with this person, or is it just you?
    - Is this difficult person a real productivity dynamo or does he or she have to be constantly pushed and reminded by others?
    - Is this difficult person seen well, or does she or he scuttles himself, from team to team, leaving a trail of low morale behind?

    Also, having an idea of the reputation of this person will help you determine what to do next.

3. *Be careful:* if you work closely with a difficult person, create an email trail or communication file.

    Never try to get close by confiding in them. It is very likely that it will backfire on you. Not everyone deserves your trust.

4. *Don't let them sap your energy:* it is absolutely exhausting to overcome a negative environment. However, to thwart, it is a question of making sure to make a positive contribution.

    Unfortunately, toxic people have a way of spreading their misery on others and can significantly damage the workplace or social morale.

    Make sure your actions and words are not contributing to an unpleasant environment.

    Strive to maintain an uplifting energy and know that your good humor will constantly upset the negative person.

5. *Re-energize:* it is difficult during encounters to deal with complainers, naysayers, or otherwise frustrating people.

    It's important for you to get away from these situations and use your free time to rejuvenate yourself, whether it's spending time with loved ones, pursuing your favorite activities, exercising, meditating, or simply resting.

Re-energize and get ready to give your best at the next meeting.

6. *Know when to ask for help:* it's one thing to have a gloomy and depressing, yet relatively harmless individual. It's quite another to have someone threatening, harassing, or intimidating you.

    If so, you should not handle such situations on your own. To do this, ask for help from one of the leaders of the organization so that he or she takes charge of the situation.

7. *Identify your limitations:* If you're stuck around someone who makes your life miserable on a daily basis despite your best efforts to cope, it might be time to make a decision.

    If no improvement is on the horizon, it's up to you to choose an environment that will allow you to shine.

    Only you can make that determination because your success depends on it.

THE MANIPULATION

We have all known manipulative people whether they are friends, family, or our spouse. These are the people who know how to push our emotional buttons.

They could frighten, coerce, compel, criticize, guilt, bribe, blame, undermine, intimidate, abuse. Or they flatter, offer sympathy, and act innocently, but not sincerely.

It's all emotional blackmail. It's manipulation!

Here we only trace an outline of emotional manipulation.

But emotional manipulation, for example, in a married life can be more complex and must be handled with great sensitivity and care.

Contact your health department even if you are the only person ready to act.

A specialized counselor can guide you in your first steps towards recovery.

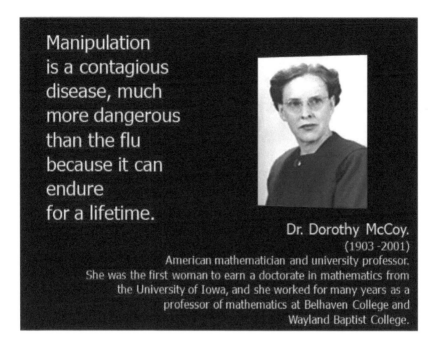

Manipulation
is a contagious
disease, much
more dangerous
than the flu
because it can
endure
for a lifetime.

Dr. Dorothy McCoy.
(1903 -2001)
American mathematician and university professor.
She was the first woman to earn a doctorate in mathematics from
the University of Iowa, and she worked for many years as a
professor of mathematics at Belhaven College and
Wayland Baptist College.

1. *What is the manipulation?*
    In short, manipulation is a dishonest way to satisfy our needs.

    We all have legitimate needs for physical survival and emotional well-being. And healthy people know how to appropriately ask for what they need and how to interact with others to achieve good results for everyone.

    However, manipulative people sneakily try to influence someone to reach their ulterior motive. And manipulation involves control and coercion.

    - *Manipulate :* to control or coerce another person by crafty, unfair or insidious, harmful, but attractive means, especially for one's own benefit.
    - *Control:* not allowing another person to choose their own action or response by controlling it in some way.
    - *Constraint:* to fulfill one's own desires by intimidating, holding back or dominating another person.

2. *Why is manipulation bad?*
    Manipulation is an attempt to take away the ability to freely determine whether to perform certain acts and to replace them with our own selfish desires or twisted motives, in order to do so in a way that completely disregards the worth and dignity of the other person.

3. *Why do people manipulate?*
    People can be manipulative because of their own hurt, pain, or
    immaturity. They tend to react with anxiety rather than being preoccupied
    with the particular situation.

    They lack the relationship skills necessary for healthy interactions. They
    never learned or denied self-awareness, humility, empathy, and a
    willingness to take responsibility for their own actions.

    Manipulation is the only way they know to relate to others.

    Then there are those who rely on others to fix things, pay for them, or
    cover them so they don't have to be responsible.

    In this sense, some people have a behavioral disorder and enjoy
    manipulating others, even to the point of hurting them.

    A conduct disorder is characterized by socially undesirable conduct, such
    as poor impulse control or an inability to maintain close emotional
    relationships, and the absence of anxiety or guilt.

    Manipulative people may have different reasons behind their actions, but
    they generally fall into three basic categories or styles:

    *   *Master:* these people pose as the one in charge and it's up to you to
        do whatever they want no questions asked because, they say, it's for
        your good.

        They tend to be pushy and easily angered. This is what we can
        commonly call brutes. Force is their primary tactic, but they can also
        coax you into submission with a mesmerizing charm.

    *   *Savior, facilitator, messiah:* these people have done something for
        you, and it is believed that because they « saved » you from anything,
        you owe them a debt of gratitude forever and you should do things
        their way.

        To make you feel guilty and bend to their will, they usually use
        comments followed by reminders of the things they have done for you.
        And like the master, the savior personality could also benefit from the
        phrase « It's for your own good. »

    *   *Victim:* these people are often overlooked as manipulative because
        they are « poor me. » These pseudo-victims know there's a lot of
        power in appearing helpless.

Yes, something legitimately bad could have happened to them, but their main tactic is to use this as an excuse to trick you into giving in to their wishes and demands.

Regardless of the style of the manipulator, their script is the same. They command the action you're supposed to take, and you're supposed to do what they want without refuting.

If you notice this pattern in any of your interactions, you might be in an unhealthy relationship with a manipulative person.

4. *What are the signs of manipulation?*
Emotional manipulators are generally very skilled.

They start with a subtle manipulation and raise the stakes over time, so slowly, you don't even realize it's happening.

So, what should you watch out for?

- They undermine your confidence in your understanding of reality.
- Their actions do not match their words.
- They are experts at distributing guilt.
- They claim the role of the victim.
- They are an emotional bottomless pit.
- They eagerly agree to help and maybe even volunteer, then act like martyrs.
- They are always one step ahead of you.
- They know all your emotional buttons and aren't shy about pushing them.

This is not an exhaustive list.

By observing, you may find that it is not always easy to recognize when someone is trying to manipulate or control you.

Remember, the sneakier a manipulator is, the harder it is to recognize their endgame.

Still, with the manipulation being so destructive, it's important to have a general idea of what to look for.

But be careful not to assume that someone loud and, lively is trying to coerce you, it could just be an outgoing personality.

5. *What are the impacts of manipulation?*
    Having another person takes or try to take your freedom through retaliation, projections, or abusive behavior that makes you question your sanity can have an extremely negative impact on you, whether physically, emotionally, and spiritual.

    You can develop:

    - Increased mental stress and physical fatigue.
    - Depression or anxiety.
    - Compromised self-confidence, which can cause you to doubt yourself.
    - A threatened sense of reality that can make you feel if you're going crazy.
    - Feelings of helplessness or shame.
    - Unhealthy behaviors to try to cope with stress and fatigue.

    There is no place for manipulation:

    - In the form of threats or physical violence.
    - Verbal denigration or insults.
    - To try to make you feel guilty for doing what they want.
    - A covert type of emotional abuse where the bully or abuser deceives the target, creating a false narrative and causing them to question their judgments and reality.

    Here, the important thing for your health and your success is to put an end to it.

6. *How to stop being manipulated?*
    If you think you are in a relationship with someone who tries to manipulate you or if your work environment is polluted, we suggest you follow these steps:

    a. *Be conscious and open-minded:* ask yourself, is this person really trying to override my choice and make me act the way they want?

        Remember that there is a difference between sustained encouragement and manipulation.

        - *Sustained encouragement:* it is when you are honestly told the truth for your own good and then left to make your own decision. The person accepts and respects your final decision, even if they disagree.

- *The manipulation:* it's when you're told something that may be true, but it's ultimately for the benefit of the manipulator.

  Essentially, he won't let you make your own decision and won't accept or respect your decision. The manipulator will keep pushing until you make the decision, he wants you to make.

b. *Get advice from a health expert:* this is especially important if the manipulator is your spouse or a family member. A counselor can help you identify any underlying personal issues you may be dealing with and guide you through the best ways to navigate your interactions with the other person. An outside perspective can help you see things more clearly.

c. *Is this person secure enough for those around you?*
    Confronting someone one-on-one is the best way to address disagreements between two people.

    Ask yourself: is this person secure enough (physically, verbally, emotionally) to be confronted, or will there be a negative backlash against me if I do it?

    If you are unsure of the person in question, do not confront them. Under these circumstances, things will likely be thrown in your face and blamed on you. Here again, the contribution of an advisor can be important.

d. *Set and enforce healthy boundaries:* stop playing the manipulator scenario. Set and enforce healthy boundaries. Boundaries keep you from being hurt, and they have consequences for people who try to cross them.

    The more destructive, the manipulation, the firmer, the boundary should be. You may need to increase the physical or relational distance between yourself and the other person, even to the point of stopping all contact until the unhealthy manipulative behaviors stop.

7. *What to expect when you stop playing?*
    When you stop playing the manipulator scenario, you can expect one of three things to happen:

a. *Discontent:* they will be upset for a while but will eventually admit their behavior and make changes in their personal life. The manipulation will stop. This is the best outcome, the one we hope for and pray for.

b.   *The person will become a worse version of themselves:* she or he will become more forceful, more verbally demeaning, or she or he will increase the pressure on you to back off, go back to the script, and do as she or he tells you.

You might even see all three styles of manipulation in the same person as they work to get what they want: the master turns into a savior who becomes the victim who turns into a master who turns into a savior and then the cycle repeats itself.

It is always possible that this person will change, but it is unlikely. This is why you need a good support strategy.

c.   *The person becomes physically and rationally dangerous:* the person becomes an aggravated version of her or himself and becomes physically and rationally dangerous.

This person may try to ruin you financially, or even file charges against you. Because you won't do what she or he wants, she or he will go out of her or his way to hurt you in some way. This person can be extremely dangerous, and you will need emotional support and possibly legal protection to weather the storm. Luckily, this type of situation isn't as common, but you still need to plan ahead to keep your surroundings and loved ones safe.

8.   *Where can I find additional help?*
We live in a broken and fallen world with people who are hurting. We need to be discerning about members of the community, our workplace, our church, our families, and our marriages.

And, as much as it depends on us, we should live in peace with everyone. However, we have to be discerning, especially when you have to rub shoulders with and even deal with a manipulative person.

Do not hesitate to talk about it at work with the boss or the human resources department and even to consult the health department in your region.

If you are experiencing discomfort at home or socially, speak with a good friend, clergy member, health counselor and if you experience or perceive verbal and emotional abuse that could lead to violence, do not hesitate to contact the authorities.

All of these contributors will certainly help you make sense of your situation and will give you suggestions for the next steps.

THE CHANGE OF MINDSET

Our state of mind plays an important role when it comes to becoming better in all areas.

Whenever we undergo training or embrace a new change, we need to have a positive mindset to achieve our goals.

Our mindset dictates most of our actions before our plans come to fruition.

When we think about success, it should start with some sort of mindset that you will achieve the things you dream of. However, certain factors can prevent this mindset from making you, successful.

These can include the type of workplace you are in, negative people around you, and personal struggles that can lower your confidence.

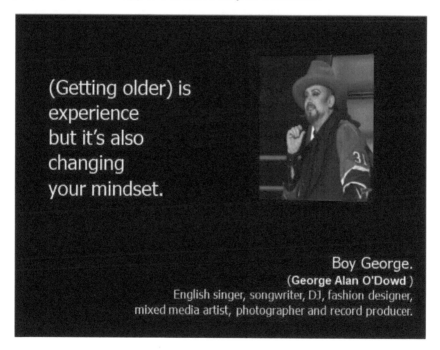

(Getting older) is experience but it's also changing your mindset.

Boy George.
(George Alan O'Dowd)
English singer, songwriter, DJ, fashion designer,
mixed media artist, photographer and record producer.

Achieving success is not an easy task, it requires hard work, perseverance and, of course, the right mindset.

Use the tips mentioned below, in order to determine a better course to become the person you always dream of.

1. *Start with generational differences:* understanding someone's generation can provide insight into how she or he thinks. It is a lens through which people view life.

The generational differences are fascinating.

Millennials (Y) often hide behind computers and voice their opinions on Twitter and blogs. They don't value face-to-face communication. Baby boomers (1945-1964), on the other hand, like to talk to someone in person.

Understanding a person's generation will help, you know, the best way to approach them to develop a relationship.

For example, if we make a deal with a generation (Y), we know there is no need to get on a plane and schedule a roundtable. They prefer a presentation via the Internet. For baby boomers, travel is necessary as well as the time to get to know each other.

Different generations value different things.

Millennials, for example, are looking for quick results. When we talk to them, we talk about fast, proven processes. Baby boomers are more conservative. When we talk to them, we go slower and talk about things like safety and risk.

The undeniable advantage for millennials (Y) lies in their ability to be open-minded to interact with baby boomers to recover their knowledge and life experiences, in order to benefit from them by reducing the periods of learnings.

However, do not limit yourself to the definition and the specified period.

For example, in certain social settings, such as at work where you are not used to meeting people, it is suggested to check for overlaps, because depending on the setting, you will meet generations (Y), more conservative who think and act like baby boomers. And, in other circles, baby boomers who have embraced a certain open-mindedness favorable to generation (X) and even (Y).

Generation (X) describes the generation of people born between 1965 and 1980, although some sources have used slightly different ranges. It has sometimes been called the « middle child » generation, as it follows the well-known baby boomer generation and precedes the millennial generation.

Members of Generation (X) generally described as being resourceful, independent, and eager to maintain a balance of work and personal life. They tend to be more liberal on social issues and more ethnically diverse than Baby Boomers.

Generation (X) people were sometimes described as slackers or whiners, particularly in the 1990s, although these descriptions have been disputed.

Note here that an important part of your successes during your life will come through intergenerational understanding. Remember the following question, it will allow you to refocus when you feel that a generational conflict is on the horizon.

Why are astronauts mostly in their fifties?

Simple, they have accumulated different techniques and experiences throughout their careers that allow them to quickly resolve a series of situations to ensure that their astronaut training is personalized and thus when making critical decisions, they can avoid irrational fear of the unknown.

Understand that astronauts during their training will not be able to simulate all situations.

However, the techniques learned throughout their respective careers mixed with the field experiences of the whole group will place them in a most advantageous position in the face of the challenges of the cosmos.

It is suggested that you put your pride and prejudices aside and take the time to listen to other generations, in order to be able to grasp their values in order to put all the chances on your side to promote your success and that of your entourage.

2. *Recognize the triggers:* another way to find out what someone is thinking is to research their pain points, which involves asking the right questions.

   To do this, it is important to establish a personal connection to find out what they consider important.

   What triggers in them an emotion?
   Where are their comfort zones located?

   Don't forget that you have to have big ears and a small mouth.

It is suggested to skip the predefined conversations and enter the relationship as a discussion. Ask open-ended questions that allow the person to share their strengths and challenges.

For your part, share what you have done and offer while contextualizing your communication strategy in relation to the needs of your interlocutor without exaggerating.

Remember that the initial goal is to get to know each other. Nine out of 10 times people will agree that they've identified a problem, which will help you, better understand what they need.

3. *Consider the personalities:* noticing and observing individual qualities can be helpful in determining who they are as people and what is important to them. Look for clues to someone's personality by paying attention, to characteristics and verbiage.

   Someone who prefers to be dominant, for example, may have too firm a handshake. People who appreciate humor often insert sarcasm into a conversation. Use these clues to determine their values and approach.

4. *Examine non-verbal communication:* non-verbal behavior is also important, and it is suggested to watch for body language cues.

   If someone leans forward, they are showing some commitment. If he backs away, looks down, or turns away, he's not sensitive to what you're saying.

   Also, it is important to develop a good ear that can listen to subtle sounds. The tone of voice can also provide clues.

   For example, if someone responds to you in a monotonous voice, chances are they aren't attached to your concept and aren't interested. However, if he looks at you while you're talking and gets closer, he values what you're saying.

5. *Be the person who listens:* listen to what someone says as well as what they don't say. Although it is more difficult when the conversation is over the phone. A committed or passionate voice is required. This is also seen when someone is frustrated. Their tone changes or you will hear a sigh. It is important to develop a good ear capable of listening to subtle sounds.

   Remember that anything critical or involving emotion should never be communicated via email or text. It's best to pick up the phone because emails are terrible at conveying the meaning behind the words. They can be a real hindrance to discernment.

6. *Change the way you see things:* your state of mind is the expression of a conviction that you embrace. It's the way you see things. If you realize that your mindset is truly an expression of a belief, then you are open to adopting that new belief.

    To change your mindset, it is important to discern the types of mindsets, so that you can navigate them.

    Here are some examples :

    a. *The victim mentality:* the world is against me; it always only happens to me and not to others.

    b. *The hero's state of mind:* you can overcome your challenges.

    c. *The scarcity mentality:* you constantly think that there is not enough for everyone.

    d. *The Abundance Mindset:* There is something for everyone and if there is more, we will do it again without evaluating logically.

    e. *The fixed mindset:* you were born that way and there is nothing you can do about it.

    f. *The growth mindset:* you can learn to become better at something if you try.

    g. *The Agile Mindset:* you embrace change.

    Changing the mindset is about checking whether each of your mindsets is truly rooted in a belief that shapes, how you see the world, how you present yourself to the world, and how you respond and react with the world.

7. *The right state of mind:* the right mindset changes everything, because it changes the way you see things. When you change the way you see things, it changes how you feel.

    When you change the way you feel, you change the way you think. And vice versa, when you change how you feel and how you think, you change what you do.

When you change what you do, you change your results. Changing your mindset changes your results.

8. *Change your mindset*: many people wish to change their mentality, but they don't know how. Once they realize that their mindset is limiting them, they want to change their mindset, but they don't know how.

You change your mindset by changing your belief. This is the challenge. We are talking about beliefs. You get what you expected. Whether you believe you can change the way you see things or think you can't, you're right.

However, a funny thing happens when you consider the possibility of adopting a new belief. Your brain can rationalize everything.

When you adopt a new belief, your mind begins to find evidence to support you. You will suddenly see a New World all around you.

We delete and filter things all day, every day. This is how our perception works. Our mindset is one of the most ubiquitous lenses in all of our perception. So, by playing with new beliefs, you're playing with your ability to see the world in a whole new way.

One of the biggest challenges of changing beliefs is when negative beliefs get in the way. You probably fought back at your parents or teachers or argued with your friends. Well, do the same, by reasoning with your thoughts.

The more you challenge your limiting beliefs, the more they will fade. You will gradually awaken your consciousness to a new level of understanding where you will find yourself taking giant leaps in your own understanding.

And that's exactly how you'll shape your new character as you battle your way through.

A great way to adopt a mindset is to simply treat it as an experience. For example, take one of your mindsets and see how it changes the way you see the world.

9. *Cultivate an abundance mentality:* If you want to cultivate an abundance mindset, there are several things you can practice that will help you.

Here are some ways to cultivate an abundance mindset.

a. *Be proactive:* the first habit of highly effective people is to be proactive. By being proactive, you anticipate and prepare for the challenges that will come your way.

    Reactive people wait for problems to arise and then try to react. They are mostly surprised. By the time they react, they are now in stress mode and operating out of fear.

    When you are proactive, you choose your response. You can't control everything that happens to you, but you choose how to react.

    The more you think about your goals and deal with the challenges you will face, the more skillfully you will learn to respond.

b. *Start with the end, in mind:* another habit of highly effective people is to work backwards from the ideal outcome. This is a great opportunity to examine and play with multiple possibilities.

    It is an opportunity to promote social inclusion, integration and to imagine a future where everyone is a winner. If you find that your goal in mind is creating a lot of losers, then you might want to rethink your possibilities.

c. *Think win-win:* another habit of highly effective people is to deliberately focus on creating a win-win solution. To think win-win is the belief that everyone can win. It's not me or you, it's the two of us.

    It is a belief that there are enough good things for everyone; it is an abundant way of thinking. Thinking that win-win is being happy for others when good things happen to them.

d. *Practice assertiveness:* don't let a lack of appreciation lead you to negative behaviors, rather support yourself positively, because when you celebrate your personal victories, you are filling the need.

    Remember that when you do well, often difficult work, you will cultivate assertiveness. Create more moments you'll be proud of. And think about those victories. They will be your juice and joy throughout your day.

e. *Adopt an attitude of gratitude:* that's really where you let the sun in. If you notice a trend among the most successful people on the planet, it's that they radiate a deep attitude of gratitude. They celebrate all that they are grateful for. They are just thankful. They appreciate everything they own.

Too often people don't know what they have until it's gone. By nurturing yourself with an attitude of gratitude, you will cultivate a powerful mindset of abundance.

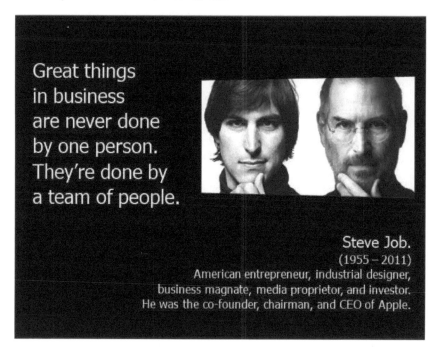

Great things in business are never done by one person. They're done by a team of people.

Steve Job.
(1955 – 2011)
American entrepreneur, industrial designer, business magnate, media proprietor, and investor. He was the co-founder, chairman, and CEO of Apple.

10. *Cultivate a growth mindset*: you can competently cultivate a growth mindset. In fact, mindsets are an important part of your personality, but you can change them.

Here are some pragmatic ways to cultivate a growth mindset.

a. *Choose a growth mindset:* Once you have decided to choose a growth mindset over a fixed mindset, you will begin to pay attention to your behaviors and thoughts.

You'll start to wonder if the words coming out of your mouth reflect someone learning new things or getting stuck in the past.

You will begin to question everything you think and everything you do. This includes your learnings and improvements in the things you are focusing on.

b. *Focus on apprenticeship rather than success:* If you're worried about your performance, you'll be resistant to stepping out of your comfort zone or trying new things.

If you embrace the idea of learning and trying new things, then it's okay to look silly, dumb or whatever. Don't judge yourself too much and embrace the apprenticeship aspect.

You can tell yourself, I know I suck when I start, so I don't focus on that negative thinking; rather, I focus on what I need to learn.

I get negative feedback, I turn to people who can give me specifics on how to change my behavior, change my results.

I am looking for people who can give suggestions and ideas in a relevant and tangible way.

c. *Appreciate the process:* when you try to figure something out, how do you feel?

Your answer will probably be that you feel uncomfortable. If so, this is what the growth looks like. Learning involves appreciating the feeling of discomfort.

It may sound counterintuitive, but it's similar to physical exercise. To advance in your physical conditioning, you appreciate the pain of a training session, because you understand that this pain is necessary to achieve the desired goal.

Think of, the saying of the US Navy Seals « Pain is a weakness that leaves the body. » Understanding the learning process will put you in perspective and thus stimulate your actions, because you will appreciate the process which will support your quest for success.

d. *Explore and develop what you are capable of:* harnessing your means is a powerful way to live and, lead with a growth mindset.

From tapping into your physical and creative abilities, you'll be surprised how much faster you can improve when you really focus on apprenticeship rather than performance.

Revisit old skills while adding new ones and you'll be surprised how changing your mindset will alter your ability to learn in a much deeper and much more effective way.

e. *The reward is your growth:* it's easy to get carried away with the rewards. It's easy to fall into the carrot-and-stick trap. Rise above it and instead focus on continuing to grow.

When you think you have achieved a mindset of abundance, remember Socrates's point of view. Any knowledge or information he possessed was likely to be insignificant, if not completely false, compared to all that was yet to be discovered.

11. *Adopt an agile mindset:* to easily identify the agile mindset, it is necessary to refer to the quotation of the Charles Darwin, English naturalist. « It is not the most intellectual or the strongest species that survives, but the species that survives is the one that is able to adapt or adjust best to the changing environment in which it finds itself. »

Simple, agility trumps being smarter or stronger or nature favors flexibility.

a. *The core belief of an agile mindset:* simple, it's about embracing change in your life. Imagine that instead of being disturbed or overwhelmed by the change, you embrace it and see it as a chance to discover something new or a new way of doing something.

You can transform your disruptive change into constructive change and create more opportunities for your growth and success.

Instead of feeling threatened by change and instead of feeling anxious, you feel excited about how you will reframe the challenge as a chance to find a better way.

With an agile mindset, you become flexible in your approach and adapt to whatever comes your way.

And the more you adapt, the better you get, like building muscle. It's a muscle you can use to go from surviving to thriving at work and in life.

Your belief that an agile mindset by its nature will become an essential means to achieving success.

b. *Cultivate an agile mentality:* flexibility will come with practice. One of your biggest challenges will be your self-image. You might say to yourself, « I'm not an artist, » or « I'm not a musician, » or « I can't do this, » etc.

You cultivate an agile mentality by reassessing your thoughts to confront them with challenges, in order to prove, if necessary, their opposite point by point. To cultivate an agile mindset is to learn to move forward.

Once mastered, you will realize that the key to all of these possibilities is your ability to adapt to change through your agile mindset.

With that in mind, here are some pragmatic ways to cultivate an agile mindset:

1. *Choose to be more flexible in your approach*: we unconsciously hold onto ways of doing or ways of thinking or ways of being, because it is unconscious, and it is a habit.

   By becoming more aware, you give yourself the opportunity to choose to be more flexible and you will even find yourself resisting change.

   Challenge yourself and ask yourself, « If I were someone who embraced change, how would I handle it differently? » Then act accordingly!

2. *Create more possibilities:* a great way to do this is to use the phrase « Imagine if... » and then fill in the blank. It's a simple way to explore and expand possibilities throughout the day.

   It's a powerful way to practice creative thinking during your daily routines.

   Don't get stuck in what is or the way things are, that's the current state. Instead, focus on the future. Imagine how things might be, play with the possibilities and gradually learn how to reshape the future.

   Some people just predict the future. An agile mindset will create and shape that future.

3. *Practice scenario planning:* expect the unexpected. Futurists know how to plan for the future, because they don't bet on just one possibility. They take multiple paths because they learn to look for how trends intersect with everyday life. Additionally, they balance market and user demands to determine the most likely scenarios.

   However, the real power is that the more scenarios you explore, the readier you are for whatever happens.

Even if you didn't predict exactly what the scenario would be, you have several ideas of how things might unfold.

Instead of reacting in the moment, take the time to put your ideas into perspective and then respond. You will feel more in control because you will be better prepared.

4. *Reframe your problems:* it is a very simple, yet subtle practice. We all have problems that we face on a daily basis.

    The first thing to do is to reframe even the idea that there are problems. Reframe your problems as « challenges » because that will make them fun. And then turn your « challenges » into « changes. »

    These are opportunities for you to learn something new, improve your skills, meet new people, etc.

    Expand the challenge in ways that are beyond you. This is how you explore and develop what you are capable of accomplishing.

    This way of proceeding becomes a source of inspiration every day, in order to encourage you to practice your agile mentality.

5. *Do the opposite:* it's a technique that really helps if you get really stuck. Whatever you normally do, try doing the reverse. If you plan too much, try to do more. If you're jumping into things too quickly, try stepping back and coming up with a mini-plan. If you tend to say, no to new things, try saying yes.

    There are many variations on this, but this is the basic approach. Just try the opposite of your normal answers. This will help you practice learning to adapt.

    As you go along, you might ask people you trust, what you would do if you were me, in this particular situation.

    Gradually, this way of proceeding will help you to penetrate the most difficult or complex problems.

12. *Change someone's opinion:* life is full of conflict. Have you ever had an argument with someone where they refuse to change their mind?

No matter how much evidence you give them, it's never enough. By nature, we hold tight to our beliefs and are stubborn to change our minds.

But how do you convince someone that they are wrong?

Below you will find ways to change someone's mind.

a. *Keep calm:* when trying to get someone to reconsider, it's important to avoid being aggressive. Aggression instantly distracts the other person from your points and puts them in a defensive state of mind, they just want to defend themselves.

   Instead, try to raise your points civilly in a meaningful conversation, not an argument. Listen to their arguments and try to understand where they are coming from before making a statement. Not only will this make you more persuasive, but it will also be a lot less stressful for both parties.

b. *Have them come to conclusions:* have you ever tried to convey an idea to someone, without success?

   You keep citing facts and providing evidence, but they still don't believe you. Maybe try to get them to come to the same conclusions. People are more likely to change their minds when they are able to apply an idea to themselves and make their own decision.

   Instead of inundating them with information, ask them questions so they can analyze their knowledge on the subject. Ask them about the circumstances and the pros and cons of each decision. Once they are able to break down your argument and apply it themselves, the more likely they will be convinced.

c. *Ask them to explain their point of view:* as individuals we like to think we know it all, when in reality there is a lot, we don't know.

   Often, however, we don't realize how little we know about something until we are asked to explain it.

   The next time you get into a debate with someone, try asking them to fully explain their point of view and see what happens.

   Chances are they will reach a point where they cannot continue. On the other hand, make sure that you are ready, on your side.

d. *Ask yourself a few questions:* when trying to persuade someone to change their mind, you need to ask yourself some perspective questions.
What are your motives?
What do you want them to believe?
What do you hope will happen?

These questions are great ways to start. On the other hand, don't forget to do your "homework" to establish your goals and understand why you think a change of mind is important. When trying to change someone's mind, it's important to know why your point of view is adequate.

e. *Have long responses:* long, thoughtful answers are more persuasive than short statements.

Being able to dissect an idea as well as back it up with evidence will make you seem more knowledgeable about a certain topic, as it will allow you to prove that you have actually thought about the problem at hand and educated yourself about it.

It's important to avoid insulting people, as this undermines your main point.

f. *Be sensitive:* it is important to know why someone has a particular belief when trying to discuss it.

People tend to keep their beliefs and values close to them for personal reasons. It is important to know these reasons when discussing them.

When trying to present a different point of view, it helps to be able to find common ground or a common point that you agree on before addressing a point.

Ask them questions trying to emphasize that they are right, for example, in an area to value their contribution.

Again, it's essential to have a conversation, not an argument.

g. *Know your audience:* it is essential to know who you are talking to, when you bring up different opinions. Having empathy and knowing where the other party is coming from is key to getting your point across.

Knowing how to speak to them calmly and politely will also help keep the conversation going. You'll be especially compelling if you can tie your ideas to something they deeply value.

This will help find common ground that you can agree on, which will lead to a productive conversation.

Remember that conflict is part of normal life. It is important to know how to speak civilly about our points of view in order to be able to convince the other person.

However, sometimes, no matter how hard we try, we can never really convince someone to change their mind, which we have to agree to disagree on.

So, the best we can do is engage in productive conversation and share new ideas.

Recommended reading and references

We suggest that you consult the works identified below in order to learn more about the particularities contained in this chapter.

BERNSTEIN, Albert J., PhD. DINOSAUR BRAINS: DEALING WITH ALL THOSE IMPOSSIBLE PEOPLE AT WORK. Wiley & Sons. ISBN0-471-61808-X.

COHEN, Dan S. THE HEART OF CHANGE FIELD GUIDE.
Harvard Press. ISBN 1-59139-775-8.

COSETTE, C. et al. COMMUNICATION DE MASSE.
Les Éditions Boréal Express. ISBN 0-88503-046-X.

DARMON, LAROCHE & PETROF Ph.D. LE MARKETING : Fondements et applications.
McGraw-Hill. ISBN 0-07-082723-0.

DASTOT, Jean-Claude. LA PUBLICITÉ : Principes et méthodes.
Marabout service. MS219, 1973.

DECKER, Bert. YOU'VE GOT TO BE BELIEVED TO BE HEARD. St Martin's Press.
ISBN: 0-312-06935-9

DELMAR, Ken. WINNING MOVES: The Body Language of Felling.
Warner Books. ISBN 0-446-32997-5.

DRUCKER, Peter F. MANAGING IN TURBULENT TIMES.
Harper Business. ISBN 0-88730-616-0.

MAURER, Rick. CHANGE WITHOUT MIGRAINES: Solving the Middle Manager's Dilemma. www.beyondresistance.com

MACKAY, Harvey. HOW TO BUILD A NETWORK OF POWER RELATIONSHIPS.
Conant. ISBN 0-7435-2659-7.

Take time
to deliberate,
but when
the time
for action
has arrived,
stop thinking
and go.

Napoléon Bonaparte.
(1769 – 1821)
As Napoleon I,
he was Emperor of the French from 1804 until 1814 and
again in 1815. Napoleon's political and cultural legacy has endured,
and he has been one of the most celebrated and
controversial leaders in world history.

DECISION-MAKING MEANDERS

Life is full of choices. Some are easy, like, what should we eat for dinner, and others, which have more consequences, for example, choosing a career.

No matter how important a decision is, good decision-making skills come in handy in life, especially if you're feeling undecided about something and feeling discouraged.

People make decisions throughout their day, most of which are simple and don't require much thought.

However, when situations are more complicated and have longer-term repercussions, it is easy to feel uncertain or hesitant.

Facing a difficult decision, it is normal to feel overwhelmed, stressed, or anxious, nervous, pressured, confused, distracted, tired.

Because indecision can have a negative impact on how you feel, it's important to learn strategies for making positive decisions in difficult situations.

Although you can't guarantee the outcome of a decision until you make it, you can at least know that you've thought about it very carefully.

Here are some tips to help you in your decision-making process:

1. *Don't let stress get the better of you:* it's easy to feel stressed and anxious when faced with a tough choice. You may tend to rush decisions without thinking about them or avoid making a decision because stress has discouraged you.

    If you're feeling anxious about a decision, try to manage your stress so that it doesn't cloud your thinking. To do this, go for a walk or go out with friends.

2. *Give yourself some time, if possible:* it's hard to think clearly under pressure, and sometimes your first idea isn't always the best one.

    Give yourself the chance to sit on a problem for a while, so you can work through your options and feel confident about the course of action you choose.

3. *Weigh the pros and cons:* when faced with an important decision, we sometimes lose sight of the big picture. Write a list of the pros and cons of each course of action, then compare them.

    Sometimes the downsides aren't as bad as we imagine them to be, or the upsides can make your options more obvious.

4. *Think about your goals and values:* it is important to be true to ourselves and what we value in life.

    When you factor into a decision on the things that are important to you, the best option may become apparent. Either way, you're more likely to end up with a result that works for you.

5. *Consider all the possibilities:* making a decision can lead to several different outcomes and not all of them are necessarily obvious.

    When considering each option, don't only list the positives and negatives; write down all the likely consequences.

6. *Talk about it:* it can be helpful to get another person's perspective on your issue, especially if they've faced a similar decision in their own life.

7. *Note*: If you feel as if you're on an emotional roller coaster, it can be helpful to keep track of your decision-making process and feelings by writing them down.

8. *Plan how you will tell others:* if you think someone may have a bad response to your decision, consider what their reaction is likely to be. Put yourself in their shoes to help you find a good way to handle the situation.

9. *Rethink your possibilities:* if you're under a lot of pressure on a decision, or if there are new factors to consider, re-examine your options. You might decide that your initial decision be still the best, but you give yourself the option to change course.

    If a decision no longer seems appropriate to you, repeat the steps to find a better solution.

If you are going through a difficult time:

If you're feeling overwhelmed by negative feelings because you're facing a tough decision, it's important to take care of yourself. Take time to relax or do something you enjoy.

If you find that your indecision about a situation is affecting the way you live day to day, it's a good idea to talk to someone you trust or see a counselor. They will be able to help you through the decision-making process and guide you through different strategies.

THE COGNITIVE BIAS

You need to make an unbiased and rational decision about something important. You do your research, make pros and cons lists, consult with experts and trusted friends. When it comes time to decide, will your decision really be objective!

Maybe not, because it's because you're analyzing information using the complex cognitive machine that is your brain that has processed your every life experience.

During your life, like any other person, you have developed some subtle cognitive biases. These aspects and perspectives influence what information you pay attention to, what you remember about past decisions, and what sources you decide to trust when researching your options.

A.   What is cognitive bias?

A cognitive bias is a flaw in your reasoning that leads you to misinterpret information from the world around you to arrive at an inaccurate conclusion.

Because you're inundated with information from millions of sources throughout the day, your brain develops filing systems to decide what information deserves your attention and what information is important enough to store in memory.

It also creates shortcuts intended to reduce the time it takes to process information.

The problem is that shortcuts and ranking systems aren't always perfectly objective, as their architecture is uniquely tailored to your life experiences.

B.   What are the most common types of cognitive biases?

Researchers have cataloged over 175 cognitive biases.

Here are some of the more familiar ones that can affect your daily life:

1. *Actor-observer bias:* actor-observer bias is a difference between how we explain the actions of others and how we explain our own.

   People tend to say that another person did something because of the distinctive marks of their character or some other internal factor. In contrast, people usually attribute their own actions to external factors such as the circumstances they were in at the time.

2. *Anchoring bias:* anchoring bias is the tendency to rely heavily on the first information you learn when evaluating something. In other words, what you learn at the start of an investigation often has a greater impact on your judgment than information you learn later.

3. *Attentional Bias:* attentional bias probably evolved in humans as a survival mechanism. To survive, humans must dodge or avoid threats. Among the millions of pieces of information that bombard the senses daily, they must identify those that could be important for their health, happiness, and safety.

   This highly adapted survival skill can become biased if you start to focus your attention too much on one type of information, while neglecting other types of information.

4. *Availability heuristic:* a heuristic is a mental shortcut that allows people to solve problems and make judgments quickly and efficiently. This experiential and observational thinking shortens decision-making time and allows people to function without constantly stopping to think about their next course of action.

   However, there are both pros and cons of heuristics. While heuristics are useful in many situations, they can also lead to cognitive biases. For example, if you can immediately think of several facts that support a judgment, you might be inclined to think that judgment is correct.

   Another common bias is the tendency to give more credit to ideas that come easily to mind. When information is readily available around you, you are more likely to remember it.

   Easily accessible information in your memory seems more reliable. For example, if a person sees several headlines about shark attacks in a coastal area, that person may think that the risk of shark attacks is higher than it is.

5. *Validation bias:* similarly, people tend to seek out and interpret information in ways that confirm what they already believe. Validation bias causes people to ignore or invalidate information that conflicts with their beliefs.

   This trend seems more prevalent than ever, as many people get their news from social media, which follows and searches for « likes, » which provides information based on your apparent preferences.

6. *Overestimation bias:* a cognitive bias whereby people with limited knowledge or skill in a given intellectual or social area grossly overestimate their own knowledge or skill in that area relative to objective criteria or the performance of their peers or people in general.

7. *False, consensus effect:* just as people sometimes overestimate their own skills, they also overestimate the degree to which others agree with their judgments and approve of their behaviors.

   People tend to think of their own beliefs and actions as familiar, while the behaviors of others are more deviant or unusual.

   An interesting note: false beliefs based on consensus are appearing in many cultures around the world.

8. *Functional fixity:* this is a type of cognitive bias that involves a tendency to view objects or people as only functioning in a particular way.

   When you see a hammer, you probably think of it as a tool for hammering nail heads. This function is what hammers were designed for, so the brain effectively affixes the function to the word or image of a hammer.

   But functional fixity does not only apply, to tools. People can develop a sort of functional fixity with other human beings, especially in work environments.

   For example, Hannah = IT and Alex = Marketing.

   The problem with functional fixity is that it can strictly limit creativity and problem solving. In many cases, functional fixity can prevent people from seeing the full range of uses for an object and the people around them. It can also impair our ability to find new solutions to problems.

9. *Aureole effect:* refers to the tendency to allow a specific trait or our general impression of a person, company, or product to positively influence our judgment of their other related traits.

If you are under the influence of a halo effect, your overall impression of a person is unduly shaped and influenced by a single characteristic, such as beauty. People regularly perceive attractive people as more intelligent and conscientious than their actual performance indicates.

10. *Misinformation Effect:* when you remember an event, your perception of it may be altered if you later receive false information about the event.

In other words, if you learn something new about an event you saw, it may change how you remember it, even if what you are told is unrelated or wrong. This form of bias has enormous implications for the validity of testimonies.

So, if the witnesses to the event practice repeating statements about themselves, especially those that focus on the strength of their judgment and memory, the effects of the misinformation diminish, and they tend to remember events more accurately.

Refer to Mark R. Levin's book (Unfreedom of the Press) to understand the role of the press in misinforming the public.

11. *Optimism bias:* an optimism bias can make you believe that you are less likely to encounter difficulties than others and more likely to experience success.

Whether people are making predictions about their future wealth, relationships, or health, they typically overestimate success and underestimate the likelihood of negative outcomes.

This is because we update our beliefs selectively, adding an update when something is going well, but less often when things are going wrong.

12. *Selfish Bias:* when something goes wrong in your life, you may tend to blame an outside force for causing it.

But when something goes wrong in someone else's life, you may wonder if that person was in some way blamed, if some internal characteristic or flaw caused their problem.

In the same way, a selfish bias can lead you to credit your own internal qualities or habits when something good comes your way.

C. How does cognitive bias affect you?

Cognitive biases can affect your decision-making abilities, limit your problem-solving abilities, hamper your career success, affect the reliability of your memories, challenge your ability to react in crisis, increase anxiety and depression and damage your relationships.

D. Can cognitive biases be avoided?

Probably not. The human mind seeks efficiency, which means that much of the reasoning we used to conduct our day-to-day decision-making relies on near-automatic processing.

But researchers believe we can better recognize the situations in which our biases are likely to operate and take steps to uncover and correct them.

Studying cognitive biases can help you recognize them in your own life and counter them once you identify them.

Here's how to mitigate the effects of bias:

1. *Learn:* studying cognitive biases can help you recognize them in your own life and counter them once you identify them.

2. *Ask questions:* if you're in a situation where you know you might be susceptible to bias, slow down your decision-making and consider expanding the range of trusted sources you consult.

3. *Collaborate:* bring together a diverse group of contributors with different areas of expertise and life experience to help you envision possibilities you might otherwise overlook.

4. *Remain blind:* to reduce the risk of being influenced by gender, race, or other easily stereotyped considerations, restrict yourself

from accessing information about these factors. It would also be nice to suggest others do the same.

5. *Use checklists, algorithms, and other objective measures:* they can help you focus on relevant factors and reduce the likelihood that you will be influenced by irrelevant factors.

Cognitive biases are flaws in your way of thinking that can cause you to draw inaccurate conclusions.

They can be harmful because they cause you to focus too much on certain types of information while neglecting other types.

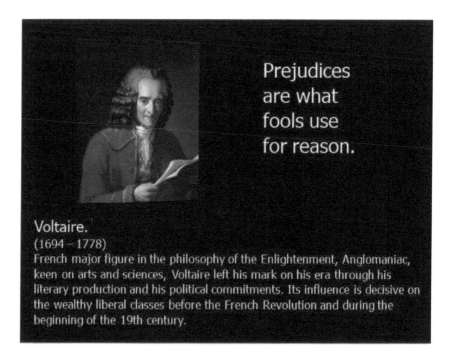

Prejudices are what fools use for reason.

Voltaire.
(1694 – 1778)
French major figure in the philosophy of the Enlightenment, Anglomaniac, keen on arts and sciences, Voltaire left his mark on his era through his literary production and his political commitments. Its influence is decisive on the wealthy liberal classes before the French Revolution and during the beginning of the 19th century.

It's probably unrealistic to think that you can eliminate cognitive bias, but you can improve your ability to spot situations in which you'll be vulnerable to it.

By learning more about how they work, slowing down your decision-making process, collaborating with others, and using checklists and objective processes, you can reduce the chances of cognitive bias leading you astray.

INTUITION

Have you ever had a gut feeling about something and couldn't explain why you had to do what you did, but, in the end, you found yourself happy because you listened to your inner voice?

It's your intuition, it's a powerful tool that we all have, but unfortunately, we don't use to its full potential.

Ordinarily, we tend to follow guidelines that evidence drives decisions, and that's partly true.

However, combining your rational mind with your intuitive mind can bring innovation that will support you in your quest for success while promoting success in your workplace, social, and home environment.

When we take the time to listen to our intuition, we are rewarded. The messages that are given and the force of attraction in one way or another, help guide us on the path to success.

There are many reasons why you should trust your instincts.

From a work, personal or social perspective, here are some of the many reasons why you, your family, your friends, your work team, and the entire organization can benefit from listening to your internal navigation system:

1. *Listen to your intuition:* intuition at work and in private life helps you identify your goals and missions as your priorities.

    When you tap into your intuition, you open yourself up to new ideas that your rational mind may have closed off.

2. *Build links:* your instincts can help you connect with others on a much deeper level.

    Being in harmony with yourself, your family, your friends, your colleagues, your employees, and your clients can help you build stronger relationships.

    Noticing that someone may be saying one thing but feeling another allows you to change your approach and determine what is best for both parties.

Intuition in the workplace lets you know when something is wrong. An essential component of business is understanding risk. The ability to follow your gut when it tells you to stay away from something is priceless.

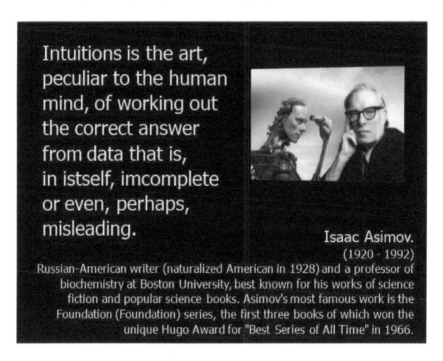

Intuitions is the art, peculiar to the human mind, of working out the correct answer from data that is, in istself, imcomplete or even, perhaps, misleading.

Isaac Asimov.
(1920 - 1992)
Russian-American writer (naturalized American in 1928) and a professor of biochemistry at Boston University, best known for his works of science fiction and popular science books. Asimov's most famous work is the Foundation (Foundation) series, the first three books of which won the unique Hugo Award for "Best Series of All Time" in 1966.

Your success depends on the use of your faculty of intuition combined with rational thought.

By using intuition, you open yourself up to all the possibilities we are endowed with. Our inner voice is powerful and helps steer every decision on the path to great success.

A. *How to take advantage of intuition and make better decisions?*
    Decision-making is part of life. We move from moment to moment depending on how we react when choices are presented.

    The process is evolutionary, sure, but it stays largely the same no matter how heavy the decision is, because we tend to go through the same series of steps when making a choice.

    We will explore the decision-making further below. However, here is the model that is generally followed for decision-making:

1. Identify the decision to be made.
2. Gather relevant information.
3. Identify alternative solutions.
4. Evaluate the options.
5. Choose an action plan.
6. Implement the decision.
7. Review the result.

This is a rational approach, but intuition ignores the fact that decision-making is not necessarily a sequential process. If we want to include all available data, we need to look at things from both a rational and intuitive perspective.

B. *Rational versus Intuitive:* our brain is made up of two parts: the conscious and the subconscious. When we approach a problem through a rational decision-making process, we access our conscious mind and work sequentially, following a logical progression that relies on analysis of the facts to make a carefully reasoned decision.

Intuitive decision-making comes into play when we experience what is called a « gut feeling, » a feeling that often goes against what logic might suggest.

Instead of recognizing and integrating these intuitive flashes into the decision-making process, unfortunately, we often tend to dismiss them as an « emotional response » and deem them immaterial. In doing so, we limit the scope of relevant information we use when making choices.

C. *Why is intuition useful?*
Throughout our lives, our brain is constantly processing information, storing it in the subconscious for future applications. This creates learning patterns called schemas that allow us to approach problems with a convenient frame of reference.

When called into action, the brain uses schemas by engaging its predictive processing framework, comparing current information and experiences with previously obtained knowledge and memories.

So, when you make a « gut decision » it is not based solely on feelings or emotions, but on logic created from experience.

You don't identify it as such because you are using applied knowledge rather than immediate data.

D. *Why are we not listening to intuition?*
    There is a cultural bias towards intuition, which mocks the idea that humans have some kind of « special sense » that can help guide their decisions. People are uncomfortable following their instincts and fear being called out for considering alternatives that don't follow the data.

    But let's call intuition what it really is, a pattern recognition mechanism. Once refined and developed, it is a key component of effective decision-making.

E. *How to develop one's intuition?*
    Intuition exists for all of us, but some people are better than others at accessing the information it provides.

    Here are some tips to help you recognize the signs that intuition gives you:

1. *Pay attention to physical cues:* we often have a physical reaction to decision-making, so when considering your options, it's a matter of being mindful of such a reaction.

    The saying « listen to your gut » has scientific validity because there are neurotransmitters in your gut that help maintain homeostasis in your body.

    - Is that feeling in your stomach nausea or nervous excitement?
    - How does each of the alternatives affect your energy levels?
    - Does the potential workload produce feelings of exhaustion or euphoria?

2. *Document your information flashes:* intuition can come to mind in little "AHA" moments as we weigh alternatives.

    These flashes of insight can suggest resources that aren't immediately obvious but will support a less likely alternative and increase its chances of success. Be sure to write down these ideas and weigh them as part of your data set.

3. *Take time to listen to yourself:* is intuition always good?

    No, but it's a legitimate tool in your decision-making toolbox. Suppress the urge to ignore a feeling you have about the decision you are making and assess the basis of your impression.

Sometimes we confuse fear or apprehension with intuition, for example, « I have a bad feeling about this! »

But sometimes those feelings are rooted in the real, quantifiable evidence of past experiences. Put aside that part of your self-esteem, or the ridicule you might face from others, to examine what intuition is telling you.

Decision-making is not a situation where you can or must use both logic and intuition when making choices. These two elements are not opposed, they are simply two sides of the same coin. Recognizing the value of both gives you access to a wider range of information to help you make the best decision.

PROBLEMS SOLVING

Dealing with issues that can be daunting can leave you feeling paralyzed and out of control. Regardless of the extent of your problems, there are steps you can take to feel more in control.

And even if you don't always make the right choice, you can learn to feel comfortable with the decisions you make.

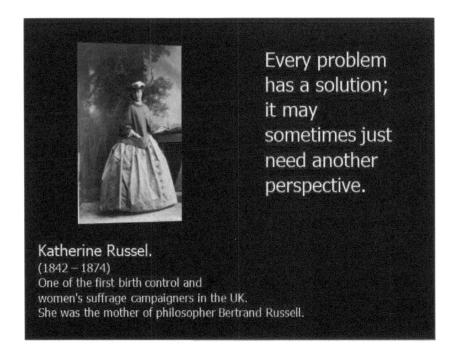

Every problem has a solution; it may sometimes just need another perspective.

Katherine Russel.
(1842 – 1874)
One of the first birth control and
women's suffrage campaigners in the UK.
She was the mother of philosopher Bertrand Russell.

Whether you are at a crossroads with a decision or have a problem that is draining you, if you approach the problem proactively, you can avoid such negative feelings of self-doubt and hopelessness.

Focus on what you can do, rather than things that are out of your control, and feel satisfied that you did your best.

Here are a few tips to help you in your problem-solving process:

1. *Define the problem:* what is happening exactly?
    Sometimes a problem simply seems too big to solve.

    However, if you make a list and break it down into smaller parts that you can start solving, it will seem more manageable.

2. *Set goals:* focus on the steps you can take to solve the problems, rather than just thinking about what you would like to happen.

3. *Think about possible solutions:* be creative and find as many solutions as you can imagine. Some ideas may be far from well known, but don't bother evaluating them yet.

    Keep an open mind and list everything that comes to mind, plausible or not.

4. *Rule out all the obvious mediocre options:* evaluate your list of ideas and eliminate those that are unrealistic or unnecessary.

5. *Consider the consequences:* review the options you have left and for each, write down a list of their pros and cons.

6. *Identify the best solutions:* now is the time to make a decision. Review your list of options and pick the ones that are the most convenient and useful. There may be an obvious solution, or some may work in combination.

7. *Put your solutions into practice:* be confident in yourself and commit to trying one of your solutions.

8. *How did it go?*
    So, you tried it.

    What happened?
    If you had more than one solution and the first one didn't work, move on to another.

9. *What if you can't solve the problem?*
   Despite your best efforts, you may still not be able to fix something. If you've tried a few strategies but haven't been successful, you might try focusing on your coping skills instead, to help you deal with things as they are.

   If you're having a lot of negative feelings about your problem, it's important to take care of yourself. Take the time to do something you love.

   You might also find it helpful to talk to someone you trust who can provide moral support. If your situation is interfering with your day-to-day life, it's a good idea to seek professional help.

THE RIGHT QUESTIONS

People ask questions for a variety of reasons. They help us learn more about each other, our ideas, and various topics.

Learning to ask questions can help you become a better communicator and increase your chances of success.

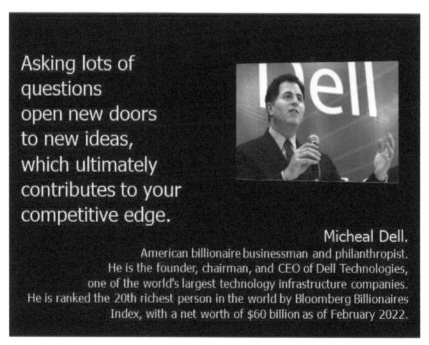

Asking lots of questions open new doors to new ideas, which ultimately contributes to your competitive edge.

Micheal Dell.
American billionaire businessman and philanthropist.
He is the founder, chairman, and CEO of Dell Technologies,
one of the world's largest technology infrastructure companies.
He is ranked the 20th richest person in the world by Bloomberg Billionaires
Index, with a net worth of $60 billion as of February 2022.

Why is it important to ask the right questions?

It is important to ask the right questions to help you receive the information you seek. It is important to ask specific questions as you wish, in order to listen to a specific answer. Asking the wrong question can get you the wrong answers, which can lead to confusion or other problems.

Learning to ask the right questions is important in developing skills for effective communication.

Excellent communication skills can help you share information and educate others, thereby improving your interpersonal skills, building better relationships, or enabling you to manage people more effectively.

A.   Here are some tips to help you ask the right questions:

1. *Think about what you want to know:* think about what you hope to learn. More specific questions can often elicit more specific answers.

    Deciding what you want to know, can help ensure you ask the right questions.

2. *Determine the subject of your question:* determine why you want to ask this question.

    Think about the type of response you will receive. Ask yourself if you want advice, an answer based on facts, or someone else's opinion or point of view.

3. *Develop an open-ended question:* create an open-ended question related to what you want to know. Open-ended questions are any question that a person cannot answer with a simple « Yes » or « No. »

    Also, open-ended questions can help the person you're asking feel more comfortable because you're not limiting their answer.

    Make sure your question is easy to understand. Evaluate your question to determine if it is unbiased. Be sure to focus your question on a single topic to avoid confusion.

4. *Find the right person:* select the right person to answer your questions. The ideal person depends on what you hope to learn.

    Contact the person and ask if they would be available and willing to answer some questions you have. Consider letting them know why you want to talk to them.

5. *Determine the right moment to ask them the question:* it is important to choose the right time to ask questions. Avoid tense or stressful situations and reduce distractions as much as you can.

   Try to plan and set aside time for the conversation to ensure you have enough time to ask your questions without worrying about rushing.

6. *Let them answer your question:* give the person plenty of time to answer your question and avoid interrupting their response.

   Although you may have good intentions, an interruption may lead the person to think that you don't care about their response.

   Instead, wait until they have finished their response and prepare questions to ask for clarification.

7. *Ask follow-up questions:* ask follow-up questions to learn more about the situation. However, it is important to be friendly and to choose questions that will not cause the person to become defensive. Ask questions that bring out your natural curiosity and sincere desire to learn more.

8. *Thank the person for his or her time:* thank the person for their time and response. Make sure they understand how much you appreciate their help. This is important, as you may need their help again in the future.

B. Here are a few tips to help you narrow your questions:

1. *Avoid rhetorical questions:* a rhetorical question is a question or statement asked without expecting an answer. People often ask rhetorical questions for dramatic effect or to emphasize a point.

   However, these questions rarely provide useful answers. Instead, focus on developing questions designed to receive answers and new information.

2. *Be understanding:* Show understanding to the person answering your questions. Avoid asking questions that put the person in a position of failure or an awkward position.

   Instead, make sure you have good intentions for your questions and ask them in the appropriate frame.

3. *Practice active listening:* make sure the person knows you are listening. Use non-verbal cues like nodding, smiling, and maintaining eye contact to show your commitment.

   Ask probing follow-up questions to clarify any misunderstandings and paraphrase what they told you to check that you understood correctly.

4. *Use silence:* use silence to your advantage. Allow time between your questions to allow the other person to relax and prepare for your next question. It also allows you to process the information you have received and think about follow-up questions.

5. *Think about how you would like to be asked questions:* think about how you want other people to ask questions. Think about how much time you would like to have to think about a question before providing an answer or how much time you would need between questions.

   Also, think about every question you ask. If you think you don't feel comfortable answering the question, consider rephrasing it or not asking it at all.

6. *Ask questions that encourage discussion:* it's important to have a specific intent with your question. However, it's important not to be so specific or direct that you limit the answers you receive. For example, avoid questions that force a person to choose between two options, such as « Do you think we should create an email marketing campaign or a social media campaign? »

   Instead, choose questions that ask for similar answers in a different format, like « which channel do you think will be most effective in reaching our target market, and what should the campaign include? »

THE NEGOTIATION

Negotiations can conjure up images of trade delegations, hostage takings, and big business mergers.

However, the truth is that negotiation is also all around us, it is a fundamental part of life and business.

Knowing the basics will come in very handy whether it's deciding your vacation plans or negotiating your salary.

If you stick to the following tips, you'll likely find that you and the other party will walk away feeling as if you got a bargain.

1. *Prepare and know exactly what you want:* any good guide to negotiation stresses the importance of preparation.

   However, anyone who has ever tried to prepare for it knows that it is trickier than it looks, as it is almost impossible to imagine all the potentialities that can arise in a rapidly changing situation.

Why fight when you can negotiate? All one needs is proper leverage.

Captain Jack Sparrow.
Fictional character and the main protagonist of the Pirates of the Caribbean film series. The character was created by screenwriters Ted Elliott and Terry Rossio and is portrayed by Johnny Depp. The characterization of Sparrow is based on a combination of The Rolling Stones' guitarist Keith Richards and Looney Tunes cartoon character Pepé Le Pew.

   To prepare yourself, as well as you can without getting overwhelmed, follow this next list of things to do:

   a. *Define your attainable maximum, not the likely outcome:* rather than focusing on the terms you think the other party will agree to, identify what success looks like to you, so you don't set the bar too low.

   b. *Define your start point:* some trade-offs will simply not be acceptable to you or your organization and these should be made crystal clear in advance.

   c. *Define your interests:* know your priorities and what you can trade to achieve them.

    d.   *Define the stakes and conditions:* measure what you can use when negotiating and think about new factors you can introduce.

It is best to identify specific measures for success. Of course, if you were to consider every negotiable condition in a complex negotiation, you could end up dealing with millions of possible combinations.

But you should at least look at the main items on your list to determine the value and thus inform your process.

This will help minimize psychological effects and streamline decisions on both sides, increasing the likelihood of acceptance.

2.   *Focus on potential:* negotiation, as opposed to haggling, can create new value rather than simply distribute it. New value is created by substituting something you want by offering something in return.

Having multiple negotiation items to trade ensures that you can increase the potential for success, rather than reduce it in the process.

3.   *Establish an atmosphere of trust and transparency:* At the start of every negotiation, reveal your priorities and ask the other side to be open about theirs.

This seems counterintuitive, as many people don't want to share this information because they fear the other party will misuse it.

Some research suggests that full transparency can lead to manipulation tactics.

However, revealing your interest can signal cooperation and elicit reciprocity. If the other party also offers information, you should feel empowered to share more.

Your counterpart's priorities will provide you with important information that you may not have acquired during preparation and can lead to the discovery of potential compromises and concessions.

This is often overlooked in negotiations, as both parties tend to think that they want to get, for example, a better price and just focus on that.

In such a situation, to generate the optimal result, do not talk about the price at the start of a negotiation. Leave the more difficult elements for the end.

Good negotiation starts with building rapport with the other party. Trust is essential. Trust is a human trait used by great negotiators to establish ground rules when opening a denial as well as when seeking mutual gains.

If a negotiation starts to go wrong, you can always refer to the goals set out at the start of the process as a way to ease the tension.

4. *Know how to dispel intimidation attempts:* at some point, you will likely encounter a negotiator who will try to assert value in a hostile manner. The person may try to intimidate you and may even threaten you.

    When this happens, fear usually kicks in and the prehistoric part of the brain that manages your experiences and emotions takes over, shutting down the creative parts of the mind and preparing you for fight or fleeing. You will need to give yourself time to emerge from this state.

    By using simple and practical tools such as questions, you can begin to guide the conversation and regain your ability to think clearly.

    For example, if your counterpart mentions, « This delivery schedule is not realistic! » It may be useful to take the last words of the statement and turn it into a question, for example, « Isn't the timetable realistic? »

    Even if you are afraid at the time, he will now have to explain himself. This gives you time to reposition yourself.

    On the other hand, when the tension rises during an attack or when someone raises their voice you could simply mention, « I feel tension in the air. » This can help defuse the situation by getting the counterpart to end their tirade and start explaining themselves.

5. *Advanced negotiation tactics:* once you've mastered these basics, including knowing how to build trust and relationships, you can focus on some advanced tactics.

    Although they can be effective ways to gain an advantage, you should use them with caution.

    For example, the benchmark tactic. A reference point can be a price, an object, a service, or a favor.

    Even though establishing a benchmark for trading seems like a simple tactic, it should be used with caution as it can also backfire.

If you're wondering if you should make the offer first or let the other party go first, a good rule of thumb is that the party with the most information to put in, should go first.

However, it is necessary to evaluate before starting. If this is you, should your request be realistic, or should you ask for a lot more than expected and meet in the middle?

Remember that your point of reference can damage the relationship you have carefully established, generate hostility, or force your counterpart to drift away.

On the other hand, you will have to consider the fact that there are negotiations where the other party asked for much less than they could have had, which becomes a costly mistake for you, if you offer first.

However, if you are presented with an « unrealistic » point of reference, it is best to communicate that it is a failure and ensure that both parties realign their strategy before making another offer.

6. *Tough guys don't win:* a good negotiation creates an agreement in which both parties feel good. A win-win negotiation above all, does not consist in winning only for oneself.

   The advantages of a win-win attitude during agreements make it possible to carry out the post-agreement successfully.

   More importantly, your reputation will be much better if you trade fairly and with respect.

7. *Listen:* the key to a successful negotiation is to fully understand the other party wants, needs and motivations. You can only achieve this by listening and learning from what they tell you.

   The adage that 2/3 should be devoted to listening and the other 1/3 to speaking is good to follow.

8. *Find out what really matters to the other party:* finding out the other party's motivation can allow you to retain the advantage for the latter part of the negotiation.

   For example, as a seller, you offer a free warranty. This is probably a marginal cost to you here, but it can give your customer peace of mind when things go wrong.

9. *Put on the scene:* the environment and the climate make all the difference in the negotiation. Choose the venue carefully, as it will reflect how the negotiation may unfold.

   For example, cold and informal meeting rooms can inspire hostility, while a more informal setting can promote warmth and understanding.

10. *Announce your colors:* at the beginning of a negotiation, you must define the terms of engagement. For example, everyone should agree to conduct a productive and respectful negotiation.

    This is useful for clarity, but also allows you to backtrack if someone strays. For example, if a person becomes stubborn and acts tough, you can remind them that they have agreed to be respectful.

11. *Bargaining Power:* Bargaining power comes in many forms, and you can often have more of it than you think. It is essential to understand where your strengths and weaknesses lie.

    Bargaining power is not just the obvious measure such as marketing power, but can be more subtle such as political, social or relationship power.

12. *Some offers just don't work:* some negotiations can hit a wall. It may be a good idea to pause and regroup, or to be open and frankly discuss the impasse. If all else fails, then maybe the deal can't be done. Some offers are not meant to be.

    However, new information may appear a little later which will change the whole equation. If so, remember that there's nothing to be ashamed of, if you can't reach an agreement.

13. *Enjoy:* negotiation can be tense, drawn-out, and stressful. Learn how to make it an enjoyable experience and everyone will thank you for it.

14. *Remember win-win:* if there's one suggestion to take away, it's a win-win.

    Negotiating is about getting a good deal and aiming to destroy the other party will do you no favors, as the cost associated with your long-term reputation could be most damaging.

THE CONFRONTATION

Unless you're a robot, it's almost inevitable that at some point you'll have to approach someone about something they might have done intentionally or unintentionally.

Most people feel an intense discomfort in the act of confronting people, in order to discuss a problem and reach common ground.

We hesitate to confront for many reasons:

- We hold painful memories of past confrontations that went wrong.
- We don't want to confront for fear of hurting or disappointing others.
- It's hard to be assertive in highly power-laden or political environments, like many of our workplaces.
- We find it difficult to control our emotions effectively when talking about something difficult because it induces fear in us.
- We guess, question, and doubt our motives for confrontation.
- We don't want to be perceived as malicious or demanding.
- We prefer this to resolve magically.

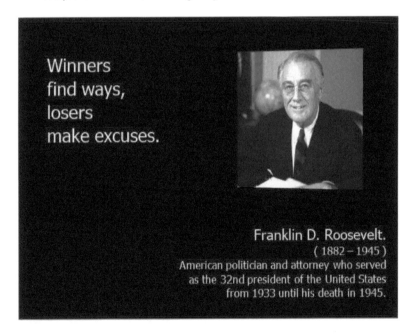

Winners find ways, losers make excuses.

Franklin D. Roosevelt.
(1882 – 1945)
American politician and attorney who served as the 32nd president of the United States from 1933 until his death in 1945.

However, the most important reason to confront someone is psychological because, you matter, your opinion matters, and having the opportunity to express yourself is well worth a little discomfort for you and those around you.

Here's how to do it peacefully and productively:

1. *Ask yourself, is this worth mentioning?*
    The first thing you should do is ask yourself if the issue is worth reporting. If you answer this question in a state of sadness or anger, then the answer will almost always be yes.

    Give yourself some time to experience your initial emotional reaction, and in doing so, make sure you have all the information and that it is reliable and truthful.

    You never want to get into a confrontation with hasty accusations. The confronted person will immediately withdraw into a state of defense, and you will move away from possible common ground.

    If someone has done something to you directly, like saying something that offended you, and you have all the information you need, just ask yourself, should I let it go?

    Or, will I feel better if I confront about this?

    If the answer to the second question is yes, then you should proceed to the next step.

2. *Pick the right moment:* confronting someone should always be done privately and never in front of people who are not involved. Not only is this very unpleasant, but it makes other people extremely uncomfortable.

    Also, don't do it in a place where you might be interrupted. Confronting someone privately allows attention to be focused on the issue at hand without interruption, embarrassment, or interference from someone not involved.

    Depending on the seriousness of the situation, you can choose to do so by SMS or email. But keep in mind that tone, meaning, etc. can be easily misinterpreted when there are no non-verbal questions or instant clarification when the confrontation is in person.

    Also, it may take longer to settle, when constantly typing answers back and forth. For best results, muster up the courage and do it in person.

3. *Choose the best introduction:* it will set the tone for the conversation. Think about how you would like someone to confront you. Here, one should not think of anger-induced rage.

This should be done in a calm, rational way that draws a comfortable parallel for information and clarification to be conveyed between two people. The opening of this parallel must be done in a well-thought-out way.

Here is how to proceed:

    a. *During the opening of the confrontation:* Rather than saying something like « I need to talk to you about something » or « I can talk to you, » so as not to create discomfort and sometimes even a feeling of panic, rather say something like « hey, do you have a minute? » or « Hey, can I ask you a quick question? »

       These questions are both vague and offer no insight into the nature of the conversation, which will prevent their immediate « guard » from getting up.

    b. *Do not use a strong, insolent, or accusatory tone:* how you say something is as important as what you say. If you heard about it from a third party, do not go into details about the source. Rather than saying, « So-and-so told me that... » or « I heard so-and-so that you..., » say something like « I was told that... »

       So, they could specifically ask who said something, and you don't have to, nor should you tell them who it was. If they insist, just say, « I just heard it. »

    c. *Leave the possibility to react:* don't rush out saying, « I heard you said XYZ about me, and that made me really angry. » « I can't believe you can say that about me! »

       Instead, give them a chance to react to the new information before telling them how you felt.

       By doing so, you give them the opportunity to clarify what was said or done, or to take immediate responsibility for it.

    d. *Use the « three-step » method:* start with a positive affirmation, state the problem, end the conversation with a positive affirmation.

4. *Wait for their reaction, here is what they could do:* offer clarification, then wait for a response.

    • Prepare for new information that may cause you to reconsider your position. Enter the situation with an open mind, a desire to communicate clearly, and a willingness to find a solution, if possible.

- If their clarification improves the situation, but still deserves you to be reasonably upset, explain that despite everything, it still made you feel to the point where you felt you should talk to them about it.

5. *Is the action justified?*
   If the person tries to justify what they did or mentions an invalid reason to defend themselves or save face, stick to the facts.

   She's or he's the one who doesn't take responsibility for what she or he did or said that hurt you. Offer a brief summary of how she or he made you feel.

6. *The irrational defense:* Usually, when someone feels « stuck, » they get too defensive and start by trying to reverse the script.
   For example, « I only said that because you started acting like one. »

   If he tries to reverse the script by saying their action was retaliation for something you did, ask him why he didn't just come and talk to you directly insisting that you thought you had a relationship where communication was open.

7. *The idiot's game:* this is obviously a very juvenile tactic to play dumb. In a perfect world, the person would simply take responsibility for what they said or did.

   But since she chooses to go this route, she's not going to magically remember what she did. If the person is playing dumb or denying their actions, just say something like, « Oh thank God, because when I heard or saw that, I was really upset for a minute or two. I thought you really said that, and I didn't want to believe it. »

8. *Put the pride aside:* at best, what most rational adults should strive to do is put their pride aside and take responsibility for the fact that what they did or said provoked a reaction negative enough to create a situation they had to deal with.

   If they apologize, you can either forgive them and move on, or tell them how you felt before forgiving them.

   Either way, depending on the severity of the situation, you should consider whether they take responsibility for their actions, want to actively rectify, and hope for sincere forgiveness.

Life is short, you must not forget, but for your own well-being it is better to forgive people in order to move on.

9. *Screaming is irrational:* whatever they do, don't raise your voice, even if they do, keep your tone calm and smooth, even if your heart races.

   Yelling is irrational and unnecessary to get a point across. Soon they will realize that they are throwing a tantrum and just looking ridiculous.

   Similarly, for swearing, you're a professional, stay that way even when things get out of hand.

10. *Keep them in the past:* bringing back, things that you have already put behind you is not productive. If you have forgiven them and moved on, keep the situations in the past.

    But always remember past situations to make better future decisions.

11. *Irrational and erratic behavior:* sometimes people resort to irrational and erratic behavior, especially in tense situations.

    If it gets out of control and you're not going anywhere with that person, just say, « Well, I thought it would be easy and you'd take responsibility for your bad decision, but I guess not, so see you later. »

    Use this situation as an indicator that this person is difficult, self-centered, or childish. Limit any contact in the future, you don't need their negativity.

12. *Think about what happened:* take a minute to decompress and think about what happened. No matter the outcome, move on.

    Reassure yourself that you are grateful to be a successful and likable person. You have done your part by approaching them peacefully and simply bringing them up, you have forced them to reflect on their actions. You did everything right, let them live now with their evil deeds.

However, be prepared for the possibility that this does not go well.

If you've done all of these things, but the person isn't listening or responding, the next step is to set boundaries.

If there is an ongoing pattern of disrespect, your next thought will be more about clarifying what your response will be the next time the behavior occurs.

Serious issues such as alcohol, substance abuse, or not respecting your physical boundaries of your personal space may require human resources intervention if you are in the work environment, healthcare professional during a personal or marital situation, including mental health professionals, clergy or even authorities.

Recommended reading and references

We suggest that you consult the works identified below in order to learn more about the particularities contained in this chapter.

BRIDGES, William. MANAGING TRANSITIONS.
Perseus Group. ISBN −13: 978-0-7382-0824-4.

CARDIN, Josée. L'ACCUEIL, MIROIR DE L'ENTREPRISE.
Éditions ARC. ISBN 2-89022-167-9.

COHEN, Herb. YOU CAN NEGOTIATE ANYTHING.
Bantam Book. ISBN 0-553-23455-2

COHEN, Herb. NEGOTIATE THIS! Warner Books. ISBN 0-446-52973-7

DECKER, Bert. YOU'VE GOT TO BE BELIEVED TO BE HEARD.
St Martin's Press. ISBN 0-312-06935-9.

HINDLE, Tim. NEGOTIATING SKILLS. Fenn Publishing. ISBN 1-55168-172-2.

LAMARCHE, J. LES REQUINS DE LA FINANCE. Éditions du jour, 1962.

LEVIN, R. MARK. UNFREEDOM OF THE PRESS.
THRESHOLD EDITIONS. ISBN: 978-1-4767-7309-4

LITTERER, Joseph A. ORGANIZATIONS: Structure and Behavior.
Wiley & Sons, New York.

MACHIAVELLI, Niccolo. THE PRINCE.
Penguin Classics. ISBN 0-14-044107-7

Happiness can be found,
even in the darkest of times,
if only remembers to turn on the light.

Albus Dumbledore.
(Richard Harris) (1930 -2002)
A fictional character in J. K. Rowling's Harry Potter series.
Dumbledore was portrayed by Richard Harris in the film adaptations of
Harry Potter and the Philosopher's Stone (2001) and
Harry Potter and the Chamber of Secrets (2002).

HOW TO ACHIEVE WELLNESS

Wellness is an experience of health, happiness, and prosperity. This includes good mental health, high satisfaction with life, meaning or purpose, and the ability to handle stress. More generally, well-being is simply about feeling good.

Well-being is something almost everyone seeks because it includes so many positive things like feeling happy, healthy, socially connected, and useful.

Unfortunately, well-being appears to be declining, at least in North America. And increasing your well-being can be difficult without knowing what to do and how to do it.

You probably already know that if you stop eating healthy and start eating junk food again, you will find yourself back where you started. It turns out the same is true for different types of wellness.

If you want to maintain the benefits you gain, you will need to continue to engage in wellness-promoting practices to maintain your body of knowledge.

It is therefore very useful to have strategies and tools that help you stick to your long-term goals, for example, a happiness and well-being plan or a well-being-boosting activity that you can use throughout your life.

Where does wellness come from?

Well-being emerges from your thoughts, actions, and experiences, most of which you have control over. For example, when we think positively, we tend to have greater emotional well-being. When we seek out meaningful relationships, we tend to have better collective well-being.

And when we lose our job or just hate it, we tend to have lower well-being at work. These examples begin to reveal just how broad wellness is and how many different types of wellness there are.

Because wellness is such a vast experience, let's break it down into its different types:

1. *Emotional well-being:* the ability to practice stress management and relaxation techniques, to be resilient, to stimulate self-love, and to generate the emotions that lead to good feelings.

2.   *Physical well-being:* the ability to improve the functioning of your body through healthy living and good exercise habits.

3.   *Collective well-being:* the ability to communicate, develop meaningful relationships with others, and maintain a support network that helps you overcome loneliness.

4.   *Well-being in the workplace:* the ability to pursue your interests, values, and life purpose in order to gain meaning, happiness, and professional enrichment.

5.   *Societal well-being:* the ability to actively participate in a thriving community, culture and environment.

To develop your overall well-being, you need to make sure that all of these types work to some extent.

Remember that having skills like a growth mindset or a positive attitude can actually help you develop your other wellness skills more easily.

This is why it is encouraged to develop these skills first, after which you may be able to increase the other types of well-being more easily.

Additionally, developing wellness skills is even more beneficial for people, who struggle, the most, especially if they've recently been through something stressful.

It may be more difficult to create wellness during this time, but the impact may be greater because there is more room for improvement.

Keep in mind that it takes time and effort to develop a new set of skills, including wellness skills. It's important to be realistic with yourself about what you can realistically accomplish in a given time frame.

Having unrealistic expectations can cause you to give up before you've reached your wellness goals.

So, it's essential to create a realistic plan for your well-being, stick to it, and take small steps each day that add up to big improvements over time.

Remember that developing your well-being is a lifelong pursuit, but it is worth it for your success in life.

STRESS

We all face stress at some point in our lives. The triggers are probably your job, a family illness, a tumultuous social life, or money problems.

Sometimes a small amount of stress can help us complete tasks and feel more energized. Not all stress is necessarily bad. It can make you more aware of things around you and allow you to stay more focused. In some cases, stress can give you strength and help you achieve more.

However, stress can become a problem when it lasts a long time or is very intense. In some cases, stress can affect our physical and mental health and even cause emotional reactions.

I stress about stress before there's even stress to stress about!

Minions (film).
American computer-animated comedy film produced by
Illumination Entertainment and distributed by Universal Pictures.

Stress can be felt in different circumstances:

- *As an individual:* when you have many responsibilities that you find difficult to manage.

- *As a group:* if your family is going through a difficult time, such as bereavement or financial problems.

- *In your community:* if you belong to a religious or political group that has been discriminated against.

- *As a member of society:* during natural disasters or major events, such as a flood, a blizzard, or a pandemic.

If you are feeling stress as part of a larger group, you can all experience it differently. This can happen even if the cause of your stress is the same.

1. *Symptoms of stress:*

    a. *Acute stress:* you may sometimes feel stressed for a short time. In general, there is nothing to worry about. Like when you have to hand in a project, or you have to speak in front of a group of people.

    You may feel « butterflies » in your stomach and the palms of your hands become sweaty. These types of positive stressors are short-lived and are your body's way of getting you through what could be a difficult situation.

    b. *Chronic stress:* you might experience this if you are often under pressure.

    You can also experience chronic stress if your daily life is difficult, for example, if you are a caregiver or if you live in poverty.

    If you let your stress skyrocket for too long, it can have detrimental effects on your body, mental, and emotional health, especially if it becomes chronic.

    You need to be aware of the warning signs of chronic stress so you can take care of it.

2. *Physical effects of chronic stress:*

    - Headache.
    - Sleep disorder or excessive sleep.
    - Muscle pain or tension.
    - Digestive problems.
    - Change in libido.
    - High blood pressure.

3. *Emotional effects of chronic stress:*

    - Feeling that you can't get things done.
    - Bad mood.
    - Anxiety.
    - Worry.
    - Lack of motivation.
    - Irritability.
    - Sadness or depression.

4. *Manage stress:* sometimes you may feel as if you have too much stress to handle. If you think you just can't handle it, you might want to get help from a specialist.

    Talk to your GP to see if they can help you determine if what you're feeling is stress or an anxiety disorder. They can also refer you to a mental health expert and provide additional resources and tools. Signs of stress overload include:

    - Panic attacks.
    - Worry all the time.
    - Feeling under constant pressure.
    - Drinking or taking drugs to cope with your stress.
    - Overeating.
    - Smoking.
    - Depression.
    - Isolation from family and friends.

5. *The causes of stress:* stress is different for everyone. What stresses you may not bother your best friend, and what bothers your friend may not necessarily bother you.

    However, many causes of stress can have a negative impact, including:

    - When bullied.
    - Working too hard.
    - Losing a job.
    - Marital or relationship problems.
    - Recent breakup or divorce.
    - Death in the family.
    - Difficulty at school or at work.
    - Family issues.
    - Busy schedule.
    - Recent move.

Much the same way our bodies react to stressors. Of course, the answer is how your own body copes with difficult or demanding situations, as it causes hormonal, respiratory, cardiovascular, and nervous system changes.

For example, stress can make your heartbeat faster, cause you to breathe quickly, sweat, and become irritated. It can also give you an energy boost.

This is called the « fight or escape » response of the body. It is this chemical reaction that prepares your body for a physical reaction because it thinks it is under attack. This type of stress allowed our human ancestors to survive in the wild.

6. *Stress Diagnosis:* if you are having difficulty managing your stress or if your reaction to a certain event is more intense and lasts longer than usual, it is a good idea to speak with a specialist who can help you.

They will likely ask you questions related to the following:

- If a traumatic life event has occurred in the last three months.
- If your level of stress is higher than usual when reacting, to situations at home or at work.
- If your stress may be related to bereavement.
- If you suffer from a mental disorder that may be related to your stress.

Based on your answers to these questions as well as other areas you talk about, the specialist may recommend some things that can help you.

7. *Stress and mental health:* stress is not normally considered a mental health issue. But it is linked to our mental health in several ways:

- *Stress can cause mental health problems:* if you feel a lot of stress, it could cause you to develop a mental health problem like anxiety or depression. Or a traumatic period of stress can lead to post-traumatic stress disorder (PTSD).

- *Mental health issues can cause stress:* you may find it stressful to deal with the day-to-day symptoms of your mental health problem. You may also feel stressed about managing your medications, medical appointments, or other treatments.

- *Recreational drugs and alcohol:* you may resort to recreational drugs or alcohol to cope with the stress. It could also affect your mental health and cause additional stress.

8. *Stress management:* stress doesn't have to affect you negatively if you learn to manage it.

   Here are some tricks you can try:

   a. *Look for the cause of the stress:* recognize what causes you stress at home or at work and find ways to avoid these situations.

   b. *Prioritize:* try not to take on too much and systematize your goals. Give yourself a break and be more forgiving when you're not getting anywhere.

   c. *Self-criticism:* criticizing yourself can add to your stress. Replace negative thoughts with positive thoughts. Tell yourself « I think I can » rather than « I know I can't. »

   d. *Find support:* create a network of close friends and co-workers you can turn when stress begins to build up. A hobby or a cause to volunteer can be good opportunities.

   e. *Stop smoking and drinking:* although alcohol and tobacco are said to help you relax, they can actually make you more anxious.

   f. *Eat well:* a balanced diet can help keep your body healthy and handle stress better. Dark chocolate and foods high in vitamin C, such as oranges and grapefruits, can lower stress hormones.

   g. *Take time for yourself and do some exercise:* a 15–20-minute walk three times a week can break up your day and help relieve stress.

   h. *Relax:* meditation, deep breathing, guided imagery, or other relaxation techniques can help calm your mind.

   i. *Sleep well:* In order to get a good night's sleep, you may need to reduce your caffeine intake during the day and your screen time in the evening. Before going to bed, develop a to-do list for the next day that will help you get a more restful night's sleep.

   If these steps don't help you manage your stress, talk to your doctor about seeing a specialist.

   If your stress has reached the point where you think you are hurting yourself or someone else, go to the nearest emergency room or call the local emergency service.

FATIGUE

Fatigue is a feeling of constant weakness that can be physical, mental or a combination of both. It can affect anyone, and most adults will experience this feeling at some point in their lives.

Fatigue is a symptom, not a condition.

For many people, fatigue is caused by a combination of the lifestyle, social, psychological, and general wellness issues rather than an underlying medical condition.

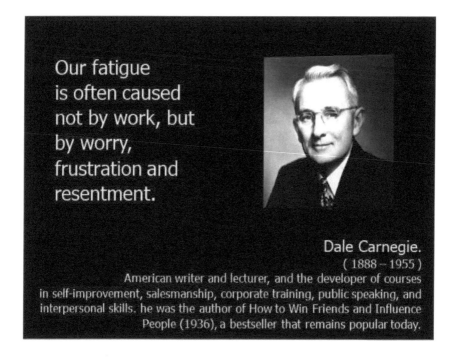

> Our fatigue is often caused not by work, but by worry, frustration and resentment.

Dale Carnegie.
(1888 – 1955)
American writer and lecturer, and the developer of courses in self-improvement, salesmanship, corporate training, public speaking, and interpersonal skills. he was the author of How to Win Friends and Influence People (1936), a bestseller that remains popular today.

Although fatigue is sometimes described as a lack of strength and energy, it is different from feeling weak or drowsy.

Everyone feels tired at some point, but this is usually resolved with a nap or a few nights of good sleep. A drowsy person may also feel temporarily refreshed after physical or mental exercise.

If you get enough sleep, eat well, and exercise regularly, but still have trouble performing your daily activities, concentrating, or being motivated at your normal level, you may be feeling fatigue that requires further analysis.

1. *Symptoms of fatigue:* fatigue can cause a wide range of other physical, mental, and emotional symptoms, including:

   - Chronic fatigue or drowsiness.
   - Migraine.
   - Dizziness.
   - Aching muscles.
   - Muscle weakness.
   - Slowed reflexes and responses.
   - Impaired decision-making and judgment.
   - Mood swings, such as irritability.
   - Hand-eye coordination disorders.
   - A loss of appetite.
   - Reduced immune system function.
   - Blurry vision.
   - Short-term memory problems.
   - Poor concentration.
   - Hallucinations.
   - Reduced ability to pay attention to the situation at hand.
   - Unmotivated.

2. *Causes of fatigue:* Causes of fatigue mainly include:

   a. *Medical:* persistent exhaustion may be a sign of an underlying condition, such as a thyroid disorder, heart disease, or diabetes.

      In addition, several diseases, and disorders trigger fatigue. If you experience prolonged bouts of fatigue, consult your doctor.

   b. *Emotional concerns and stress:* fatigue is a common symptom of mental health issues, such as depression and grief, and can be accompanied by other signs and symptoms, including irritability and lack of motivation.

   c. *Lifestyle related:* everyday lifestyle factors that can cause fatigue include:

      - *Lack of sleep:* generally, adults need about eight hours of sleep each night. Some people try to get by with fewer hours of sleep.

      - *Too much sleep:* adults who sleep more than 11 hours per night can lead to excessive daytime sleepiness.

      - *Sleep disorder:* Disturbed sleep can occur for a number of reasons, for example noisy neighbors, young children waking up at night, a snoring partner, or an uncomfortable sleeping environment like a stuffy bedroom.

- *Alcohol and drugs:* alcohol is a depressant that slows down the nervous system and disrupts normal sleep patterns. Other drugs, such as cigarettes and caffeine, stimulate the nervous system and can cause insomnia.

- *Lack of regular exercise and sedentary behavior:* physical activity is known to improve fitness, health, and well-being, reduce stress and increase energy levels. It also helps you sleep.

- *Bad nutrition:* low-kilojoule diets, low-carb diets, or energy-dense foods that are nutritionally poor do not provide the body with enough fuel or nutrients to function at its best.

  Quick-fix foods, such as chocolate bars or caffeinated beverages, only provide a temporary energy boost that quickly wears off and worsens fatigue.

- *Individual factors:* illness, personal situations or too many obligations. For example, working two jobs or financial problems can cause fatigue.

d. *Work related:* Common workplace issues that can cause fatigue include.

- *Shift work:* the human body is designed to sleep at night. This pattern is defined by a small part of the brain known as the circadian clock.

  A shift worker disrupts his circadian clock by working when his body is programmed to sleep.

- *Poor Workplace Practices:* they can increase a person's level of fatigue. The most commonly observed are long working hours, heavy physical labor, irregular work schedules such as rotating shifts, a stressful work environment such as excessive noise or extreme temperatures, boredom, working alone with little or no interaction with others or a fixed focus on a repetitive task.

- *Workplace stress:* it can be caused by a wide range of factors, including job dissatisfaction, heavy workload, conflicts with bosses or co-workers, bullying, constant change, or threats to job security.

- *Professional exhaustion:* it can be described as trying too hard in one area of life while neglecting everything else.

  Workaholics, for example, put all their energy into their careers, which throws family life, social life, and personal interests out of balance.

- *Shortage of work:* financial pressures, feelings of failure or guilt, and emotional exhaustion from a prolonged job search can lead to stress, anxiety, depression, and fatigue.

e. *Psychological:* studies suggest that psychological factors are present in at least 50% of cases of fatigue. These may include:

- *Depression:* this disease is characterized by severe and prolonged feelings of sadness, depression and hopelessness. People who are depressed usually suffer from chronic fatigue.

- *Anxiety and stress:* a chronically anxious or stressed person keep their body in overdrive. The constant flow of adrenaline exhausts the body and fatigue sets in.

- *Sorrow:* the loss of a loved one brings on a wide range of emotions, including emotional shock, guilt, depression, despair, and loneliness.

Fatigue is a symptom, something you can feel and describe, not a condition or disease. To reduce your fatigue, you must first understand the underlying reasons for your fatigue.

If fatigue is negatively affecting your quality of life or causing you distress, consider seeing a healthcare professional. By asking questions, they'll help you understand why you're feeling tired and offer suggestions on how to find relief.

If necessary, your doctor may suggest certain medical tests if there is a reasonable likelihood that the cause of your fatigue is an undiagnosed medical condition, such as anemia or thyroid dysfunction.

Fortunately, for most people, fatigue will subside on its own over time or with a few simple, practical lifestyle changes.

ANXIETY

Feeling nervous is a natural reaction to something that instills fear in us, perhaps a formal presentation, a business opportunity, or a promotional meeting you have arranged with your boss.

Anxiety's like a rocking chair. It gives you something to do, but doesn't get you very far.

Jodi Lynn Picoult.
American writer. Picoult has published 27 novels, accompanying short stories, and has also written several issues of Wonder Woman. Approximately 40 million copies of her books are in print worldwide.

Simple, fear makes you nervous and this state of psychological excitement can prevent us from giving the best of ourselves.

A. *What causes nervousness?*
Nervousness is a mental and physical condition that is caused by your body's stress response system.

It's the same system that kicks in when you feel stressed or anxious, but nervousness tends to occur in response, to very specific events, like a special encounter or a military operation.

Basically, nervousness is caused by your body releasing stress hormones, for example, adrenaline, cortisol.

And the results of nervousness, panic, stress, and anxiety can all cause the following symptoms:

- « Butterflies » in the stomach.
- Pains in the chest.
- Sleep disorder.
- Extra alertness or nervousness.
- Faster, shallower breathing.
- Feeling of weakness.
- Headaches.
- Inability to concentrate.
- Inability to relax.
- Increased irritability.
- Increased heart rate.
- Irregular heartbeats.
- Loss of appetite.
- Nausea and want to vomit.
- The worry.
- Sweat.
- The tears.
- Visit the toilet more frequently.

Also, after your period of nervousness, you may feel relieved or tired, because your body will have consumed much more energy than usual. Be sure to give yourself the opportunity to rest and refuel when you experience it.

B. *How do you calm your nerves?*
    Although nervousness may seem beyond your control, there are many simple, easy, and effective tasks you can follow that will reduce the difficult aspects of nervousness and, in fact, improve your performance.

    1. *Try deep breathing:* breathing exercises are one of the simplest and easiest activities you can do to reduce the symptoms of nervousness, such as slowing your heart rate, improving oxygen exchange, and thus reducing the effects of combativeness.

    2. *Channel your nervous energy into positivity:* It may sound difficult, but there is a distinct link between feelings of motivation and eagerness, and fear and nervousness.

        These two states are called eustress and distress, the two sides of the stress coin. You will experience similar reactions to both, such as an elevated heart rate.

        So, if you can put the upcoming activity into perspective in a positive way, you may find that your « positive » nervous energy actually improves your performance.

If you find yourself in a particularly difficult situation, ask yourself, « What can I learn from this situation that will help me in the future? »

3. *Explore the task that makes you nervous:* if you have time, try to practice what makes you nervous.

    Going through your presentation, speech, or meeting will demystify much of the process and identify areas where you can improve before proceeding.

4. *Listen to music:* especially tunes that remind you of positive times or cause happy feelings.

    Music can have a distinct effect on calming the body and mind, and this technique can work even if you only have a few minutes to calm down.

5. *Talk to someone you trust about how you feel:* talking about mental health at work and in society may seem taboo, but it fosters a more open culture, where support can be given more freely. As the old saying goes, a problem shared is a problem halved.

6. *Realize that it's okay to be vulnerable:* feeling nervous can actually demonstrate a number of positive qualities that you may not have thought of.

    Caring about your job role and wanting to do a good job can only help you understand.

7. *Get some fresh air:* getting away from the current environment that makes you nervous and taking a walk around the block can give you the opportunity to get your normal heart rate back, stabilize your stream of thoughts, and also give you a moment of peace.

8. *Get there early:* if you are planning to attend a meeting or interview and you are feeling nervous, try to be early to familiarize yourself with the premises.

    Simply sitting down for a while will help you visualize the process before it happens. Plus, you can guarantee you'll arrive on time.

9. *Drink a glass of water or even take an herbal tea break:* combining something mundane and keeping your mouth from going dry are two brilliant ways to reduce nervousness.

10. *Practice mindfulness:* it's something that big blue-chip companies actively promote within their teams, and if practiced regularly, it can provide you with the tools to feel calmer in your work.

    Mindfulness can range from writing down how you feel to meditation for a few minutes.

11. *Know that you are not alone:* many people feel nervous in similar situations, and you may even find colleagues who share your nervousness as well.

PSYCHIC VAMPIRISM

Along your path to success, you are going to meet people who will try to pump your energy in any way they can, with the result that you will feel tired, even drained.

If you scratch a little in your memories, you will surely remember having already suffered such situations before.

To achieve an experience of health, happiness, and prosperity, you must recognize the different types of people who will try to rob you of your well-being throughout your life. Doctor Stéphane Clerget psychiatrist has identified them for you.

Below, you will find a series of excerpts from interviews and comments concerning the book « Psychic vampires, how to recognize them, how to escape them » by Doctor Stéphane Clerget psychiatrist, available from Arthème Fayard. I suggest you get this book.

Have you ever had the feeling of having been « vampirized » by a colleague, a stranger, a relation, or a parent?

You then feel tired, even drained. You come to understand that you are being used by this person, and that you give them, or they take you, without receiving anything in return. You are the victim of a psychic vampire.

Psychic vampires need to feed on your physical and emotional energy, whether it's a vital need related to their psychological functioning or simply out of opportunism.

For the one who is a victim, it is a kind of mental drainage that begins. Unlike narcissistic perverts, vampires don't want to destroy you. On the contrary, they need you.

So, faced with their voracity, you have to be able to adopt defense strategies.

And since they can adopt very different appearances and personalities, which makes it difficult to identify them at first glance.

So, it is suggested to try to understand them to protect yourself from them.

However, upon informing yourself of this psychic situation, you realize that you may also sometimes be a psychic vampire yourself.

Stéphane Clerget « The psychic vampire deprives its victim of all energy. » They drain our energy, ask for advice and services, but give nothing in return. In the family, at work or as a couple, « psychic vampires » are psychologically and emotionally exhausting.

How to live with them?
They do not suck our blood but suck our vitality. In both professional and personal life, « psychic vampires » take advantage of us, monopolize our ideas, exhaust us with all kinds of demands.

Psychiatrist Stéphane Clerget's comparison seems most relevant for several reasons. With a psychic vampire as with a « real » vampire, the victims feel exhausted, drained of their energy. The vampire is a universal myth. There are also, psychic vampires everywhere and at all times.

One can also wonder if these personalities did not inspire the myths. Finally, psychic vampires can't stand being exposed. When they are discovered, they lose all power.

1. *What are the salient personality traits of the psychic vampire?*
    We speak of « casual vampirism » when a person particularly likes to attract attention, by talking loudly in a restaurant or at work, for example.

    There is a deeper form of vampirism. Within the couple, in the family, the vampire uses our energy for his benefit. It perverts a central notion in human relations, that of exchange. She or he takes without ever giving back.

2. *What warning signs should be kept in mind?*
    Bear in mind that psychic vampires do not want to harm us. They even have every interest in preserving us.

    They will therefore constantly seek to capture our attention, our listening. They « ask to be reassured » and things often have to be done for them.

When one systematically gives up one's needs and one's personal pleasure for someone else's benefit, one must be concerned.

3. *Why do these people need to « steal » their loved ones?*
Some just don't like to give. They are selfish. These cases are rare. Psychic vampires are more often very dependent people, unable to rejuvenate themselves emotionally and intellectually.

This may be the result of a childhood when the parents gave too much because they did not learn affective autonomy. The result is a « profound lack of self-confidence. » Still, this is in no way an excuse to « vampirize» others!

« Psychic Vampires must have a seductive personality for you to be able to give in to them... » Indeed, some of them have a great power of seduction. They use their charms to « vampirize » us, especially in the couple. We are increasingly wary of these people, who are often mistaken for « narcissistic perverts. »

The majority of psychic vampires play on our natural tendency to compassion, humanity and tenderness. More than great seducers, they behave like little children whom we would like to take care of.

4. *What is the ideal victim's personality type?*
These are people who naturally have a lot of empathy, a propensity for affection. They think they can give endlessly.

Some even feel valued by these incessant requests. They feel as if they're important in this « vampire-vampirized » relationship.

They may be people who fear that they will not be loved or who feel that they have been spoiled by life, that they have received too much.

This imagined guilt leads them to want to « fix » others. It gives meaning to their lives.

5. *Should we then be wary of everyone to avoid being « vampirize? »*
Of course not!
We must not conclude that we must not help anyone, but in order to give, we must preserve ourselves.

Some people get eaten alive without even realizing their relationships aren't healthy.

To avoid getting there, it is important to learn to say stop in time.

6. *How to get out of anxiety-provoking relationships with a psychic vampire?*
   Being aware of this is already a first step. Of course, we can continue to give, but not as much. It is better to « measure » what you transmit and what you keep for yourself.

   The main thing is to bring things to light, to talk to those around you to make the power of the psychic vampire inoperative.

   In addition, we can express his feelings to him, explain the effects produced by his behavior, bearing in mind that he will probably continue to cling, by pressing where it hurts: whether it is our tendency to guilt, the need to be loved, the debt that we feel we have towards him, etc.

   Finally, if the break is obviously not mandatory, you have to allow yourself to come to this conclusion if you can no longer do otherwise.

7. *Can the psychic vampire, him, regain autonomy?*
   It is often difficult.
   If we feel in this case, we can try to understand why we are there, how our childhood has conditioned our behavior?

   Vampirism can be treated very well with psychotherapy. Its analytical dimension makes it possible to delve into the roots of evil in order to become independent and, finally, to be free.

8. *How do you recognize an affective vampire?*
   Incapable of recharging their batteries emotionally and intellectually, having no affective autonomy, they do not know how to give or listen.

   Often egocentric, in the position of victims, overstretching, in search of the slightest attention, they exhaust those around them, miserly of reciprocity and gratitude.

   Whether it is a colleague who appropriates the work of another and steals the show, a hierarchical superior who arrogates the ideas of his collaborators, a loved one or a romantic partner in constant demand, psychic vampires, present several typical profiles:

   - The depressive or the plaintive: he tells his misfortunes all day long, seeing everything in black.
   - The tragedian or the victim: his life is a permanent tragedy, a succession of dramas.
   - The critic: he already knows everything. Nothing is good enough for him. He criticizes everything.

- The tireless speaker: he pours out his thoughts, his emotions, his feelings without being interested in those of others perceived as simple receptacles.
- The egocentric or the narcissist: he seeks to be admired, to make the world revolve around him.
- The indifferent: he closes in on himself and lets the other, exhaust himself questioning him, making him feel guilty.
- The snooper or interrogator: he questions everything. He has an unhealthy curiosity. He is jealous of everything.
- The aggressive or the bully: he constantly complains, threatens, imposes, attacks, oppresses.
- The sarcastic or the ironic: it ridicules everything. For him, nothing matters. It reduces all action to nothing.

9. *What are the consequences for their victims?*
   The most empathetic, the great helpers, the very attentive people are their ideal victims.

   Pouring their fear, hatred, unhappiness, bitterness, endless questions or demands on their victims, psychic vampires exhaust them on all levels (physical, emotional, or psychological).

   From headaches to back pain to symptoms of depression without the sadness, the negative consequences are many.

   Dragging their victims into a negative spiral, they end up draining them of their positive energy or « converting » them to the forms of this ordinary vampirism (criticism, negativity, derision, etc.).

10. *How to guard against it or detach yourself from it?*
    A few elementary principles, although difficult to apply in the first instance, should govern professional, friendly, or romantic relationships:

    - Remain lucid about the nature of relationships. Listen to your intuition, realize the emotional, psychological, and physical consequences of each relationship.
    - Do not trust appearances (kindness, seduction, victims…).
    - Become aware of flattery, not constantly finding excuses or being careful not to open the door to harmful relationships out of naivety, fear, desire to please, need for attention or guilt.
    - Maintaining a critical sense, remaining firm and true to oneself.
    - Maintain self-respect and self-esteem.
    - Stay pragmatic, set limits and balance.

- Limit contacts or end one-way relationships.
- Surround yourself with positive people.
- Prioritize harmonious and balanced relationships.

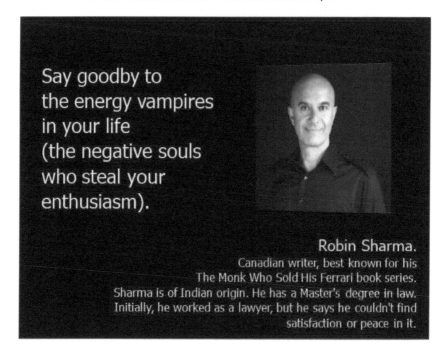

Say goodby to the energy vampires in your life (the negative souls who steal your enthusiasm).

Robin Sharma.
Canadian writer, best known for his
The Monk Who Sold His Ferrari book series.
Sharma is of Indian origin. He has a Master's degree in law.
Initially, he worked as a lawyer, but he says he couldn't find
satisfaction or peace in it.

Do not overvalue others, stop devaluing yourself, forgive past mistakes, renounce perfection, and opt for authenticity, harmony and balance are necessary for the development of confidence and self-esteem.

This can be instrumental, in not being drawn into or seduced by toxic personalities that can cause severe emotional, psychological, and physical damage.

Psychic energy is invisible energy that can be channeled and shielded to its full potential, but also risks being « vampirized » or spent for nothing.

11. *How do I know if I am a psychic vampire?*
Psychic vampires are not easy to recognize because they mean us no harm, so we don't worry about them, yet it is indeed a « toxic relationship» in which our energy is fully absorbed.

- *It feeds on everything that can be brought to it:* whether on an emotional, affective, or energetic level. You feel weak without any more energy and vivacity both physically and psychologically.

- *He is always asking for attention:* he is in demand of the slightest attention he can receive. In short, he sucks the oxygen out of the other.

- *It depends on you:* he systematically solicits you at the slightest difficulty... So beware, you may be « vampirized. »

  It is up to you to consider the limit between simple help or persistent solicitation. The psychic vampire needs you and tends to overstretch you, it's up to you to determine your limits so as not to be overwhelmed.

- *He places himself in the position of victim:* he does this to arouse your empathy so that you always give him more.

- *He does not feel empathy:* the day he can no longer feed on the other, he abandons it. He turns to empathetic people, who invest a lot in others.

  If you are this type of person, you may be dealing with a psychic vampire.

12. *Psychic vampires or narcissistic pervert, how to tell the difference?*
   We hear a lot about « narcissistic perverts, » but the psychic vampire is another type of toxic profile, which is much less rare. According to psychiatrist Stéphane Clerget, the latter are not only more numerous, but also very different from the famous narcissistic perverts.

   The psychic vampire does not seek to manipulate the other with the intention of destroying him. On the contrary, he must be able to continue to suck the energy of the other, so he will never wish him harm.

   Moreover, we feel pity for the psychic vampire, but we do not pity the narcissistic pervert. On the contrary, we expect empathy from him.

13. *How do you cure a psychic vampire?*
   It is often difficult. If we feel like this, we can try to understand why we are here, how has our childhood conditioned our behavior?
   Vampirism can be treated very well with psychotherapy.

Remember that by recognizing such behaviors and trying to stop them, you are protecting yourself, your health, and your overall well-being. No one deserves to be mistreated or used in this way. It's definitely not your fault.

There will always be some people who refuse to take responsibility for their own emotional maturity. You don't have to carry that burden.

Know how to perceive this psychic dimension, so that you can adjust the shot to ensure that it does not harm your well-being and your path to success.

GRIEVING AND LOSS

No matter what kind of loss, you've suffered, there's no right or wrong way to grieve. But by understanding the stages and types of grief, you can find healthier ways to deal with it.

Grieving is a natural response to the loss. It is the emotional pain you experience when something or someone you love is taken away from you.

Often the pain of loss can seem overwhelming. You may feel all kinds of difficult and unexpected emotions, from shock or anger to disbelief, guilt, and deep sadness.

The pain of bereavement can also disrupt your physical health, making it difficult to sleep, eat, or even think properly.

These are normal reactions to a loss and the greater the loss, the more intense your grief will be.

Coping with the loss of someone or something, you love is one of life's greatest challenges.

You may associate grief with the death of a loved one, which is often the cause of the most intense type of grief, but any loss can cause grief, including:

1. A divorce or relationship breakdown.
2. Loss of health.
3. Loss of employment.
4. Loss of financial stability.
5. A miscarriage.
6. Retirement.
7. The death of a pet.
8. The loss of a cherished dream.
9. Serious illness of a loved one.
10. The loss of a friendship.
11. Loss of security following trauma.
12. The sale of the family home.

Even subtle losses in life can trigger feelings of grief. For example, you might be grieving after leaving home, upon graduation, or a job change.

Whatever your loss is personal to you, so don't be ashamed of what you're going through or believe it's somehow appropriate to grieve some things. If the person, animal, relationship, or situation was important to you, it is normal to grieve the loss you are experiencing.

Whatever the cause of your grief, there are healthy ways to deal with the pain that, over time, can lessen your sadness and help you come to terms with your loss, find new meaning, and eventually move on.

A. The approach:
   Grieving is a highly personal experience. There is no right or wrong way to grieve.

   How you grieve depends on many factors, including your personality and coping style, your life experience, your faith, and how important the loss is to you.

   Of course, the grieving process takes time. Healing takes place gradually and cannot be forced or rushed. There is no « normal » time for mourning. Some people start to feel better after a few weeks or months.

   For others, the grieving process is measured in years. Whatever your grieving experience, it's important to be patient with yourself and allow the process to unfold naturally.

B. *Myths and realities:*
   1. *Myth:* The pain will go away faster if you ignore it.
      Reality: Trying to ignore your pain or prevent it from happening will only make it worse in the long run. For true healing, it is necessary to confront your grief and actively deal with it.

   2. *Myth:* It is important to be « strong » in the face of loss.
      Reality: Feeling sad, scared, or lonely is a normal reaction to loss. Crying doesn't mean you're weak. You don't need to « protect » your family or friends by showing courage. Showing your true feelings can help them as well as you.

   3. *Myth:* If you're not crying, it means you're not sorry for the loss.
      Reality: Crying is a normal response to sadness, but it's not the only one. Those who don't cry can feel pain just as deeply as anyone else. They may just have other ways to show it.

4. *Myth:* mourning is expected to last about a year.
    Reality: There is no specific time limit for mourning. The time it takes differs from person to person.

5. *Myth:* Moving on means forgetting your loss.
    Reality: Moving on means you have accepted your loss, but it is not the same as forgetting. You can move on and keep the memory of someone or something you lost as an important part of you.

    In fact, as we go through life, these memories can become more and more integral to defining who you are.

C. *Dealing with the process:*
    While grieving a loss is an inevitable part of life, there are ways to help deal with the pain, come to terms with your grief, and eventually find a way to pick up the pieces and move on.

    1. Accept your pain.
    2. Accept that grief can trigger many different and unexpected emotions.
    3. Understand that your grieving process will be unique to you.
    4. Seek face-to-face support from people who care about you.
    5. Support yourself emotionally by taking care of yourself physically.
    6. Know the difference between grief and depression.

D. *The stages.*
    In 1969, psychiatrist Elisabeth Kübler-Ross introduced what is known as « the five stages of grief. » These stages of grief were based on her studies of the feelings of patients dealing with terminal illness, but many people have generalized them to other types of negative changes and loss of life, such as the death of a loved one or a breakup.

1. *Denial:* « It can't happen to me. »
2. *Anger:* « Why is this happening? Who is to blame? »
3. *Negotiation:* « Make sure this doesn't happen, and in return, I'll ___. »
4. *Depression:* « I'm too sad to do anything. »
5. *Acceptance:* « I am at peace with what happened. »

If you are feeling any of these emotions following a loss, it can be helpful to know that your reaction is natural and will heal over time.

However, not everyone who cries goes through all of these stages and that's okay.

Contrary to popular belief, it is not necessary to go through every stage to heal.

In fact, some people resolve their grief without going through any of these steps.

And if you go through these stages of grief, you probably won't experience them in a neat, sequential order, so don't worry about how you « should » feel or what stage you're supposed to be in.

E. *Symptoms.*
Although loss affects people in different ways, many of us experience the following symptoms when we are grieving.

Remember that almost everything you experience at the start of grief is normal, including feeling as if you're going crazy, having a bad dream, or questioning your religious or spiritual beliefs.

1. *Emotional symptoms:*
    a. *Shock and skepticism:* immediately after a loss, it can be difficult to accept what has happened.

        You may feel numb, find it hard to believe the loss really happened, or even deny the truth.

        If a pet or someone you love has died, for example, you can still expect them to show up, even though you know they're gone.

    b. *Sadness:* deep sadness is probably the most universally experienced symptom of grief.

        You may have feelings of emptiness, despair, longing, or deep loneliness.

        You may also cry a lot or feel emotionally unstable.

    c. *Guilt:* you may regret or feel guilty about things you did or didn't say or do. You may also feel guilty about certain feelings.

        For example, feeling relieved when someone dies after a long and difficult illness.

        You may even feel guilty for not doing more to prevent your loss, even though it is completely out of your control.

    d. *Fear:* a major loss can trigger a host of worries and fears. If you have lost your partner, your job, or your home, for example, you may feel anxious, helpless, or uncertain about the future. You may even have panic attacks.

    The death of a loved one can trigger fears about your own mortality, about facing life without that person, or about the responsibilities you now face alone.

    e. *Anger:* even if the loss is no one's fault, you may experience anger and resentment.

    If you've lost a loved one, you might be angry with yourself, God, the doctors, or even the person who died for abandoning you.

    You may feel the need to blame someone for the injustice done to you.

2. *Physical symptoms:*
We often think of grief as a strictly emotional process, but grief often involves physical issues, including:

    a. Tiredness
    b. Nausea
    c. Decreased immunity
    d. Weight loss or gain
    e. Aches and pains
    f. Insomnia

F. *Seeking support:*
The pain of bereavement can often cause you to want to withdraw from others and withdraw into yourself.

But having face-to-face support from other people is essential to healing from loss.

Even if you are not comfortable talking about your feelings under normal circumstances, it is important to express them during your grief.

While sharing your loss can ease the burden of grief, it doesn't mean that every time you interact with friends and family you should talk about your loss.

Comfort can also come from simply being around other people who care about you. The main thing is not to isolate yourself.

If you follow a religious tradition, embrace the comfort its mourning rituals can bring you.

Spiritual activities that are meaningful to you, such as prayer, meditation, or going to church, can bring you comfort.

If you question your faith as a result of the loss, speak to a member of the clergy or others in your faith community.

Grieving can make you feel isolated, even when you have loved ones around you.

Sharing your grief with others who have experienced similar losses can help.

To find a bereavement support group in your area, contact local hospitals, hospices, funeral homes, and health service centers.

SMILE

Your smile has the power to light up a room and connect with people without saying a single word. They say a picture is worth a thousand words, but I like to say a smile is worth a thousand words. Happiness, optimism, and love to name a few.

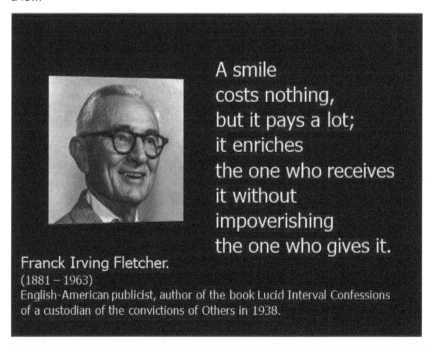

A smile costs nothing, but it pays a lot; it enriches the one who receives it without impoverishing the one who gives it.

Franck Irving Fletcher.
(1881 – 1963)
English-American publicist, author of the book Lucid Interval Confessions of a custodian of the convictions of Others in 1938.

Many things can be resolved with a smile. You can break down barriers, automatically put someone at ease, express your cheerful mood, convey confidence, and thousands of other actions, feelings, and emotions.

Not only can a smile improve your mood and that of those around you, but it also increases your likability and has tremendous health benefits.

Many see smiling simply as an involuntary response to things that bring you joy or make you laugh.

While this is certainly true, it overlooks an important point: smiling can be a conscious and intentional choice.

Whether your smile is genuine or not, it can affect your body and mind in a variety of positive ways, providing benefits for your health, your mood, and even the mood of those around you.

1. *Smiling helps you live longer:* perhaps the most compelling reason to smile is that it can lengthen your overall lifespan. Overall, happy people seem to enjoy better health and longevity.

    Maintaining a happy and positive mood can be an important part of a healthy lifestyle.

2. *Smiling reduces stress:* stress can permeate our entire being and it can really show on our faces. Smiling not only helps prevent us from looking tired, exhausted, and overwhelmed, not only it can actually help reduce stress.

    Believe it or not, smiling can reduce stress even if you don't feel like smiling or even if you fake it with an insincere smile.

    When you're stressed, take time to smile. You and those around you will reap the benefits.

3. *A smile lifts the mood:* next time you're feeling down, try smiling. Chances are your mood will improve.

    The physical act of smiling actually activates pathways in your brain that influence your emotional state, which means that by adopting a happy facial expression, you can « trigger » your mind into a state of happiness.

    This is true whether your smile is real or not. Think of smiling as a natural antidepressant.

4. *Smiling is contagious:* how many times have you heard that a smile has the power to light up the room?

   While it's certainly a beautiful sentiment, it contains a hint of truth. Smiling not only has the ability to uplift your mood, but it can also change other people's moods for the better.

   Your brain automatically notices and interprets other people's facial expressions and sometimes you can even imitate them.

   This means you might notice someone else's smile and unknowingly smile at you.

   Yes, it's scientifically proven that smiling is contagious.

5. *Smiling stimulates the immune system:* smiling can also improve your overall health by helping your immune system work more efficiently.

   It is believed that when you smile, immune function improves because you are more relaxed due to the release of certain neurotransmitters.

6. *Smiling can lower blood pressure:* smiling could have a beneficial impact on your blood pressure.

   Laughter specifically appears to lower blood pressure, after causing an initial increase in heart rate and breathing.

7. *Smiling decrease pain:* studies have shown that smiling releases endorphins, other natural pain relievers, and serotonin.

   Together, these brain chemicals make us feel great, from, head to toe.

   Not only do they improve your mood, but they also relax your body and reduce physical pain. Smiling is natural medicine.

8. *Smiling makes you attractive:* we are naturally drawn, to smiling people.

   While harsher or negative, facial expressions like frowns and grimaces work in the opposite direction, effectively repelling people, smiling is seen as more attractive, and people may even assume you have more positive personality traits, if you smile.

   Not only smiling can make you more attractive, not only it can also make you look younger.

The muscles we use to smile also lift the face making a person look younger.

So instead of opting for a facelift, try smiling throughout the day, you'll look younger and feel better.

9. *A smile suggests success:* research has shown that people who smile regularly appear more confident are more likely to be promoted, and more likely to be approached.

Try to smile at meetings and business appointments. You might find that people react differently to you.

Remember that smiling can influence your feelings of positivity, even if it seems unnatural or forced.

Whether your smile is genuine or not, it always sends the message that life is beautiful to your brain and, ultimately, to the rest of your body!

HUMOR

A sense of humor can be an amazing line of defense when it comes to dealing with stress. Unfortunately, stress is inevitable, and you cannot eliminate it, no matter how hard you try.

However, you can better prepare for stress with several coping techniques.

Developing a sense of humor in the face of life's challenges is a great place to start.

A sense of humor will help build your resilience to stress and improve your overall physical and emotional health.

It will also allow you to:

- Connect with others.
- See things in a different way.
- Normalize your life experience.
- Keep your relationships strong.

Fortunately, developing a healthy sense of humor isn't too difficult, but it does take some practice.

Laughter is the best medicine. But if you're laughing for no reason, you might need medicine.

Minions (film).
American computer-animated comedy film produced by Illumination Entertainment and distributed by Universal Pictures.

Humor is the quality of being amusing or comical. More specifically, the humor effect is a cognitive bias that causes people to remember information better when they perceive it as humorous.

For example, when students learn a new concept in a humorous way, such as through a funny story, they are generally more likely to remember that concept, compared to non-humorous teaching.

The effect of humor can be very beneficial, and humor in general provides a wide range of benefits, such as increased interest and increased energy levels.

1. *The benefits of humor:* one of the main advantages of humor is that people are generally better able to remember information that they perceive as humorous, compared to information that they do not perceive as humorous.

    This benefit, called the humor effect, extends to different types of memory, such as recognition memory, which involves the ability to recognize things one has encountered, and recall memory, which involves the ability to retrieve past information.

    Similarly, humor can also improve people's memory when it comes to verbal information, such as words and sentences, as well as when it comes to visual information, such as pictures, and mixed information, such as cartoons and videos.

Moreover, in addition to improving memory, humor has various other benefits. More specifically:

a. *Humor increases energy levels:* reading or watching something funny, has a positive and energizing effect. This is beneficial for people's general well-being and can help improve people's memory.

b. *Humor reduces negative emotions:* humor can distract from negative emotions, such as anger or anxiety, that may be felt when processing certain information.

   This can be attributed, among other factors, to the fact that processing humor places a heavy cognitive demand on working memory, which means that people focus on humor rather than the negative emotions they would experience otherwise.

c. *Humor leads to increased interest:* adding humor to the information you present can make it more interesting and appealing to others.

   For example, ads that use humor get more attention from people, and are more memorable and compelling.

d. *Humor can make others see you in a more positive way:* Humor, when used correctly in the right circumstances, can improve the impression others have, of you.

   For example, including humor in a speech can have a positive impact on how listeners perceive the speaker.

   Likewise, using humor can improve people's perception of your friendliness and competence, especially when you combine it with negative information that you need to update.

   Additionally, humor and laughter, have additional social, mental, and physical benefits, in a wide variety of areas.

Overall, the humor effect represents a noticeable advantage, where humorous information is remembered better than non-humorous information.

Additionally, humor provides a variety of other benefits, such as increased interest, increased energy levels, and reduced negative emotions.

2. *Situations where humor can be beneficial:* as we have seen above, humor can be beneficial in various ways.

   As a result, there are many situations where humor can be beneficial, such as:

   - When you want to cheer someone up.
   - When you want to establish a relationship with others.
   - When you want to make a speech more interesting.
   - When you want a project, you've worked on, to stand out and grab people's attention.

   In addition, specifically regarding the benefits of humor on memory, there are various situations where humor can be beneficial, such as:

   - When trying to learn new material.
   - When teaching a subject to others.
   - When you create a slogan that you want people to remember.
   - When you formulate a key message that you want your audience to remember.

3. *How to use humor effectively:* in order to make your humor effective, you must pay attention to the following elements:

   - *The type of humor:* you generally want to avoid hurtful humor aimed at people directly, as such humor can alienate them.

   - *The style of humor:* you will often want to avoid, very subtle, shocking, or radical humor, as such humor may be less effective than more cautious humor.

   - *The amount of humor:* you will often want to avoid using humor too often, as it can be boring and make you look like a clown.

   - *Humor timing:* even good humor can end up being inappropriate and ineffective if you deliver it poorly.

   - *The delivery of humor:* even good humor can end up being inappropriate and ineffective if you deliver it poorly.

4. *Adopt the right kind of humor:* To use humor effectively, it's important to pay attention to the type of humor you use.

- *Positive Humor:* the use of positive humor is associated with a relaxed learning environment, better retention of information, increased motivation, increased participant satisfaction.

- *Negative humor:* the use of negative humor, and particularly aggressive humor, is associated with poorer, learning outcomes, an anxious and uncomfortable learning environment, more distractions, and reduced participant satisfaction.

This indicates that it is important to use humor that is perceived as positive, while avoiding humor that might be perceived as negative, as the latter type of humor can harm your goals.

Although it can sometimes be difficult to distinguish between the two types of humor, it is generally better to err on the side of caution and avoid using humor that your target audience is likely to find insulting or offensive.

Also, remember that what is perceived as appropriate, will depend on the context and the audience to which you are presenting information.

For example, a joke that's appropriate to tell your friends while you're sitting in a bar may not be appropriate during a work session or other social gathering.

Remember when you use humor incorrectly, in case it negatively affects people's opinion of you, even if they find the humor itself amusing. This may be the case, for example, if you come across as a « clown, » as a result of inappropriate or overly cheap humor, or if you use humor too frequently.

5. *Adopt the right style of humor:* when it comes to using humor effectively, the style of humor matters. More precisely :

- *Humor generally works best, when it's not too poignant:* often, restrained humor can be more beneficial than humor that goes beyond the ordinary measure, for example, when it comes to improving people's memories, and in many cases even simple humor, such as a funny pun, can help people to remember the transmitted information more.

  Also, over-the-top humor can often lead to various problems, such as leaving an unpleasant impression of you.

- *Humor generally works best, when it's not too subtle:* while you don't want to use radical humor, you should generally avoid using humor that is too subtle, as some people just won't notice it, rendering it ineffective.

Remember that the optimal style of humor depends on factors such as the context and audiences.

For example, in some situations you can be sure your audience will respond well to subtle humor but not overly poignant humor, while in other cases you might know that the audience won't notice subtle jokes at all.

6. *Humor as an effective reminder:* there are also some things to consider when using humor specifically as a way to draw people's attention to information and improve memory of it.

    - *Humor generally works best, when tied to the information at hand:* so try to use humor that is relevant, and especially humor that relates directly to the information you want to emphasize.

    - *Humor can serve as a better aid to attention and memory when it is unexpected in some way:* therefore, try to avoid information that might be perceived by your audience as too predictable.

    - *Attention to humorous information at the expense of related non-humorous information:* it is mainly a problem if two important pieces of information are presented one after the other. Keep in mind if you use humor in a presentation or conversation that it is a memory enhancer.

Remember that there is no one right way to use humor, as the relevance and effectiveness of humor depend on factors such as the circumstances you are in, the people whom you talk to and the goal you hope to achieve. This is up to you when deciding when and how to use humor.

THE BEAUTIFUL LIFE

« Life is short, enjoy it while it lasts. »

This kind of statement is common to those who believe that the essence of life is personal pleasure, fulfillment, and enjoyment. Therefore, many seek to achieve the « good life » with this mindset.

1. *What is a good life?*
    A good life can be described as a satisfying and fulfilling life. It is characterized by personal joy, accomplishment, and the enjoyment of life's little pleasures.

    When someone says their life is good, it means they can access the basic things that give them comfort and pleasure.

2. *The qualities of a good life:* a good life is a combination of experiencing goodness in different areas. So, when you have a good life, it can be said that you are healthy, happy, contented, blessed, and have a good reputation.

    a. *Health:* health is a state in which one feels, looks and is healthy. It refers to a state of complete emotional and physical well-being and is also referred to as a resource for daily living.

        Health is not just the absence of disease, but also the ability to perform your daily activities without the limitations of health.

        Without good health, it would be virtually impossible to do or accomplish the things that ensure a good life.

    b. *Happiness:* happiness is a state of satisfaction with what you see and the experience you have. Although happiness is usually short-lived, it plays an important role in sparking the enthusiasm needed to achieve and live a good life.

    c. *Pleasure:* pleasure is an experience that makes us feel good. Different things give people pleasure.

        For some it may be money, for others it may be a loving and caring spouse, children, or the ability to access whatever they want at any time.

        Although something is most pleasant does not mean that it is good, people often seek different pleasures in order to feel good.

d.   *Peace:* peace is a state of calm, physical, mental, and emotional as well as the feeling of being safe.

Peace does not necessarily mean the absence of challenges, but the ability to stay afloat despite the storms. When one is at peace, the mind is freed from worries and anxieties.

e.   *Money:* money is an indispensable good in life. Lack of money can create stress but having enough money to support yourself can create the experience of a good life.

The idea that pleasure is a component of the good life already means that there is a measure of satisfaction that can be obtained by the availability of money.

f.   *Good reputation:* a good life is not only characterized by what you do or value for yourself, not only by how others perceive you.

Integrity and character are necessary to earn a good reputation with people and it is also a very important component of a good life.

3.   *How to make the transition from a good life to a beautiful life?*
Living a good life is not enough; you may be living an average life. Indeed, unless you continue to grow, the things you cherish now may begin to slip away from you without continued growth.

Moreover, the true essence of life is not just in personal happiness, but also in continually growing, being the best version of yourself, and having a meaningful impact on others. Therefore, to turn a good life into a beautiful life, you must begin to look beyond your personal pleasure and convenience.

Here are some tips you can use to go from a good life to a beautiful life.

a.   *Be committed to growth:* never settle for the level of success you can achieve. This is because success can stand in the way of progress.

The biggest enemy of progress is your latest success, you might become so proud of what you have already achieved that you will stop moving forward towards what you can still achieve.

Therefore, to rise to greatness, you must keep up the pace of progress. Go from one level of achievement to another and from medium achievements to greater achievements.

b. *Discover your passion:* to accomplish greater accomplishments in life, you must discover and ignite your passion. Your passion represents your true desire and what you are programmed for. Your greatest source of motivation will undoubtedly come from your passion.

Passion creates a « burning desire » within you and produces the energy and drive needed to live a beautiful life. When you focus on what releases the energy within you, there is no limit to what you can accomplish.

c. *Find your purpose in life:* life is measured by its impact and not just by its achievements. Your purpose is the reason for your existence. This is the impact you are meant to have in life. The purpose is unique in the sense that it is not selfish, but in the service of people.

Therefore, the goal of life should not only be to indulge oneself, not only to do everything possible to help others, advocate for a cause, and transform society. Most great people in history are not remembered for what they accomplished for themselves, but for the impact they had on the world.

A good life is when you smile often, dream big, laugh a lot and realize how blessed you are for what you have.

Charles "Charlie" Brown.
Created by Charles M. Schulz.
Charlie is the principal character of the comic strip Peanuts.
First appearance October 2, 1950.

d. *Cultivate your personal discipline:* average people revel in delight at the slightest success, but great people celebrate their victories and keep spurring themselves on to, greater accomplishments.

If you wish to turn your goodness into greatness, you must cultivate personal discipline. Be moderate with pleasure and focus your energy and resources on, building bigger dreams.

e. *Set more ambitious goals*: set yourself ambitious goals, big goals that will take you out of your comfort zone. To reach a higher level of success, you need to set bigger goals that can stretch your abilities. You cannot recognize your abilities until you place greater demands on yourself.

Therefore, turn goodness into greatness by constantly pushing your limits. Set ambitious goals, enterprising goals that will take you out of your comfort zone.

So, don't feel comfortable living a good life, but turn goodness into greatness by continuously developing yourself, pursuing your passion, setting higher goals, making a meaningful impact on society. Then you can tell yourself that you are living « a beautiful life. »

Recommended reading and references

We suggest that you consult the works identified below in order to learn more about the particularities contained in this chapter.

BOYES, Alice, PhDs. THE ANXIETY TOOLKIT. Perigee Book. ISBN: 978-0-399-16925-0

BRIDGES, William. MANAGING TRANSITION.
Perseus Books. ISBN: 13-978-0-7382-0824-4

PETER, L. J & HULL, R. LE PRINCIPE DE PETER ; Pourquoi tout va toujours mal ?
Éditions Stock, 1970. ISBN 70-11-682-850-1580.

DR STÉPHANE CLERGET : Les vampires psychiques.
Fayard. ISBN 782213704371

SELYE, Hans, Dr STRESS SANS DÉTRESSE. La Presse. ISBN 0-7777-0095-6

SILLS, Judith. OSER CHANGER. Stanké. ISBN: 2-7604-0481-1

THE NEW YORKER. THE COMPLETE CARTOONS OF.
Black Dog Press. ISBN 1-57912-322-8.

Keep away from people who try to belittle your ambitions. Small people always do that, but the really great make you fell that you, to, can become great.

Samuel Langhorne Clemens (Mark Twain).
(1835 – 1910)
American writer, humorist, entrepreneur, publisher, and lecturer. His novels include The Adventures of Tom Sawyer (1876) and its sequel, Adventures of Huckleberry Finn (1884), the latter of which has often been called the "Great American Novel".

SUCCESS THANKS TO THOSE AROUND YOU

The people you surround yourself with, on a daily basis, have a significant influence on your life. Choose the people around you wisely, as they will have a significant impact on your potential for success.

If you surround yourself with wise people who are trying to improve themselves, their characteristics will help you improve.

On the other hand, if you associate with people who engage in self-destructive habits, those habits will affect you negatively. Stay away from people who try to downplay your ambitions, especially in these unprecedented times.

According to Mark Twain, little people always do that, but great people make you feel that you too can become great. Being around like-minded people will help you achieve your goals, and in doing so, help you become extraordinary.

Whether you are a leader, a boss, an employee, a social worker, or a politician, it is important to understand that the path to success is above all the people around you.

Depending on your game plan for achieving success, you will have to understand the circumstances and the people to get there.

If you are a boss, for example, you will have to make every effort to ensure that you are logically able to act for your success and those around you, because otherwise you will not achieve the expected success.

If you are an employee, your success is tied to the organization you work for. Simple, success is a matter of collaboration and teamwork!

Take the time to explore the different types of stakeholders in your potential success, to identify and get to know the people around you, and then understand their interests in participating.

Thereafter, you will have to execute your plan for success and if necessary, insert it into a larger vision and mission.

However, none of this will happen, because your success depends foremost on your ability to imagine, but above all on being a visionary.

To reach this state, you will have to transform yourself. A visionary is not just someone with a fertile imagination, but someone who has a clear idea of what the future should be like and who can outline concrete steps to achieve that particular vision.

So, your success is definitely linked to the people around you who want their own success. For some, it will be a question of being part of the development team and for others, of imagining and carrying out the management in part or all of a project.

Below, you will find the different points of view that will lead you to understand the position of the various stakeholders, so that you can participate in all conscience in the success of the people around you and thus ensure your own success.

THE VISIONARY

Management is about persuading people to do things they don't want to do, while leadership is about inspiring people to do things, they never thought they could do. (Steve Job)

If you're working on something exciting that really interests you, you don't need to be pushed. The vision attracts you.

Steve Job.
(1955 – 2011)
American entrepreneur, industrial designer, business magnate, media proprietor, and investor. He was the co-founder, chairman, and CEO of Apple.

Are you a visionary?
I'm always dumbfounded when I read about people being able to see what no one else sees. It gives me goosebumps every time because great leaders have this gift of communicating a vision so vividly that everyone in the organization is

excited about its possibilities. They inspire their team to believe that they can accomplish the impossible.

They recharge people with positive energy due to their positive attitude and surround themselves with positive people willing to help them achieve a common vision.

Remember, the greatest gift God has ever given us is not the gift of sight, but the gift of vision. Sight is a function of your eyes, but vision is a function of your heart.

Below, you will find some tips to help you put into perspective what a visionary leader is.

1. *Leadership and people:* leadership is a matter of human consideration. It's not about organizations. It's not about projects. It's not about strategies. It's about motivating people to do the work; you have to be people centered.

    No one said leadership was easy, and it's certainly not for the faint-hearted. To become one of the greats of leadership, you have to make very difficult and unpopular decisions:

    a. You have to accept responsibility when things go wrong while giving credit when things go well.
    b. You have to run headfirst into the heat of the moment when everyone else is running in the opposite direction.

    Leadership can be tough, but when you really think about it, leading people is one of the most fulfilling and rewarding experiences you can have since you have the opportunity to change people's lives every day.

    People look to you for guidance, strength, hope, inspiration, motivation and more.

    Leadership will have its tough days, but the satisfaction of knowing that you are having an impact and making a difference every day, far outweighs any challenge on any given day.

    Be careful, when your most passionate collaborators are silent, it is a sign that something is wrong. The leader must be aware of this and act accordingly immediately.

    When you have a passionate team inspired to help the business achieve its vision while fulfilling its purpose, you need to do everything in your power to ensure that team maintains that vibe. Otherwise, you risk pushing away great talent while settling for mediocrity.

Also, remember that a leader must transition from being responsible for the work to being responsible for the people responsible for the work.

Many people are promoted or recruited into leadership positions without understanding the fundamental philosophy of leadership which will help them produce their best work.

When you are a leader, you are no longer responsible for getting the job done, you are now responsible for inspiring, coaching, mentoring, and motivating your team to become the best version of themselves, which will help them produce their best work.

This is why many businesses and organizations are grossly over-managed and severely under-directed. It must be remembered that the talents that make a person successful in a previous, non-leadership role, are rarely the same ones that will make them excel as a leader.

When a leader can inspire and empower their team to become the best version of themselves by challenging their assumptions about what they can accomplish, a leader can now empower their team to believe in the impossible and produce incredible results to the astonishment of many.

2. *Mediocrity:* a mediocre leader can easily transform a work environment until it destroys it, causing the best employees to flee and the demotivation of others.

Many of the problems that exist in various organizations today stem from poor leadership. While great leaders encourage their employees to reach their full potential and help their organization exceed their goals, weak manager logisticians drive their employees away to the point that many jump ship.

Generally, people don't change jobs just for the money. They rarely quit on a whim or in a fit of anger. They joined the organization because they believed it was good for them and they wanted it to be good.

However, when things go wrong and people quit, you have to really take the time to dig into their real reasons for leaving to see that it's not « the company, the organization » they blame. It's not the location, or the team, or the database, or the air conditioning. In fact, it is the lack of leadership!

So, the next time a resignation happens, resist the temptation to laugh it off like a person without intelligence and common sense who doesn't stop to understand, but concludes without looking at the facts. It's not the departing employee who doesn't understand. It's not the company they're leaving, but it's the lack of leadership!

Note that a leader's job is not to do the work for others, but to help others figure out how to do it themselves, get things done, and achieve success, beyond what they thought possible.

The job of the leader is not to have all the ideas, but rather to ensure that all ideas are heard, so that the best prevails.

The best leaders know that they cannot achieve their goals alone. They need the right people doing things for the right reasons.

Leadership is about delegating the task to the right people to get the job done, and then listening to their team to make sure the best ideas are used.

3. *Teamwork*: when personal agendas become more important than team goals, more important than the team itself and especially the success of the overall mission, performance automatically suffers, and failure to follow.

   Remember you are not a team because you work together. You are a team because you respect, trust and care about each other.

   A « team » is not just people working at the same time in the same place.

   A true team is a group of very different individuals who enjoy working together and who share a commitment to work cohesively to help the organization achieve its common goals and thereby fulfill its purpose.

   Being part of a team and feeling supported by your teammates is one of the best feelings you can want at work.

   There is a capacity for achievement in a group of people working together to achieve a common goal. That's what real support is!

   The teams supported are high-performance teams.

   Leaders are as successful as their teams, and the best known that with the right team dynamics, the right decisions, and diverse personalities, everyone wins.

Germain Decelles

345

True leadership is about people who inspire people to believe that the impossible is possible by inspiring them to push beyond their normal limits.

When leaders recognize that their team is the organization's most valuable resource, great things happen and as a result, the organization can now make a difference in the life of the team, the community, the country and, by extension, the world.

4. *Develop a swarm of ideas:* the role of a leader is not to have all the good ideas. The role of a leader is to create an environment in which great ideas can emerge.

No one ever said, being a leader was easy. It's very simple to bark orders and fire someone if they're not performing, but it takes a lot of effort to coach, to accompany, to supervise, inspire and motivate a team to give the best of itself.

This is the fundamental difference between a leader and a logistician because you must be prepared to pay the price of leadership if you want to experience the benefits of leadership.

As a leader, you owe it to yourself to create a culture where people will be inspired to create big ideas, where dreamers will be encouraged to dream big dreams.

A leader lives their purpose by serving others and continually inspiring their team to elevate the organization to a higher level of performance.

5. *Don't push people:* never push a loyal person to the point where they don't care.

When an employee's performance is consistently good, it becomes expected and can unknowingly be taken for granted.

I have seen people in management positions manipulate high performers to produce more, shoulder the burden of others while nothing is done to address the significant shortfall in the performance of other team members.

At some point, these people burn out and lose all inspiration to continue performing at such a high level.

Remember that when passionate employees shut up, it usually signals that the work environment has become very dysfunctional. As a leader, this is something you need to observe and act on immediately.

Please don't push your most loyal people to the point that they don't care anymore. When you have passionate, inspired, and motivated people to help the company realize its vision while fulfilling its purpose, you need to do everything in your power to keep that team going.

Otherwise, you run the risk of pushing away great talent while settling for mediocrity.

6. *Freedom to work:* Steve Job often said, « It doesn't make sense to hire smart people and tell them what to do; we hire smart people so they can tell us what to do. »

   Bad leadership is about building a great team and doing everything in your power to stay in control. I've seen people report to their manager on everything.

   For example, why is a manager interested in a routine interaction between two colleagues? It doesn't make sense at all.

   No one can build and maintain an organization if no trust exists. It makes no sense to recruit the best and tie their hands by not giving them the freedom to excel.

   Great leaders know that the soul of their organization is their team, and they must trust their team to produce their best work, because that is why they recruit qualified and responsible people in the first place.

   If you want to be a leader, give your team the space to work, create an environment free from the shackles of toxicity, and witness significant growth in your business, but more importantly, your team.

7. *Value people:* I have found the most powerful motivator to be a simple thank you note for their outstanding work.

   Appreciation is one of life's greatest motivators, and now more than ever, all of our employees and associates need to be recognized for the incredible sacrifice and inspiring work they do every day.

   A knowledgeable leader must make it a priority to be grateful to his team, to value the importance of their commitment, to appreciate their contributions and, above all, to thank them for their excellent service.

When we take the time to let people know we value them, it encourages them to keep doing even more. This is precisely why gratitude is the ultimate gift that keeps on giving.

8. *Do not react:* get in the habit of never concluding until you know more, because it's mostly our reaction that gives power to negative situations or people's negative comments.

    If we don't react, then these situations have no power over us. When you take a moment to respond, you don't allow anyone to take away your power or evoke a reaction from you.

    Take responsibility for your own thoughts, feelings, and actions. By doing so, you will no longer cede your power, to forces outside of yourself.

    When something negative, comes your way, you'll pause and instead of reacting, you'll respond to everything and everyone. You will no longer be a victim, but rather a person aware of your inner strength and power.

9. *Above all build:* to build your success, you must view someone else's strength as a compliment to your weakness, not as a threat to your position or authority.

    No one is an expert in everything. The strongest organizations are built on the smartest people, not just one person.

    Strong leaders don't fight for the first and last word. Instead, they listen to their teams, ask the right questions, and give everyone the opportunity to contribute.

    Instead of trying to do it all, find people who can do it better.

    Then, with the right people in place, you can step back to focus on your strengths, like leading the team and planning for the future of the business.

    Great leaders are not know-it-alls who continually try to outdo everyone else. They admit when they are wrong, and they really want to learn from others.

    At the end of the day, it's not about being the smartest person in the room. It's about building a team with the smartest people available and inspiring people to believe in the impossible.

10. *Show respect:* even to people who don't deserve it, not as a reflection of their character, but as a reflection of yours.

    True leadership has always been built on a strong character. It's not just a role you play, it's a life you lead, whether you're at home or at work.

    Questionable personality and behavior can destroy a reputation in seconds. This is why leaders of good character encourage employees to think and act in ways that contribute to the well-being of their organization and society.

    It is not about an image which one draws up for the public. It's about being your true, authentic self while living your life as an example for people to follow.

    Treat people, the way you would like to be treated. Speak to people, the way you would like to be spoken to. Respect is earned, not given.

    Too many people think that having a position of authority is a right given to them by God. They feel superior to those they employ or to the so-called lower levels of the organization.

    Surely you have already seen a certain level of arrogance and entitlement from people in leadership positions who seek to bring people down instead of uplifting them.

    Leaders treat everyone with dignity and respect. They don't bore you with disparaging comments or place you in an embarrassing or demeaning position in front of others, be they co-workers or clients. Instead, they show sincere concern for others.

    The way you treat people, says a lot about you, and always remember that respect is something you deserve, it is never given, no matter what your title.

11. *Generate enthusiasm:* the way you make others feel it says a lot about you.

    How you treat people, says a lot about you and your leadership will be judged on how you inspire, influence, and motivate your associates and employees.

    Exceptional leaders are those who stand up for their people and support them through the toughest times. They also encourage and challenge their people to take on bigger challenges.

True leaders treat you as you deserve to be treated, with respect and dignity. They don't bore you with disparaging comments or intentionally try to put you in an embarrassing or demeaning position in front of others, whether co-workers or clients.

They show genuine interest for others. They ask you, « How are you? » or « How is your family? » And then they listen and express real concern.

Exceptional leaders always find time to express their appreciation for the work of their team and have this unique ability to inspire and motivate people to believe in something beyond their own limiting thinking.

12. *Have courage:* courage does not mean that you are not afraid. Courage means you don't let fear stop you. Never let fear stop you from achieving your dreams. Simple, be brave!

13. *Surround yourself:* surround yourself with a great team and build that team slowly. Your team is one of your most important investments and if you are careful to hire only the best people, it will pay dividends.

What makes you effective as a leader is not the title you hold. Instead, it demonstrates a relentless focus on helping others succeed in their collective endeavors.

Great leaders know that the soul of their company is their team, and they need to allow and trust their team to produce their best work, because that's why you recruited them in the first place.

True leadership is about people, inspiring people to believe that the impossible is possible and inspiring people to go beyond their normal limits.

It's the essence of leadership to help your people reach their full potential, help your team maximize their talents, and help people become the best version of themselves.

Leadership is a huge responsibility and privilege because you can influence the trajectory of someone's personal and professional life in positive or negative ways.

If you want to be a leader, give your team the space to work, create an environment free from the barriers of toxicity, and witness significant growth for your business, but more so, your team.

14. *Your value:* make sure you don't start seeing yourself through the eyes of those who don't like you. Who knows you're worth it even if they don't. Your worth does not diminish based on someone's inability to see your worth.

15. *Don't think too much:* overthinking will destroy your happiness and mood. It will make everything look worse than it is. Take a deep breath, exhale and trust. What must happen will happen. Thinking too much will destroy your happiness.

16. *Do you have the correct answers:* no one will have all the right answers. As a leader, you will make better decisions by having different people and perspectives on your team.

    Building a team with conflicting worldviews, even differing opinions about your industry or society, will push you to think critically even more than in the past.

    Leaders surround themselves with skilled people who can make the impossible possible and create an environment where someone can raise their hand and say « I disagree » without fear of victimization or dismissal. These are the organizations that achieve incredible feats, and these are the companies that produce exceptional people.

    If you want to build a great business, allow your team to disagree with you, listen to all their feedback, because it's not about you.

    Rather, it is about providing the best possible service and products that make a difference in the lives of those entrusted to you.

17. *Change someone's life:* as a leader, you have an incredible opportunity to change someone's life every day. Leadership is never about tearing people down; it's about helping people become the best version of themselves.

    It can be something as simple as saying hello, writing a handwritten note saying you did a great job today, or remembering the names of your employees when you greet them.

    Leadership is about people because it's about inspiring people to believe that the impossible is possible.

    It's about developing and training people to perform at unimaginable levels.

It is about having a positive impact on your community, your company, your department, your organization, your collaborators, and by extension on the world.

As a leader, you don't inspire your team by showing them how amazing you are. Instead, you inspire them by showing them how amazing they are.

18. *Learn from mistakes:* give people permission to make mistakes and an obligation to learn from them. Mistakes are essential to our growth. Also, we often put too much pressure on ourselves to pursue an unrealistic ideal of perfection.

   As a leader, let your team know that there is no shame in making mistakes and more importantly that you support them when they happen.

   I have seen people in leadership positions ducking and throwing their employees under the bus when mistakes have happened. This way of acting leads to mistrust, lack of inspiration and fear of trying something new.

   The most amazing people in their pursuit of success have made countless mistakes. They didn't give up. They persevered and inspired many to follow their example.

   As Albert Einstein pointed out, a person who never made a mistake never tried anything new.

   Leaders are humble enough to admit their mistakes. Successful people are transparent enough with themselves and with others to admit their mistakes.

   As a leader, you will make mistakes. It's inevitable. Don't beat yourself up, despise yourself, or engage in negative self-talk. All of this is a natural part of the growth process.

   Remember that one of the essential characteristics of a leader is the ability to admit mistakes. Decision makers are called upon to make countless decisions, and sometimes things inevitably go wrong.

   Many leaders may view admitting error as a sign of weakness, but for the leader, the opposite is true in many cases.

Admitting your mistakes has the potential to strengthen your relationship with your team. Admitting your mistakes powerfully communicates that you believe in the relationships you have developed.

The people around you need to know that you are human. They need to know that you trust them and your own leadership to say, « I'm sorry. I didn't handle XYZ well. I take full responsibility. Here's what we need to do to get things straightened out and back on track... »

The sign of a great leader is not that they avoid making mistakes, but when they make a mistake, they are humble enough to admit it and learn from it.

19. *Disagreements:* disagreements are inevitable and even healthy, here's why.

An environment that is not auspicious to disagreement is not a growth-oriented environment. It is a control-oriented environment.

To raise a well-balanced business or organization positioned for success, disagreements are inevitable and even healthy. The most successful teams and organizations are regularly at odds.

Yet traditional work cultures have conditioned us to think that everyone should agree with everything, and those with an opposing point of view are labeled as troublemakers or disruptors. But if everyone is always in agreement, how do you know what people are thinking?

As a leader, you are passionate about your ideas. However, it can be discouraging to hear a board member, team member or even employee disagree with your idea or strategy, please listen to what they have to say.

A leader must create safe and engaging work cultures that respect differences of opinion.

No one will have all the right answers, and it's only through conversation, debate and yes, even argument, that real insights emerge to drive better decisions.

20. *Change, evolve:* do not be afraid of change, because it leads you to a new beginning. Change is the evolution of things in a natural way. Change leads to success!

21. *Challenge:* each challenge contains a lesson. We don't grow when things are easy, we grow when we encounter challenges.

    Every difficult moment in your life contains a lesson. Please don't fall victim to « why is this happening to me » but change your mindset to « What is this trying to teach me? »

    It may be difficult, and it may seem overwhelming, but remember, that every step has a purpose. Embrace it, learn from it, and grow from it.

22. *Surround yourself with smart people:* build a great team. No one is an expert in everything, the strongest organizations are built on the smartest people, not just one person.

23. *Develop a culture:* when there are no consequences for a bad work ethic and no rewards for a good work ethic, there is no motivation.

    The culture of any organization is shaped by the worst behavior, the leader is willing to tolerate.

    When the negative behaviors of toxic employees are tolerated, it can have an extremely detrimental effect on the culture of the organization, reduce collaboration between teams, affect the way customers are treated, and much more.

    People in leadership positions will often look for a quick fix, but it's not that simple. It's easy to blame the hiring process or a single employee, but unfortunately the blame lies with you as the person in charge.

    You need to take full responsibility for low morale in your department or organization and urgently remedy the situation before all the good employees leave and you're just left with the toxic ones.

    What makes some organizations great?
    What is this magic formula used by these organizations to enthuse their employees for their work?

    Many large organizations have similar traits, and their most significant strength is their culture and the leadership's ability to develop, maintain, and retain their unique culture throughout the life of the organization.

    But fantastically, money is not the primary motivating factor for many of these employees. They are not obsessed with generating profits alone.

Instead, many of these employees enjoy the family spirit of their organization and a common purpose that motivates and inspires them to perform at their best, enabling them to continually add value to the people they are commissioned to serve.

There is no magic formula for a quality corporate culture. The key is to treat your staff as you would like to be treated.

24. *Be visionary:* if you're working on something exciting that really interests you, you don't need to be pushed. The vision attracts you. (Steve Jobs)

    I'm always dumbfounded when I read about people being able to see what no one else sees; it gives me goosebumps every time because great leaders have this gift of communicating a vision so vividly that everyone in the organization is excited about its possibilities.

    They inspire their team to believe they can achieve the impossible.

    They recharge people with positive energy due to their positive attitude and surround themselves with positive people who are ready to help them achieve a common vision.

    Remember that the greatest gift God has ever given us is not the gift of sight, but the gift of vision. Sight is a function of your eyes, but vision is a function of your heart.

THE VISION AND THE MISSION

1. *The vision statement:* a vision states what the organization aspires to become, in the future. A mission reflects the past and present of the organization by specifying why the organization exists and what role it plays in society. Objectives are the more specific goals that organizations pursue to achieve their visions and missions.

   A vision is a vivid mental image of what you want, your organization to be at some point in the future, based on your goals and aspirations.

   A vision statement captures, in writing, the essence of where you want your organization to go and can inspire you and your staff to achieve your goals.

   In the context of management, a vision is an expression that the organization wants to become what it wants to be and what it wants to be known for.

The vision comes from the leaders. This is how they express the future of the organization or its strategic direction.

A vision statement is the anchor of any strategic plan. It describes what an organization would ultimately like to accomplish and gives purpose to the existence of the organization.

A well-written vision statement should be short, simple, unique to your organization, and leave no room for interpretation.

A vision statement is important for an organization because it serves as a strategic blueprint for success. It can act as a guide when participants encounter difficulties.

Vision statements also help motivate employees and collaborators to work towards common goals. A vision statement can also help an organization identify its organizational culture.

2. *The mission statement:* a mission statement is a concise explanation of the organization's purpose. It describes the purpose of the organization and its overall intent.

   The mission statement supports the vision and serves to communicate purpose and direction to employees, customers, suppliers, and other stakeholders.

   Mission statements help employees understand the meaning and purpose of their job by giving them clear reasons why their job serves a larger purpose.

   Mission statements help employees see the positive aspects of their day-to-day activities, boosting morale and creating a long-term employee investment in the company culture.

   Therefore, a mission statement provides the basis for judging the success of an organization and its goals.

   It helps the organization to check if it is on the right track and to make the right decisions.

   It provides direction when the organization is tempted by distractions and forced to adapt to new demands.

DELEGATE

Delegating seems easy and those who can do it well make it seem easy, but passing the baton requires a lot of trust, communication, and coordination. Yet, if you learn to delegate and do it well, everyone on your team will be winners.

As a leader, it's important to delegate, because you can't and shouldn't do everything yourself.

Delegating empowers your team, builds trust, and helps with professional development. Additionally, it will help you learn to identify who is best suited, to tackle tasks or projects.

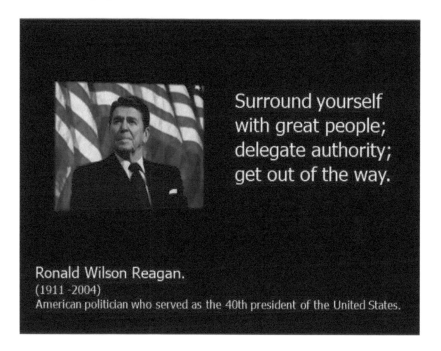

Surround yourself with great people; delegate authority; get out of the way.

Ronald Wilson Reagan.
(1911 -2004)
American politician who served as the 40th president of the United States.

Sure, delegating can lighten your workload, but delegating does more than just get rid of your tasks.

On the one hand, the people who work for you will be able to develop new skills and gain knowledge, which will prepare them for more responsibilities.

On the other hand, also delegating can be a clear sign of respect towards your collaborators and employees that you trust them and that you are sure that they will strive to have a higher level of commitment towards their work, their organization and, above all, their leader.

Although the benefits of the delegation are clear and numerous, many managers still fail to delegate effectively.

The reality being that there are several myths and misconceptions about delegation that can make some leaders reluctant to give work to others because they think that delegating is simply giving work to someone else. So, they don't, and they end up wasting their time and the organization's time and resources.

Delegation can be a chance to make workloads more manageable, but even more so, it can provide valuable learning opportunities for your co-workers and employees. Delegating is not a sign of weakness; it is a sign of strong leadership.

You will surely find that as a leader, letting go it can be difficult, but it is important to accept that you cannot do everything yourself. Do not worry too much, because it is part of the apprenticeship of any good leader.

Another common obstacle to the delegation is that leaders are unsure of what tasks they should or should not delegate. In any leader's workload, especially new ones, there are likely tasks you need to do and tasks you need to delegate.

Here are some tips to help you delegate effectively so your team shares the workload and makes progress that benefits everyone.

1. *Choose the right person for the job:* Part of being a good leader is understanding the strengths, weaknesses, and preferences of your associates and employees. If you need to delegate a task that is going to require a lot of collaboration, don't delegate it to someone who strongly prefers to work alone.

   Delegate it to someone who prefers to collaborate. Depending on the case, you might want to consider sitting down with your team, going through the task list, and letting people pick the tasks that interest them the most. Letting people choose the tasks delegated to them is another way to build trust and inspire commitment within a team.

2. *Explain why you delegate:* If you're delegating a task to someone out of the blue, it really helps to provide some context as to why you're giving them this responsibility. When selecting people to delegate to, tell them why you specifically chose them and how you hope it will help them grow. Help them see each delegated task as an opportunity to take on more responsibility or learn new skills.

3. *Provide proper instructions:* any good delegator provides basic and important information without micromanaging. Tell the person your goals or the steps you hope to achieve and let them solve the problem in their own way. Don't look for perfection or micromanagement, because that person might do the job differently than you did. The important thing is that you get the result you are looking for and not to assert your way of proceeding on a particularity.

4. *Provide resources and training:* you need to ensure that the person tasked with a job or project has the tools and resources to succeed.

5. *Delegate responsibilities and authority:* you've probably been in a situation where you were tasked with something but didn't feel fully empowered to make decisions. As a result, work stops, you end up having to ask for help, and the task takes longer from both the employee and the manager.

   Managerial logisticians who fail to delegate responsibilities in addition to specific tasks end up finding themselves reporting to their subordinates and doing part of the job, rather than the other way around. Foster an environment and culture where people feel empowered to make decisions, ask questions, and take action to get the job done.

6. *Check the work and provide feedback:* there is nothing worse than a leader who delegates something to an employee and then blames them when something goes wrong. Don't be like that. Check the work you've delegated to your employees when it's done, make sure they've done it right, and then give them the feedback they need to improve by encouraging them to move forward.

7. *Say thank you:* when someone completes a task or project you've delegated, show genuine appreciation, and point out the specific things they did well. When you take note of these details, you give people a roadmap of what they need to keep doing to be successful.

   The simplest step is to thank people, but this phase is among the hardest for many people to learn. When you say thank you, you inspire loyalty, provide real satisfaction for the work done, and facilitate future mentoring and performance reviews.

Remember, if you delegate well, you can increase trust and engagement with your employees and collaborators, improve productivity, and ensure that the right people are doing the tasks that work, best for them.

So don't hesitate to pass the baton. It may take some practice to become a great delegator, but if you work on it, you'll get closer to success.

FAMILY

The word « family » is one of the most loosely defined terms in the English language, as it means something different from everyone.

While one person may define family as the relatives who share their home, another may view the family as including extended relatives residing near and far.

For others, they see their beloved circle of friends or their pets as a family. Families are very different, but they all operate under the same premise: shared love and commitment.

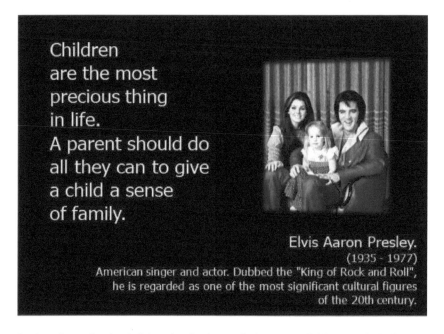

Children are the most precious thing in life. A parent should do all they can to give a child a sense of family.

Elvis Aaron Presley.
(1935 - 1977)
American singer and actor. Dubbed the "King of Rock and Roll",
he is regarded as one of the most significant cultural figures
of the 20th century.

Rather than simply defining family by a dictionary definition, each individual should seek to define a family by their own standards.

You can have multiple families in your life, or even multiple families at once, if you wish. However, if you define your family unit, whether traditional or unique, your definition is the family unit that is right for you.

As the saying goes, « Family is what you make of it. » Whether it's blood relatives, friends, pets, or a combination of these, your family can provide the support you need to thrive.

Work, social life, achieving goals are part of a hectic life. However, the element that cements all these efforts is above all the success of the family. A job is a schedule for a period, but the family is a lifetime.

The family provides emotional and psychological security, in particular through the warmth, love and camaraderie, that living together generate between the spouses, then between them and their children.

This environment balances life and rejuvenation so necessary for success.

A. *The society of the last decades:* Society in recent decades has tended to neglect the use of this important element, the family unit. For example, in many urban areas, the family unit has broken down mainly because of poverty.

To explain this social upheaval, it is necessary to take into account the lack of enthusiasm and perseverance of the educational institutions which are often undermined by a financial shortage or of the unions which want to advance their causes often to the detriment of the children.

There are also pseudo-educational theories that promote timeless pedagogy or social agendas like « American Marxism. »

For avid readers, refer to « American Marxism » author Mark R. Levin.

These theories are taken up by politicians, the media and high-tech to push us to forget our history, our traditions, our principles, and our past sacrifices, to abandon everything we know from life experience to be true, from honor to biology and from freedom to mathematics.

In other words, when others tell you what to think, stop and say no, I will remember how to think and think for myself, consider all assumptions with skepticism, give them weight which is due to them, and nothing more.

Remember that the greatest service we can render to our children is to teach them « to think » and « not what to think! »

The greatest service we can do ourselves is to humbly remember this lesson.

This may sound like common sense, but common sense is fading.

Now is a good time to remember to ensure success for your children as well as for you.

B. *Success starts with the family:* your success in life depends on the success of your family and especially your children.

Whether you're just starting your career or retired, remember that there will come a time in your life when you're sitting on your balcony on a sunny summer's day and wondering, « What is my life legacy to society? »

There will always be « turtle » parents. The male seed at sea, the female oviposits, her young, on the beach to set off again, leaving the brood to its own destiny.

There are also responsible parents who are eager to meet challenges, in order to transmit their life values to their children, so that they in turn can aspire to success.

Are you a « turtle » or a successful « parent? »

Always remember that the family gives you the support you need to flourish and that your children are the source of valuation and well-being necessary for your moral and emotional balance, and achievement of success to which you will refer at the end of life.

C. *Parenting is not easy:* good parenting is hard work. A good parent is someone who strives to make decisions in the best interests of the child.

What makes a good parent is not only defined by the action of the parent, not only the desire for success.

A good parent doesn't have to be perfect. Nobody is perfect. No child is perfect either. It's important to keep this in mind when setting your expectations.

Successful parenting is not about achieving perfection. But that doesn't mean you shouldn't work towards that goal.

Set high standards for yourself first, then for your children. Never forget the fact that you are one if not the most important role model that will shape your children.

Raising children is one of the hardest and most fulfilling jobs in the world and the one for which you may feel the least prepared.

The following parenting tips can help you feel more fulfilled as a parent.

1. *Boost your child's self-esteem:* children begin to develop their sense of themselves as babies when they see themselves through the eyes of their parents.

   The tone of your voice, your body language and your every expression are absorbed by your children.

   Your words and actions as a parent affects their developing self-esteem more than anything else.

   Praise your children's accomplishments, no matter how small, and she or he will make them proud of themselves. Letting children do things independently will make them feel capable and strong.

   On the other hand, disparaging with comments or comparing one child unfavorably to another will make children feel worthless.

   Avoid making heavy statements or using words as weapons. Comments like:

   « What a stupid thing to do! »
   Or « You're acting more like a baby! »

   Will do as much long-term damage as physical hits.

   Choose your words carefully and be compassionate. Tell your children that everyone makes mistakes and that you still love them, even if you don't like their behavior.

2. *Research your children's successes:* have you ever thought about how many times you react negatively to your children in a given day?

   Surely you will find yourself criticizing them much more often than complimenting them. What would you think of a boss who treated you with so much negativity, even if he meant well?

   The most effective approach is to surprise children doing something good:

   « You made your bed without being asked, that's great! »
   Or « I was watching you play with your sister earlier and you were very patient. »

These statements will do more to encourage long-term good behavior than repeated reprimands.

Make sure you find something positive every day. Be generous with rewards, your love, hugs, and compliments can do wonders and are often enough reward. Soon you will find that you are « cultivating » more of the behavior you would like to see.

3. *Set boundaries and be consistent with your discipline:* discipline is needed in every home. The purpose of discipline is to help children choose acceptable behaviors and learn self-control.

They may test the boundaries you set for them, but they need those boundaries to grow into responsible adults.

Establishing house rules helps children understand your expectations and develop self-control. Some rules may include no TV until homework is done, no hitting, name calling, or hurtful teasing.

You may want to set up a system. For example, a warning, followed by consequences such as « downtime » or loss of privileges.

A common mistake that parents make is not enforcing the consequences. You can't punish kids for responding one day and ignoring, it is the next. Being consistent teaches what you expect of them.

4. *Make time for your children:* it's often difficult for parents and children to get together for a family meal, let alone have a good time together. But there's probably nothing more, the kids would like.

Get up ten minutes earlier in the morning so you can eat breakfast with your child or leave the dishes in the sink and take a walk after dinner.

Children who don't get the attention they want from their parents often act badly or misbehave because they are sure to be noticed that way.

Many parents find it rewarding to spend time together with their children. Create a « special night » each week to be together and let your children help you decide how to pass the time.

Look for other ways to connect, such as putting a note or something special in your child's lunch box.

Teenagers seem to need less attention from their parents than younger children. Because there are fewer windows of opportunity for parents and teens to get together, parents should do their best to be available when their teen expresses a desire to talk or participate in family activities.

Attending concerts, games, and other events with your teen communicates caring and lets you learn more about your child and their friends.

You should not feel guilty if you're a working parent. It's the many little things you do, like making popcorn, playing cards, window shopping, that the kids will remember.

5. *Be a good role model:* young children learn a lot about how to act by watching their parents. The younger they are, the more they are inspired by you. Before you lash out or explode in front of your child, think about this: is this how you want your child to behave when angry?

Know that you are constantly being watched by your children. For example, children who hit others usually have a pattern of aggression at home.

Show the traits you want to see in your children: respect, friendliness, honesty, kindness, tolerance. Adopt a generous behavior. Do things for others without expecting a reward. Express your thanks and give compliments. Above all, treat your children as you expect others to treat you.

6. *Make, communication, a priority:* you can't expect kids to do it just because you, as a parent, « say it. » They want and deserve explanations as much as adults.

If we don't take the time to explain, children will start to question our values and our motivation, so they will doubt the basis. Parents, who reason with their children allow them to understand and learn without judgment.

Clarify your expectations. If there is a problem, describe it, express your feelings, and invite your child to work with you on a solution. Be sure to include consequences. Make suggestions and offer choices. Be open to your child's suggestions as well. Negotiate. Children who participate in decisions are more motivated to implement them.

7. *Be flexible and ready to adjust your parenting style:* If you often feel, « Disappointed » with your child's behavior, you may have unrealistic expectations. Parents who think « should, » for example, « my child should be toilet-trained already, » might find it helpful to educate themselves on the topic or talk to other parents or child development specialists.

    Children's environment has an effect on their behavior, so you may be able to change that behavior by changing the environment.

    If you find yourself constantly saying « no » to your two-year-old, look for ways to change your environment so that fewer things are off limits. This will cause less frustration for both of you.

    As your child changes, you will need to gradually change your parenting style. Chances are, what works with your child now won't work as well in a year or two.

    Teenagers tend to look less to their parents and more to their peers for role models. But continue to provide guidance, encouragement, and appropriate discipline while empowering your teen. And take advantage of every available moment to establish a connection!

8. *Show that your love is unconditional:* as a parent, you have the responsibility to correct and guide your children. But how you express your corrective orientation makes all the difference in how a child receives it.

    When confronting your child, avoid blaming, criticizing, or finding fault, which damages self-esteem and can lead to resentment.

    Instead, try to intellectually nurture and encourage your children, even when disciplining them. Make sure they know even if you want and expect better next time, your love is there no matter what.

9. *Know your own needs and boundaries as a parent:* admit it, you're an imperfect parent. You have strengths and weaknesses as the head of the family. Recognize your abilities such as love and devotion. Make a vow to work on your weaknesses, such as the need to be more consistent with discipline. Try to have realistic expectations for yourself, your partner, and your children. You don't have to have all the answers, be kind to yourself.

    Try to make parenting a manageable task. Focus on the areas that need the most attention rather than trying to solve everything at once.

Admit it when you're exhausted. Make time for yourself to do things that will make you happy.

Focusing on your needs, doesn't make you selfish. It just means that you care about your own well-being, which is another important value for your children to embody.

Recommended reading and references

We suggest that you consult the works identified below in order to learn more about the particularities contained in this chapter.

BENNIS, Warren. LEADERS. The strategies for taking charge.
Harper. ISBN: 0-06-015246-X

CROSBY, B. Philip. COMPLETENESS: Quality for the 21st Century.
Dutton Book, ISBN 0-525-993475-8.

ELGIN, S. PHD. HOW TO DISAGREE WITHOUT BEING DISAGREEABLE.
MJF BOOKS. ISBN: 10:1-56731-739-1

GREENE, Robert. THE 48 LAWS OF POWER.
Penguin Books. ISBN 978-0-14-028019-7.

HAINEAULT, Pierre. SE LIBÉRER DES GENS QUI NOUS EMPOISONNENT LA VIE.
Les Éditions Québécor. ISBN 2-7640-0889-9.

HEALD, Tim. PHILIP: A Portrait of the Duke of Edinburgh.
William Morrow & Co. ISBN 0-688-10199-2.

HÉBERT, Sylvie. LE PRIMAIRE, DES RÉPONSES À VOS QUESTIONS.
Éditions les parents d'abord.

HELLER. R. & ALL. ESSENTIAL MANAGER'S MANUAL.
DK BOOKS. ISBN:0-7894-3519-5

DRUCKER, Peter F. POST-CAPITALIST SOCIETY.
Harper Business. ISBN 0-88730-620-9.

FRIEDMAN, L. Thomas. THE WORLD IS FLAT. A Brief History of the Twenty-first Century. ISBN 1-59397-669-0.

GILBERT, Martin. CHURCHILL. Houghton Mifflin Co. ISBN 0-395-19405-9.

GIULIANI, Rudolph W. LEADERSHIP. Miramax Books. ISBN 0-7868-6841-4.

GRAY, Collin S. WAR, PEACE AND VICTORY: Strategy and Statecraft for the Next Century. Simon & Schuster. ISBN 0-671-60695-6.

JOYNER, Rick. LEADERSHIP, MANAGEMENT, And the Five Essentials for Success.
Morning Star Publications. ISBN 1-878327-33-X.

Common sense
is something
that everyone needs,
few have, and
none think they lack.

Benjamin Franklin.
(1706 - 1790)
American polymath who was active as a writer, scientist, inventor,
statesman, diplomat, printer, publisher, and political philosopher.
Among the leading intellectuals of his time, Franklin was one
of the Founding Fathers of the United States.

YOUR SUCCESS IS BASED ON COMMON SENSE

The ability to perceive, understand and exercise judgment is the most desired quality that almost everyone wishes to have in order to survive and grow in life.

As life tends to throw different challenges at each stage, people want to have the ability to do the right things and be prepared when something unexpected happens in life.

Common sense is a natural ability to make proper judgment on practical matters.

You don't need to have specialized knowledge to use common sense and make informed judgments in everyday situations. For example, common sense tells us not to jump into deep water when we can't swim.

The accumulation of do's and don'ts in all particular situations that enrich a person's common sense is a by-product of life's experiences.

Although common sense is a natural quality and does not need to be taught, there are a few steps that will help you improve your common sense.

1. *Trust yourself:* confidence is the basic step to increase your common sense. If you don't trust yourself, you won't be able to see a clear picture of situations in order to find the appropriate way to solve problems. So, trust yourself and be confident and handle life's challenges to improve your common sense.

2. *Take emotion out of the equation:* to make a good decision, you must eliminate emotion from the equation.

    When your mind is occupied with the outcome of certain situations, you cannot pay attention to every detail and find the best possible alternative to handle the situations.

    So, you have to emotionally detach yourself from situations, to find the appropriate solution.

3. *Do not complicate anything:* if you tend to overthink and overanalyze situations, it will only make situations more complicated. So, stop thinking and analyzing situations and deal with them as soon as you find the best way to proceed.

4. *Act with intelligence:* there are certain ways to perform a specific job. If you do things the way you like to do them rather than how they can be done effectively, you complicate matters. Proper handling of issues is what matters most, not how you want to handle them.

    So be smart and do things the way they can be done rather than the way you would like to do them, and your common sense will improve.

Therefore, common sense is an essential element not only for our survival, but also for growth in life. Increase your experiences of dealing with life's problems to improve your common sense rather than getting stuck at certain life stages.

So, if you want to reach the pinnacle of success in all walks of life, always be sure to discipline yourself to develop a habit of growing awareness, to enhance your common sense.

UNDERSTAND COMMON SENSE

Everyone has common sense lapses. Common sense is not a single destination. It is a way of thinking that needs constant nurturing and application.

Common sense can be learned and applied in everyday situations, regardless of your background, training, intelligence quotient, social status, or experience.

The more we are trained to think one way, by our workplace, family, culture, etc., the more likely we are to hastily use a thought or automatism to take the place of common sense.

We are human and therefore fallible.

Our brains somehow function as a way to provide shortcuts to ensure survival in a world where being chased by predators could end your life.

Things are generally not as they appear. Smart people don't always do things smart.

Sometimes smart people can do irrational things like gamble all their money on the stock market, have extramarital affairs that destroy their marriages and political careers.

While each of us creates a reality from our own experiences and makes sense of our world through this personal lens, for the most part we understand that our sense of reality is only a small part of a much larger picture.

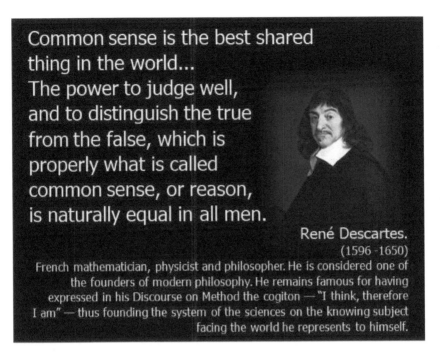

Common sense is the best shared thing in the world... The power to judge well, and to distinguish the true from the false, which is properly what is called common sense, or reason, is naturally equal in all men.

René Descartes.
(1596 -1650)
French mathematician, physicist and philosopher. He is considered one of the founders of modern philosophy. He remains famous for having expressed in his Discourse on Method the cogiton — "I think, therefore I am" — thus founding the system of the sciences on the knowing subject facing the world he represents to himself.

For some people, however, their sense of reality becomes the only sense of reality, and they believe that they can magically manipulate or transform situations to turn out as they wish. Irrational behavior for some and dementia for the less fortunate.

1. *The purpose and significance of common sense:* common sense consists in exercising « sound and prudent judgment based on a simple perception of the situation or the facts. »

    This definition of common sense depends on not over-complicating the situation by keeping it simple, and then applying general experience and knowledge to the situation with sound, careful, context-derived judgment. This is the self-confidence that this experience holds valid for future situations.

    Common sense is practical intelligence. It is the mental capacity to deal with the challenges and opportunities of life.

    Common sense is situational, and it depends on the context of one aspect of your life that may be excellent while failing miserably in another aspect of your life.

As for the purpose of common sense, it is essentially the thought that keeps you from making mistakes or irrational decisions, an approach to thinking that can open your eyes to the possibility that insisting on being right prevents you from seeing the big picture.

Common sense can also help you avoid being bound by rules, theories, ideas, and guidelines that would hinder or stifle the best decision in a particular situation.

In other words, just because someone tells you so that an enforcement rule is in place, or just because it's always been done that way, doesn't mean you have to give up the common sense in the face of current needs and new circumstances.

2. *How to use common sense:* start by examining your own emotions, beliefs, and practices to make sure they don't override your common sense. Test different scenarios in your head to try to determine the practical consequences of applying the decision or action as you wish.

Is it practical, have you considered everything, and what if things go wrong?
If things go wrong, can you fix them and if you can't, what will be the consequences?

If appropriate, if your reality is clouding your judgment too much, reach out and discuss the situation with people you trust, to better understand their views and ideas. This is especially important when you are too close to a situation and any decision or action you could take affect those around you.

Reflexive intelligence is being able to step back and see the bigger picture, so that you realistically assess the situation or environment directly around you rather than to force you to conform to its relevance or to practice wishful thinking.

After an accurate assessment of the situation, an introspective mindset allows you to set realistic goals within the parameters in which you work and take reasonable steps to achieve the goals.

Do less, think more.

Many of us suffer from « must do obsessively. » It just means that we are obsessed, with always doing more instead of thinking.

And, while we're running around being busy all the time, we're not being productive and contributing to a culture that admires busy people.

Is it common sense?
Hardly. It's about working harder and longer without taking time to think.

Give yourself time for reflection every day, even if it's only 20 minutes. After a few weeks, you will notice a considerable reduction in stress levels. And your common sense will definitely improve.

LEARN BASIC COMMON SENSE

There are things every human being should know how to do and not leave to another person, things that are central to personal survival, self-knowledge, and long-term health and safety.

To do this, you can learn common sense through practical knowledge and its applications.

So, you can be informed precisely when times are tougher or when you need to react quickly.

1. *Know how to cook and know how food arrives at your table*: for every person who proudly proclaims they cannot cook, there is a person who is easily persuaded by others that any food is good for them, no matter how unhealthy or of unethical or unproductive origin.

    It's not a badge of honor not to know how to cook yourself. It is often a sign of laziness or rebellion against so-called domesticity.

    Knowing how to cook is basic common sense, as it will ensure healthy survival in all conditions. And no matter how often you use this skill, it's enjoyable and rewarding.

2. *Know how to grow your own food:* being able to grow your own food is survival insurance. Learn the skill if you haven't already and instill it in your children.

3. *Knowing how to feed:* if you cook for yourself and maybe grow your own food, you will be more connected with your body's needs for healthy eating.

    Eat healthy most of the time, in moderation and making sure to meet all nutritional needs appropriate to your age, sex, size and personal situation.

4. *Know and respect your environment:* it makes sense to know what local conditions impact your life, from weather to wildlife.

    Take the time to get to know your local environment and respond appropriately, from properly weatherproofing your home to eliminating invasive species from your garden.

5. *Know how to budget and not spend more than you earn:* it makes sense to only spend what you have. Unfortunately, many people manage to forget about this in an orgy of frequent overspending, behaving as if bloated credit card debt completely surprises them.

    Overspending is an irrational habit, as is hiding unopened bills in the back of a closet. Controlling spending with a budget and moderation is common sense and remember to make sure you keep all important decisions, financial agreements, and other agreements in writing. Remember, we are never too careful when it comes to money!

6. *Know your body's limits:* is to identify which foods wreak havoc on your body and which ones work for you and how many hours of sleep you need without forgetting the type of exercise that benefits best, your body and your metabolism.

    Read a lot but figure out for yourself what harms and heals your body, because you are the real expert on the matter. Plus, you're not a superhero, and ignoring bodily injuries is at your peril, like continuing to carry heavy loads with a sore back or refusing to acknowledge constant pain.

7. *Knowing how to analyze situations and think for yourself:* instead of digesting the media thrown at you every day and finding yourself in a state of fear because one in two news items constitute crime, disaster, or propaganda, start thinking about the reality behind the wire news and start thinking about life and events with a healthy and open mind while maintaining a questioning mind. Help others break free from fear media by teaching them to recognize the tactics used.

8. *Know how to repair objects:* in a world that relies heavily on disposing of objects rather than repairing them, we are increasing the burden on Earth.

    And we are indebted to those who make items with built-in obsolescence because we have lost the ability to tinker and fix things ourselves.

    Learning how to repair and mend clothing, appliances, household objects, car engines, and many other items important to our daily functioning is not only liberating, not only an important way to exercise our common sense.

9. *Know how to plan:* in order not to do things haphazardly, more expensively or without any idea of the consequences, learn to anticipate. Forward thinking is always a sign of common sense, as is the ability to consider the consequences of different outcomes.

10. *Knowing how to be resourceful:* ingenuity is the art of « doing with it. » It's about taking small things and moving them forward with a little imagination and elbow grease. It's about being able to thrive in difficult conditions while still thriving and not feeling deprived.

    Ingenuity is a key part of common sense, and again, it's a skill that frees you from overconsumption.

11. *Knowing how to relate to the community:* being part of your community makes good sense.

    Unfortunately, many people prefer to hide and stay away or feel embarrassed by others around them.

    Connecting with others in your community is part of being human, part of relating and being open to sharing and generosity.

12. *Know how to protect yourself:* whether you are in public or at home, safety is a matter of common sense.

    Pushing pot handles away from you on the stove, looking both ways when crossing the street, walking with a friend or a group in dark areas of town at night instead of being alone, etc.

    All of these common sense security measures can be planned and implemented before anything harmful happens. This will often avoid problems. Think prevention, not disaster.

13. *You don't have to be very educated:* you have to be open-minded and curious. And, realize that this is a process, not a destination.

    You will have to make the mental effort throughout your life to know which messages you absorb and which people you allow to influence your way of thinking.

    Even this book is only a source of suggestions on common sense and success, analyze it, criticize its applicability to your own situation and choose, subtract, or adopt what suits you or does not suit you. After all, it is common sense.

USE COMMON SENSE

Keep in mind that manipulation and control strategies are not synonymous with common sense. These are signs of people who want to change reality and get others to adjust to their notions of reality. You can't change this type of person, so unless you're paid to hear their woes, use your common sense and keep a safe distance from them.

Listen to the people around you before you speak, especially if you have something to say that could be considered judgmental. If you can't add anything meaningful, say nothing.

It may not immediately increase or cultivate your true common sense, but it will give others the distinct impression that you do indeed possess common sense.

For example, common sense tells us that all important agreements, such as financial and marriage, should be in writing. Do not trust the vagaries of time and erroneous memories.

Learn all you can about any part of the universe that interests you before you die. This will allow you to cultivate common sense in context. « Common sense » without real knowledge is not even as good for man as animal instinct.

Common sense is learned through experience. Your friends and family will be more than happy to talk about the do's and don'ts of a given situation they're familiar with, if they know it's for your own safety.

Also, remember that popularity doesn't necessarily mean common sense.

GUIDING PRINCIPLES

A person of principle means someone who faithfully follows their set of principles rather than giving up on them when it suits them.

If the person is faced with a seemingly difficult decision in life, they will refer to their set of guiding principles and simply deduce the correct action to take.

Your principles are your compass, to refer to, when in doubt, when evaluating conflicting opportunities or priorities, or when you need to take a stand.

They will help you define your goals and values and choose between them when you are faced with conflicting problems or opportunities.

Simply put, a principle is a law that cannot be circumvented or violated. An example is the law of gravity.

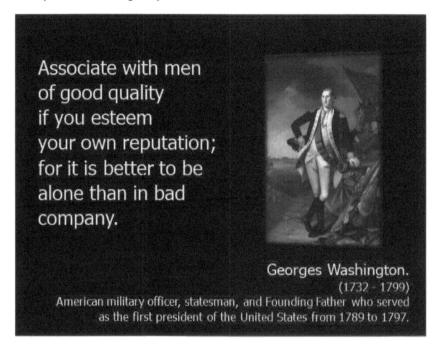

Associate with men of good quality if you esteem your own reputation; for it is better to be alone than in bad company.

Georges Washington.
(1732 - 1799)
American military officer, statesman, and Founding Father who served as the first president of the United States from 1789 to 1797.

We borrow most of our principles from those close to us. However, many stem from the fabric of our society.

You don't even really notice most of them. This becomes apparent when interacting with someone who was raised very differently from you.

To create a timeless perception of purpose and to shape the overall mission of your life, you will need to become fully aware of your principles.

Writing down your principles will make it easier for you to embody those you like and reject those you don't like.

1. *Your principles:*

    - Are your compass to which you refer, when in doubt, when evaluating opportunities or conflicting priorities, or when you need to take a stand.
    - Define your goals and values, so you can choose between them when faced with conflicting problems or opportunities.

- They serve as a handy point of reference, so you never feel uncertain or find yourself searching for an answer.
- They help you understand the differences between good and evil.

Whether you're planning your day, choosing between conflicting priorities, or setting a new goal, come back to your principles. By having well-thought-out principles, you can always feel comfortable knowing you made the right decision.

Establishing your principles is no small task, you really lay the foundation for whom you are as a person, creating the laws that govern all of your important decisions.

Some people take days, weeks or more before they can really settle on their principles. Don't be afraid to make this an iterative process.

2. *The qualities of a person of principle:*

    a. Honesty.
    b. Responsible.
    c. Care and compassion.
    d. Courage and audacity.
    e. Justice and impartiality.
    f. Gratitude and recognition.
    g. Humility.
    h. Loyalty and fidelity.
    i. Patience.
    j. Presence.

3. *A person who has principles:* simple, a person which is based on principles acts according to morality and recognition of right and wrong.

A person who has principles observes rules based on convictions or ideas which guide them. You can also say that a good ethical person has a lot of principles. In general, a principle is some kind of fundamental truth that helps you in your life. « Being fair » is a principle that guides you or should guide most people.

Success is not accidental. Living a good life will not come by accident or chance. Success will not fall from the sky. There is no magic wand. There is no quick fix.

Take responsibility for your life and you will take control of it. Take responsibility for where you are in life and accept the challenge required to get where you want to be. Successful people don't make excuses or blame others, they just focus on what they can achieve.

The good news is that there are five main principles that lead to success: concentration, strength, success, wisdom, responsibility.

If you commit to doing the things that successful people do, you will lead a life of success and happiness.

Live by these principles and you will ensure that you live a good life!

MORAL VALUES

How someone approaches ethics is fundamentally tied, to whom they are as a person. If a person has good morals, it is because of his virtues and his ethics.

Whether you are a parent, spouse, student, small business owner, worker, civil servant, politician, or professional such as a doctor, engineer, lawyer, good character is essential to successful relationships.

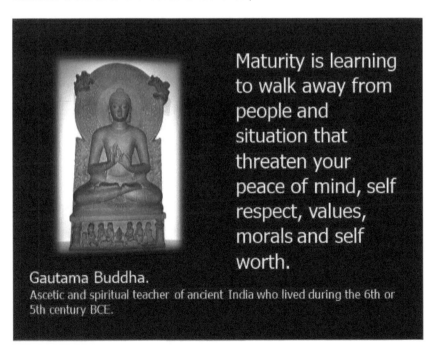

Maturity is learning to walk away from people and situation that threaten your peace of mind, self respect, values, morals and self worth.

Gautama Buddha.
Ascetic and spiritual teacher of ancient India who lived during the 6th or 5th century BCE.

To understand what constitutes a moral character, you must understand the meaning of ethics, which involves moral principles or values.

The decisions you make on a daily basis can have a positive or negative impact on many people.

To develop good moral character, an individual must analyze the consequences of exercising bad moral character and perform actions that are ethically correct.

If there is no trust between you and your family, at work or socially, miscommunication, dishonesty, conflicts can arise. An untrustworthy person keeps you in doubt while a trustworthy person reassures you.

For example, if a person lies about a particular situation, it puts you on your guard and soon you find yourself doubting everything they say. Because of his dishonesty, you are now questioning his moral character.

This also applies to how you treat others. If someone doesn't trust you, they probably won't, for example, commit to doing business with you.

If you demonstrate a sound moral character towards your relationships and treat them with respect, you are likely to retain their respect and high regard. The people who talk to you should also have these traits. For example, if your ethics are sound, but an employee disrespect or lies to your customers, it will be difficult to build customer loyalty.

Specifically, getting customers through decent prices and quality products can be easy, but how you serve those customers will determine whether you'll retain them. This also applies to employees, your family, and friends. If you treat them well, they are more likely to stay with you.

Individuals with a strong moral character have a high degree of certainty about their actions. They have, in mind, a clearly recognized objective and the methods necessary to achieve these objectives. Anxiety and nervousness are concepts that are foreign to them.

Moreover, people with a strong moral character chart their own path to success and never waste time contemplating unnecessary topics. Such individuals do not invent excuses to cover their backs.

A strong moral character is also instrumental in developing effective leadership qualities. They are visionary with a « can do » attitude.

They tackle the impossible, face problems and obstacles head-on, and make decisions that position them successfully for the future.

Humility is another trait possessed by people with strong moral character. They put aside their egos and self-interests and strive to work in ways that achieve the highest good for all.

Even if they fail or partially succeed in their endeavor, they are not deterred from achieving their goals and instead pursue them with even greater vigor.

People with strong moral character also become positive role models for others. They set the benchmark for excellence and their lives become an inspiration to others.

This is so because those who form a strong moral character conscientiously adhere to moral values through their actions and personal conduct and do not resort to a pompous and contrived style.

Simply put, moral character is perhaps best described as the set of dispositions or characteristics of a person that play a role in how the person, morally speaking, behaves. Moral character is therefore the edifice on which an individual's personal identity rests.

It is our moral character that determines who we are and what actions we take.

You might wonder why it's not always easy to admit a mistake, to persevere in difficult times, or to keep every promise you make. It is not always comfortable to convey the hard truth or to defend one's convictions.

In the short term, it may not be beneficial to distance yourself from a questionable relationship. But, in the long run, doing the right thing is the clear path to success and happiness. Morality matters!

Here are some reasons why moral character matters.

1. *Achieve peace of mind:* people with character sleep well at night. They take great pride in knowing that their intentions and actions are honorable.

   People with character also stay true to their beliefs, do good for others, and always take the lead.

2. *Build confidence:* people of character enjoy meaningful relationships based on openness, honesty, and mutual respect.

   When you have good character, people know that your behavior is reliable, your heart is in the right place, and your word speaks for itself.

3. *Build yourself a solid reputation:* people of character enjoy a solid reputation. This helps them attract interesting opportunities « like a magnet. »

4. *Reduce anxiety:* People of character carry less baggage. They are comfortable in their own skin and accept responsibility for their actions. They never have to play games, waste valuable time keeping their stories straight, or make up excuses to cover their backs.

5. *Increase leadership effectiveness:* leaders with character are very effective. They don't need to play their cards right or resort to command and control to get results. Instead, they are effective because they are knowledgeable, admired, trusted, and respected.

   This helps them secure membership automatically without requiring blatant rules or strict monitoring designed to force compliance.

6. *Build on trust:* people of character, don't mind being embarrassed if their actions are made public. This will alleviate the need for damage control or the fear of potential shame as a result of indiscretions.

7. *Become a positive role model:* people with character set the standard for excellence. They live their lives like an open book, teaching other important life lessons through their words and actions.

8. *Live a purpose-driven life:* people of character live a life they can be proud of. They are determined to make a difference and do good for others rather than trying to impress others with extravagance.

GOOD JUDGMENT

The ability to use good judgment in making decisions is one of the most important skills you can possess.

On a daily basis, you may be faced with mundane and potentially upsetting decisions.

Making good decisions applies to many aspects of your life, including work, health, education, family, and personal relationships.

Sound judgment requires a healthy mental state, a willingness to think things through, and self-confidence.

Good judgment involves considering the consequences of one's decisions, thinking before acting and speaking, and having the tools to make good decisions in various situations.

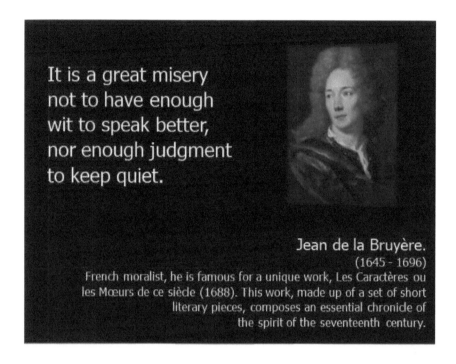

It is a great misery
not to have enough
wit to speak better,
nor enough judgment
to keep quiet.

Jean de la Bruyère.
(1645 - 1696)
French moralist, he is famous for a unique work, Les Caractères ou les Mœurs de ce siècle (1688). This work, made up of a set of short literary pieces, composes an essential chronicle of the spirit of the seventeenth century.

In order to make sound decisions, you need to break down the elements of the decision you are facing in your head. Consider your goals, the alternatives, the likely consequences of your decision, and any potential trade-offs.

Evaluate the uncertainties and all the risks that accompany your decision in a logical and coherent process. This process should help clarify the decision and point the way to the right choice.

Reframe the problem you're facing if you're still struggling to make a decision. Take the time to list the potential pros and cons, or it could be a more in-depth analysis. Reformulate your thought process using new word arrangements, different formulations, and new points of attention.

Ask other people you respect for their opinions, after describing the decision you're facing, to get some new insights. Also, if appropriate, talk openly about the process with trusted family members and friends. This can be advantageous because another person can clarify a situation by offering an unexpected perspective.

Listen to your instincts, but don't be a slave to them. Although humans are hardwired to make quick decisions and this approach can be useful in certain circumstances, it is not always the best tactic. Embracing the first ideas that pop into your head and clinging to them to the exclusion of everyone else can lead to bad decisions.

Develop the personality traits associated with people who consistently use good judgment when making decisions. Have a high tolerance for ambiguity rather than insisting on immediate gratification in your decision-making process. Have a well-ordered sense of priorities in every aspect of your life. Avoid stereotypes of all kinds, welcome feedback, and be realistic about your personal strengths and limitations.

BE RESPECTFUL

While respect should be second nature to all of us, there seems to be a major deficit in our world today. Text messages and emails with inappropriate behavior tell us that respect is clearly losing ground and that a return to normal is long overdue.

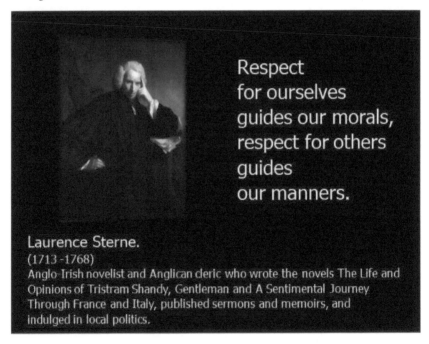

Respect
for ourselves
guides our morals,
respect for others
guides
our manners.

Laurence Sterne.
(1713 -1768)
Anglo-Irish novelist and Anglican cleric who wrote the novels The Life and Opinions of Tristram Shandy, Gentleman and A Sentimental Journey Through France and Italy, published sermons and memoirs, and indulged in local politics.

We have all heard that respect is earned. It cannot be given freely, and you have to work hard to achieve it. It is imperative that you pay attention to respect if you wish to achieve any success in your life.

You definitely want to be respected as someone valued for their professionalism, intelligence and good manners. Respect leads to trust and results in the development of better productivity at work, respect at home and in society.

Simple, it is a question of introducing basic rules to your way of life in order to gain the respect of others. For example, treat everyone the way you would like to be treated by seeking kindness and positivity, while considering that the person in front of you, has certain qualities that deserve your respect.

Remember that respect is one of the most important ingredients in any relationship for success to happen. It may sound like an idealistic statement, but we can only live peacefully with others if we learn to respect them despite our differences in culture, race, religion, and even ability.

It may be easy to say, but as you no doubt know these days, it is very difficult to do. In order to respect people who do not share the same values as you, you are invited to make compromises. This often means having to look past the mistakes of others and disregard your conflicting beliefs with them. In short, respect is choosing to see the good in others and appreciating their talents, skills, and what they can contribute beyond preconceived opinions.

If you are a person who wants to build better relationships with friends, partners, colleagues, or family members, you will find that the first step in this exercise is to respect them. Only then can you establish mutual trust.

Here are some simple ways to practice respecting others:

1. *Be kind and courteous:* understand that kindness and courtesy are the basics of respect and apply them in your daily life if you consider yourself a reasonable and respectful human being.

    Once you stop focusing on yourself and establish a moral connection to someone you are grateful for, you will automatically inspire change within yourself, for kindness and courtesy are important ways to be respectful.

    On the other hand, when you begin to recognize other people's time and point of view, you create a respectful image towards them. Be considerate of other people's feelings and be sure to treat everyone you meet with consideration.

    Remember that making eye contact, holding, or opening doors, greeting people with a sincere smile, offering help, and thanking others are ways people feel respected and valued.

2. *Listen and be present:* communication is the key to success, so take the time to listen and speak appropriately. Take the time to put people at ease by listening carefully.

    Don't look bored and in a bad mood, as this will be interpreted as rudeness. Don't interrupt someone when they're talking, even if it's very important.

    Let your interlocutor pause or finish their sentence before speaking.

    Maintain eye contact and keep a positive posture to show your respect towards your interlocutors. Don't start nodding to show some courtesy, instead process, understand and participate by listening properly.

    This will foster a sense of sharing and trust among stakeholders. Ask meaningful questions that encourage the other person to open up.

    Each of us loves to talk, so keep the conversation going if you want to find ways to be respectful.

    Remember that by listening, you make the other person feel important.

3. *Say, « Thank you! »:* even if it's just because a stranger held the door open for you. Especially if your parents gave you a present or your wife took the time to cook your favorite dish for dinner. Say « Thank you! » and let them know that their efforts are appreciated.

    It's so easy to forget that sometimes, but just imagine how happy they will feel when they hear that precious word from you. Thanking people is not just about expressing gratitude.

    It is also to show people that you respect them and that their efforts have not been wasted when they do something for you.

4. *Be polite:* politeness and good manners go hand in hand, as both fall under basic social etiquette.

    Master politeness if you're looking for ways to be respectful. Be polite to everyone, not just to people you know and admire or want to get information or a favor from them.

    If you're only being respectful to make a good impression, you're on the wrong track. Do not discriminate but treat everyone the same with respect and politeness. Remember to follow basic good manners to create a favorable impression.

For example, don't talk or text on the phone when you're in a personal conversation with someone else.

Remember to always thank everyone for their efforts and follow the rules that can make everyone's life easier. Politeness is a virtue which is admired by all and which results in the respect of each.

5. *Pay attention to other people's time:* if you're meeting a friend or client at nine in the morning, be there a few minutes before. Being aware of other people's time is a very underrated quality. People will be grateful that you show up on time for a meeting, for dinner, and especially for special events.

   Time is our most precious resource as human beings. It doesn't come in endless amounts, so make sure you don't waste, other people's time by just being mindful.

6. *Be humble and considerate:* be patient in your dealings with others. Sometimes you may come across rude and disrespectful people.

   Yes, it will test your patience, but don't stoop to their level, instead maintain your dignity and composure.

   Do not encourage what is considered disrespectful, such as speaking loudly, rolling your eyes, interrupting, or looking at your mobile device repeatedly when you are on a conversation with someone else.

   Be mindful of other people's feelings if you're looking for ways to be respectful.

   Remember that everyone deserves respect, so don't create unnecessary situations by being disrespectful.

7. *Be honest:* being honest and truthful about how you feel will be much desired by anyone in your life. If you respect a person, you know they deserve the truth and nothing less.

   Lying never does any good, so drop that attitude. However, there is a thin line between honesty and tactlessness.

   First think about the words you are going to say.
   Are your thoughts biased?
   Will it sound wrong if you say that?

Effort and courage are not enough without purpose and direction.

John F. Kennedy
(1917 – 1963)
American Navy officer and politician who served as the 35th president of the United States.

Practice honesty, but never use it to hurt others. You can be right about something, but wrong about how you say it.

Be honest and show people that they can count on your honesty. If they know you're honest, they'll learn to trust you.

8. *Give a helping hand or lend a listening ear:* be prepared to offer help to someone in need if you are looking for ways to be respectful. If you see someone in distress, strike up a conversation and listen. This will give the other a chance to share their issues with you.

Don't overlook opportunities to help, because a cry of distress is genuine and should be heard by a compassionate person.

Take responsibility and help out if you want to feel respected. Don't wait for someone to approach you and ask for help. You can help by doing simple things like helping an elderly person cross the street, helping another employee with their workload or simply donating your clothes to a shelter for disadvantaged people.

Be ready to change. We all have something good and bad in our habits and behavior. Encourage the good and be prepared to change the bad if you are looking for ways to be respectful.

Remember that the stubborn nature can prove your downfall, so it is best to put in the effort to learn and try something that can improve your life for the better.

Give up bad habits, especially anger and resentment, because both are negative emotions that can cause moral, spiritual, intellectual, psychological damage to your interlocutors.

Forgive and forget people for their transgressions. Move on and put situations behind you for your own peace of mind.

On the other hand, don't make excuses for bad choices. Admit you made a mistake, and it won't happen again. Rectify your mistakes with a positive mindset if you want to be respectful.

Talk to the disrespected person and admit your mistake and sincerely apologize for it. You will find inner peace and the joy of having done well with this action.

Your actions show your caring nature and people will respect you for it. It is important to respect your fellow human beings if you want to be recognized as a respectful person.

9. *Avoid gossip:* don't gossip because it can come back and cause you serious distress.

   Remember that the person you are gossiping about is a human being with real feelings and when someone murders their character or behavior, it can cause them harm.

   Avoid gossip at all costs as people will not be respectful towards people who tend to engage in such activities. Simple, you avoid gossip if you look for ways to be respectful.

   Be polite in your objections, if you recognize someone who is participating in gossip, politely remind them of the possible repercussions of such actions.

10. *Do not abuse your power:* if you're in a position of authority, don't abuse it if you're looking for ways to be respectful. Do not speak disrespectfully to people who are below you in position or monetary matters.

    Be kind, polite and courteous to everyone, regardless of their situation or circumstances.

    Remember that a really successful person is one who makes a viable effort to bring everyone along without devaluing their efforts.

    Sympathize, with their situation and try to understand their position. Understanding leads to empathy and results in respectful behavior.

11. *Respect physical boundaries:* everyone's body is their own and everyone has the right to decide the level and type of physical contact with which they are comfortable.

    For example, some people like to be greeted with hugs, others don't, and that's normal!

    Respecting people's personal preferences is of utmost importance.

    Always validate how the other person wants to be treated and how they should insist that others respect their boundaries as well.

It all starts with self-respect, the most important thing you will learn to do.

If you respect yourself, you have to be in tune with how you feel and be honest about it.

If you ever fail, say sorry and respect yourself enough to be kind to yourself. People who respect themselves tend to practice respect better, because they know their worth, their abilities, and what they can accomplish.

If you learn to appreciate yourself as a person, you will certainly learn to find the good in others as well.

Always remember that in this big world of ours, there are a billion different ways to live a life, and that's what makes life interesting!

As long as everyone is respectful and no one is hurting anyone else, it's important to take a step back and accept the fact that there's no one right way to exist on this planet.

So live and let live!

OBJECTIVITY

Objectivity is one of those character traits we all like to think we have. After all, the best course of action in any given situation is to consider the facts and circumstances and then make the best decision possible.

In reality, we all have prejudices. If left mismanaged, then we can pay in lost opportunities, money, relationships, and other ways.

We constantly make cognitive errors. We perceive something, and in an instant we project our mental models, our experiences, our antecedents, onto anything, a person, a situation or an event and often end up deceiving ourselves.

Whenever you think you know, everything there is to know about a subject, it's time to check your point of view for the sake of objectivity.

Your lack of objectivity could cost you dearly in more ways than one. Shake off your biases and get a clearer picture by addressing these important steps.

1. *Understand the limits of objectivity:* if you think you are really objective, you are wrong. Remember that we all have luggage.

This baggage blurs our perception which naturally leads us to have biased options. Once you realize that you are not objective by nature, you can take steps to get, closer to it.

2. *Find your weak points:* we all leave behind clues when we are less objective.

    - Are there any subjects on which you are particularly argumentative, or which irritate you?
    - Are there situations where you regularly overreact?

    If you become restless or very emotional, you are probably not thinking rationally or objectively. It may be because you are emotionally invested in the subject or because you have particular beliefs that do not allow you to see other points of view clearly.

    Remember to be aware of yourself, but in the moment, you need to be aware of your triggers and do the opposite.

3. *Become more objective:* the best way to become more objective is to broaden the input you receive. Develop a network of people you respect, whose viewpoints usually differ from yours to seek out their opinions on various topics.

    They can be, colleagues, professionals from other companies and organizations, social or spiritual advisors.

    Ideally, these are people who care about you, but also have the ability to say something clearly in a way that you will actually hear.

4. *Check your personality type:* your natural way of being, can lead to certain prejudices. If you naturally like to please people, you may make decisions based at least in part on your desire to avoid conflict or disagreement with others.

    This is another form of bias and can prohibit you from weighing facts strictly on their merits.

5. *Check your personality type:* whenever you think you know everything about a subject, be it social, political, religious, or commercial, it's time to check your point of view for the sake of objectivity.

    A good way to do this is to solicit new viewpoints from other sources such as reference materials, reliable and verified news outlets, etc.

Specifically ask people you trust to share how their views differ from yours.

The important thing is to be clear about your opinion and inviting others to share theirs in a non-threatening way. Only then will you be able to compare points and see where you might be missing something.

Remember, let the people helping you know that you want to know how their views differ.

WISDOM

We associate wisdom with old age, the accumulation of knowledge of the hardships and tribulations of life.

However, life experiences should not be confused, and age does not necessarily condition us towards wisdom.

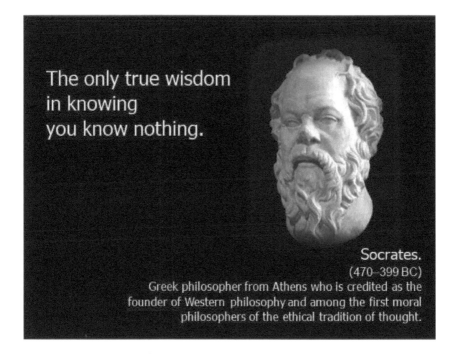

The only true wisdom in knowing you know nothing.

Socrates.
(470–399 BC)
Greek philosopher from Athens who is credited as the founder of Western philosophy and among the first moral philosophers of the ethical tradition of thought.

Wisdom is not just the result of sorting out experiences.

It is also the product of learning a variety of essential ways of seeing our life and the world around us as we go along.

Here is a list of both the characteristics and the stages of its realization.

1. *Be honest with yourself:* surely, a simple statement, but in reality, more complicated than it seems. In fact, to reach the state of wisdom, there are a few steps to consider.

    One is to have some level of self-awareness, to realize and be able to define one's emotions, to no one's values, one's own priorities of what is important in life and what it means to be a « good » person.

    It's also knowing what you want, being able to use your instinctive reactions and instincts, rather than the rules in your head, to let you know what you need.

    And if that's not enough, the next step is to use that self-awareness as the basis for realizing when you're making a mistake and admitting that you did, taking full responsibility for your decisions and actions, rather than to blame others.

2. *Be honest with others:* honesty with yourself is the basis for being honest with others. To be honest with others is to reveal yourself, and for that you obviously need to be able to articulate what that self is.

    Many people are able to take the first step, but then encounter a bigger hurdle. Even if they know what they think and believe, they cannot intervene and speak out.

    Instead, they don't feel safe, they worry about other people's reactions, and so they sugarcoat their complaints to their co-workers, they bite their tongues not telling their partner what is bothering them or what they want them to change. They just hold back.

    The danger is that you start to feel isolated because no one really knows you. The issues that bother you come back over time, leading to outbursts or depression.

    The antidote is to replace your old coping style, then develop the courage to step up even if your gut tells you to quit.

3. *Focus on the process rather than the result:* While the first two suggestions are about honest dialogue with yourself and others, this step is more about your behaviors and how you approach work.

    The issue obviously concerns the result, the goal, the end. We tend to think of the process as just a means to that end.

But those who are considered wise, reverse this equation, and make the process, an end in itself, this is all about mindfulness, the secret to enlightenment.

Instead of focusing on the outcome, focus your attention and energy on the process itself, let go of expectations.

By doing this, you are able to stay focused on the present, rather than living in the future, the possible outcome. Not only is the present where life is, not only the current process is the only thing you can control, say the wise. The result is out of your reach, it is simply the future.

Those who only focus on the outcome often feel frustrated or pushed. They develop tunnel vision that erases what is happening now. They lose sight of the day-to-day pleasures of managing their lives and dislike the process of action itself.

Instead, they easily end up measuring their happiness by measuring themselves against others and what others say about them, and in doing so, they give up their power and self-esteem.

4. *Listen to the changes in yourself:* if you're driven and results-focused, if life is a forced march from one goal to another, not only can you miss out on what's good in everyday life, but you're also missing out on those subtle changes that naturally evolve naturally within you.

    What is often seen in people who take this forced march approach is depression or eventual crisis. They suddenly realize that too much of themselves, has been compromised and left by the wayside, that their life is one-dimensional, all because those inner voices have been drowned out by their myopic focus or fear of others.

    The obvious antidote is to periodically slow down, take stock of the state of your life, pay attention to those silent inner voices telling you your needs are changing, and then have the courage to speak up.

5. *Learn from your mistakes:* at the heart of the problems are lessons to be learned. Once you learn the lesson the problem is trying to teach that you shouldn't rant at your boss or your partner that you should check the oil in your car, the problem goes away. If you don't, the problem keeps popping up.

    Older people and especially wise people generally have an easier time managing their lives because life is a process of eliminating problems.

They have learned enough lessons from them that only a smaller batch remains.

Where it's easy to get stuck it is not taking this approach. Instead, you see life or others as attacking you, blaming you, feeling like the perpetual victim, and so instead of learning the lesson the problem can teach you are still left with the same problem either that you can't trust other people, that they want to hurt you, that life is unfair.

Or you don't blame others, but rather blame yourself and see mistakes not as lessons, but as endless sources of regret, guilt, self-flagellation.

This way of thinking allows you to live forever in the past, which in turn blackens the present, in addition, this abuse of yourself destroys self-esteem and leads to depression.

6. *The power of time itself:* or the ability to step back, to put what seems like big issues and events into perspective, to sort out priorities so that everything doesn't seem so important and overwhelming.

   It is also about realizing that what seems so important today, this month, this year is subject to change over time, because whether you like it or not, you will change, because of the power of time itself.

7. *Believe that you have a contribution to make:* a defining existential problem that we all have to grapple with in our own way is my life purpose. Without a sense of purpose, life is just a thing to go through, a mere drudgery, a treadmill you walk on forever until you die.

   For example, your goal might be to shape a child's life, as well as you can, to make a small difference in your community, to start a business that will change millions of people.

   But « what it is » doesn't really matter. What matters is having something. And the starting point for having that something is having blind faith, a raw belief that you actually have a purpose, that there is something you are here for, that you have unique talents that can make an impact, no matter how big or small, on others and on the world.

8. *Be kind to others:* yes, it sounds like the platitude that everyone knows. But what's behind it isn't just how you treat others, but also how you see the world.

Kindness is a by-product of you and others being connected in some way, realizing that even though we are different, we all struggle in our own way, with that filter in place you can be whatever the others feel.

Without it, life is a competition, a hunger game where others cannot be trusted, where it's every man for himself. Sure, you might be the one to get away with it, but that comes at the cost of a life filled with anxiety, paranoia, and loneliness.

Remember every day of your life, you are developing your wisdom. It's not something that comes to you later in life. Conditioning yourself towards wisdom is above all a way of living your life.

RELIGION AND SPIRITUALITY

Today, religion as an institution is set aside by many for various reasons. One of them being exploitation through possible commercialization.

Therefore, this type of so-called modern religion should be eliminated from a person's life, as this type of religion can only lead nowhere.

Human beings can live without religion, but they cannot live without spirituality. They are two different entities but intertwined due to people's lack of awareness.

The only possibility of giving meaning to one's existence is to elevate one's natural relationship with the world to the height of a spiritual relationship.

Albert Schweitzer.
(1875 -1965)
Alsatian-German/French polymath. He was a theologian, organist, musicologist, writer, humanitarian, philosopher, and physician.
A Lutheran minister, Schweitzer challenged both the secular view of Jesus as depicted by the historical-critical method current at this time, as well as the traditional Christian view.

It is a matter of fact that we humans are trivial in this universe. Therefore, spirituality should be accomplished in the good deeds of a person by being humble in nature.

It is in this gratitude to nature for giving so abundantly that a person feels satisfaction and contentment.

It is unfortunate that the earliest forms of every religion, whether polytheistic or monotheistic, brought these points into stark relief.

It's time for people to take a look at scriptures like:

- *The Bhagavad-Gita:* Hindu scripture of 700 verses which is part of the epic Mahabharata.
- *Vedas:* a large number of religious texts from ancient India.
- *The Quran:* the central religious text of Islam.
- *The Bible:* a collection of religious texts or scriptures in Christianity, Judaism, Samaritan, and many other religions.
- The Torah: according to the tradition of Judaism, the divine teaching transmitted by God to Moses.

To consult them independently, in order to learn from them ethics and universal values.

Human beings can surely live happily without religion as an institution, but without rejecting the ideologies that form the ethical foundations.

RELIGION:

Religion today has taken on a very institutionalized form. Its origin has always been debated and discussed and today researchers are delving into it.

In sociological terms, « Religion is a system of sacred beliefs and practices in both tangible and intangible form. » Religion can play the dual role of ideology as well as institutions.

Today, religion has assumed a narrower approach. However, understanding religion broadly highlights the following important points about it in society:

1. *Cultural identity:* religion plays a crucial role for a person by giving him a cultural identity. Each religion has festivals, traditions, mythologies which are part of the material and immaterial heritage of the country.

    Thus, religion helps to protect this heritage and also adds to the diversity of the country.

2. *The values and ethics:* religion helps to create an ethical framework and also a regulator of values in everyday life. This particular approach helps in shaping a person's character.

    In other words, religion acts as an agent of socialization. Thus, religion contributes to the construction of values such as love, empathy, respect, and harmony.

3. *The Spiritual Bond:* people are always looking for economic and material achievements in today's world.

    It is religion that plays a crucial role in establishing our connection to the divine and developing the belief that there is a supreme energy that acts as a regulator in our daily lives.

    Thus, the components of prayer, songs, canticles, etc. create the spiritual bond.

4. *The idea of wellness:* each religion promotes its philosophy, and the main thing has always been the well-being of the people.

    For example, in Sanatana Dharma there are ideas like Vasudaiva Kutumbakam (the whole world is one family), Sarve Sukhina Bhavantu (Let everyone be happy) which nurtures and cultivates love and compassion in society.

SPIRITUALITY:

We must remember that spirituality involves the recognition of a feeling or a sense or a belief that there is something greater than oneself, something more to be human than an experience sensory, and that the greater whole of which we are a part is of a cosmic or divine nature.

1. *Spirituality means:* knowing that our lives have meaning in a context beyond a mundane daily existence with respect to the biological needs that lead to selfishness and aggression. It means knowing that we are an important part of a conscious unfolding of Life in our universe.

2. *Spirituality entails:* to explore certain universal themes such as love, compassion, altruism, life after death, wisdom, and truth, knowing that certain people such as saints or enlightened people have reached and manifested levels of development higher than the ordinary person.

Aspiring to manifest the attributes of such inspiring examples often becomes an important part of the journey through life for spiritually inclined people.

3. *Spiritual journeying involves:* first the healing and affirmation of the ego, so that positive states are experienced with secure self-esteem, self-confidence and a capacity for love and generosity, so that the person becomes less constrained by ego defenses. Openness of heart is an essential aspect of true spirituality.

4. *The development of spirituality: it* is generally accepted as requiring some kind of practice or discipline in order to progress. It may challenge the neophytes of opinions that run counter to common opinion such as non-effort, doorless pass, in Chinese Wumen Guan, in Japanese Mumen, that is to say, the problem of death and of the meaning one wants to give to one's life or the return one expects from it.

Contemplative practices such as prayer and meditation are the common denominator of many religions and the foundation of spirituality. Without them, personal development is much slower and more random. A teacher or mentor is usually recommended.

Spiritual development often involves spontaneous events which cannot be explained scientifically, and which can be attributed to an external force, for example, grace or angelic or divine interventions. The conversion of Saul of Tarsus on the road to Damascus is a dramatic example.

Development may not necessarily be an instantaneous event, but may occur more gradually, such as during an experience of severe illness or terminal diagnosis, when the fragility of life is revealed, and a person reassess the meaning of their life.

5. *Religion formalizes:* certain aspects of spiritual awareness in a coherent belief system that can be taken on trust, even if the person has no direct experience of the Divine.

For example, one person might believe that Jesus is the son of God because that is what the Bible teaches, while another person may have had a vision of Jesus himself telling him that he is the son of God.

Religion's belief systems extend beyond the individual's experience to their role in society and morality-based rules are formulated to govern relationships and activities.

Usually, the religion manifests as a collective through the church, mosque, synagogue, or temple, and is involved with the community as much as with individuals.

It provides a real framework through which the « greater than self » can begin to be experienced.

Recommended reading and references
We suggest that you consult the works identified below in order to learn more about the particularities contained in this chapter.

BOYES, Alice, PhDs. The Healthy Mind Toolkit. Simple Strategies to Get Out Your Own Way and Enjoy Your Life. Tarcher perigee. ISBN: 978-0-14-313070-3

COLLARD, Nathalie. À LA RECHERCHE DU BONHEUR.
Le Quotidien la Presse. Forum, avril 2007. ISBN 0317-9249.

GLOTTIER, Agnes & Henry et al. 1,000 YEARS, 1000 PEOPLE.
Ranking the Men and Women Who Shaped the Millennium.
Barnes & Nobles. ISBN-13: 978-0-7607-8349-8.

HOWARTH, David & Stephen. NELSON: The Immortal Memory.
Conway Classics. ISBN 0-85177-720-1.

INGLE, Sud. QUALITY CIRCLES MASTER GUIDE.
Prentice-Hall. ISBN 0-13-745000-1.

KENNEDY, John F. PROFILE OF COURAGE.
Harper Classic. ISBN-13: 978-0-06-085493-5.

MONTEFIORE, Simon Sebag. 101 WORLD HEROES: Great Men and Women Who Changed History. Metro Books. ISBN-13: 978-1-4351-0509-5.

OSTEEN, Joel. BECOME A BETTER YOU. 7 Keys to Improving Your Life Every Day.
Free Press. ISBN-13: 978-0-7432-9688-5.

WEISS, David S. & LEGRAND, Claude P. INNOVATIVE INTELLIGENCE. The art and practice of leading sustainable innovation in your organization.
Wiley. ISBN: 978-0-470-67767-4

Germain Decelles, O.S.J.

ABOUT THE AUTHOR

In addition to writing, Germain Decelles acts as a strategist and facilitator of change management.

Each year, he offers several seminars and training sessions on change management, transformation, and business innovation. Additionally, he serves as President of WebTech Management and Publishing Incorporated.

Germain Decelles has over 40 years of business and consulting experience in local and international markets, particularly in sectors such as retail, distribution, information and communications technology, transportation, manufacturing, financial services, and government organizations.

He attended the campuses of Ford Motors Management Institute, Chrysler Leasing Institute, International Forecasting Institute, McGill University, Kappa Institute and Digital Equipment Computer Institute. He holds a master's degree in business administration from Concordia College & University and a certificate in business management and organization from Hautes Études Commerciales de Montréal.

He is a member of the Canadian Coast Guard, retired (S.A.C.S.M.), secretary of the General Assembly and international adviser. He received the Admiralty Service Award in 1990 for promoting the service internationally. He is also a member of the Sovereign Order of Saint John of Jerusalem.

Germain and his family live in Montréal, Quebec, Canada. You can contact him at: gdecelles@webtechmanagement.com

ISO POUR TOUS - ISBN : 978-0-9783667-0-4
Le guide de préparation ISO - ISBN : 978-0-9783667-1-1
Le Manuel d'information ISO - ISBN : 978-0-9783667-0-4
La Gestion de projet en affaires - ISBN : 978-0-9783667-2-8
La gestion du changement en affaires - ISBN 978-0-9783667-3-5
Le changement POUR TOUS - ISBN 978-0-9783667-4-2
CHANGE Your Future, Now! - ISBN 978-0-9783667-7-3
MY SUCCESS IS YOUR SUCCESS - ISBN 978-1-7388000-0-1
MON SUCCHS EST VOTRE SUCCÈS - ISBN 978-1-7388000-1-8

Information: **www.webtechpublishing.com**

MY SUCCESS IS YOUR SUCCESS - ISBN 978-1-7388000-0-1
MON SUCCÈS EST VOTRE SUCCÈS - ISBN 978-1-7388000-1-8

MANAGEMENT and PUBLISHING